Accrington's Pals

Accrington's Pals
The Full Story

The 11th Battalion, East Lancashire Regiment (Accrington Pals) and the 158th (Accrington and Burnley) Brigade, Royal Field Artillery (Howitzers)

Andrew Jackson

Pen & Sword
MILITARY

First published in Great Britain in 2013 by
Pen & Sword Military
an imprint of
Pen & Sword Books Ltd
47 Church Street
Barnsley
South Yorkshire
S70 2AS

Copyright © Andrew Jackson 2013

ISBN 978-1-84884-469-8

The right of Andrew Jackson to be identified as Author of this Work
has been asserted by him in accordance with the Copyright, Designs and
Patents Act 1988.

A CIP catalogue record for this book is available from the British Library.

Typeset in 11/13 Ehrhardt by Concept, Huddersfield, West Yorkshire
Printed and bound in England by CPI Group (UK) Ltd, Croydon, CRO 4YY

Pen & Sword Books Ltd incorporates the Imprints of Pen & Sword Aviation,
Pen & Sword Family History, Pen & Sword Maritime, Pen & Sword Military,
Pen & Sword Discovery, Wharncliffe Local History, Wharncliffe True Crime,
Wharncliffe Transport, Pen & Sword Select, Pen & Sword Military Classics,
Leo Cooper, The Praetorian Press, Remember When, Seaforth Publishing and
Frontline Publishing.

For a complete list of Pen & Sword titles please contact
PEN & SWORD BOOKS LIMITED
47 Church Street, Barnsley, South Yorkshire, S70 2AS, England
E-mail: enquiries@pen-and-sword.co.uk
Website: www.pen-and-sword.co.uk

Contents

List of Plates

List of Maps

Preface

More than twenty-five years have passed since the publication of William Turner's *Accrington Pals*, the first book to provide a detailed account of the history of 11/East Lancashire, the Kitchener battalion founded and raised in the early weeks of the First World War by John Harwood, then mayor of the Lancashire textile and machinery town of Accrington. While a reappraisal of the Accrington Pals' story is anyway timely – with much fresh material having emerged in the intervening years – Turner's book told only part of the remarkable contribution made by Harwood to Britain's war effort. Less than twenty weeks after recruitment for the Accrington Pals had been completed, Harwood took on the responsibility for raising a local artillery formation, the Accrington and Burnley Howitzers. Harwood himself was quoted after the war as saying 'it was only matter for regret that the Howitzers were broken up into six-gun batteries and that their career could not be followed'. In this he was mistaken; although the Howitzers' gun batteries were dispersed early in 1917, the careers of the two Accrington batteries can be traced through to the end of the war. Moreover, by bringing together the stories of the Pals and the Howitzers, it becomes possible to follow, through their experiences, every major campaign in which the British Army took part on the Western Front from 1916 onwards.

Lists of those who enrolled into the Pals and the Howitzers on their formation can be found on the author's website at www.pals.org.uk/palslist.htm and www.pals.org.uk/howitzers/list.htm respectively.

I hope my friends in Burnley and Chorley will forgive the title of the book, for Harwood was able to raise his two local formations only with the support of those towns and their communities; truly they were Accrington's Pals.

Acknowledgements

I owe my interest in Accrington's role in the First World War to my father, Maurice, with whom I made the first of many visits to the battlefields of the Western Front and beyond in the early 1970s.

Of those who have given generously of their time, help and knowledge throughout my work, I would like particularly to thank John Garwood, David Ingham, Mike Townend and the late Denis Otter.

For information on the Harwood family, the help given by Mike Harwood, Nin and Pen Harwood, André and Justine Gernez, Heather Fereday, Anne and Paul Willett, and Jayne Waring has been invaluable.

I am grateful to staff at the following archives for allowing me access to collections for which they are responsible and, where requested, for their permission to quote from documents: British Library, The National Archives, Royal Geographical Society, Imperial War Museum, Lancashire Infantry Museum, Royal Artillery Museum, Liddle Collection at the University of Leeds, North West Sound Archive, Accrington, Burnley and Chorley public libraries.

I should also like to thank all of the following who have contributed to this book, and apologize sincerely to anyone whom I may have inadvertently overlooked: Nelly and Jacquie Ainslie, Bob Ashton, Anthony Battersby, Peter Bell, David and Derek Bent, Enid and Stuart Briggs, Gillian Brown, Malcolm Bury, Ross Davies, Neil Erskine and Bindy Wollen, Elnora Ferguson, Tracey Gardner and Dorothy Parkinson, David and Barbara Gay, John and Honor Gorst, Gerald and Pam Hargreaves, Kit Harvey, Dennis Hounsell, Hardy Huber, Pat and Roger Kay, Judy Langton and John Sayer, Marjorie Lloyd-Jones, Jane Maclean, Barry McAleenan, Frances Morris, Diccon Nelson-Roberts, Steven Owen, Jane Ramagge and Michael Ritzema, Robert and Tony Robinson, Barbara Rogers, John Slinger, Walter Slinger, Sue Baker Wilson and Steve McGreal, Hannah Sloane, Diana Stockford, Ian Thomas, Terry Whittaker.

Last, but not least, special thanks go to my wife, Alyson, without whose help, encouragement, support, patience and cartographic skills this book could not have been completed.

While every effort has been made to trace and acknowledge the holders of all copyright material, I trust that anyone whose copyright I have unwittingly infringed will accept my sincere apologies.

Abbreviations and Terminology

The following abbreviations are used in the text and notes:

AFA	Army Field Artillery
Anzac	Australian and New Zealand Army Corps
BEF	British Expeditionary Force
CCS	Casualty clearing station
DCM	Distinguished Conduct Medal
DFC	Distinguished Flying Cross
DSO	Distinguished Service Order
FOO	Forward observation officer
GOC	General Officer Commanding
GHQ	General Headquarters
GS	General Service
HE	High explosive
KCB	Knight Commander of the Order of the Bath
KOYLI	King's Own (Yorkshire Light Infantry)
MC	Military Cross
MM	Military Medal
NCO	Non-commissioned officer
OC	Officer Commanding
RAMC	Royal Army Medical Corps
RFA	Royal Field Artillery
RFC	Royal Flying Corps
RGS	Royal Geographical Society
TNA	The National Archives
VC	Victoria Cross
YMCA	Young Men's Christian Association
YWCA	Young Women's Christian Association

Throughout the book, the coalition between Germany, Austria-Hungary, Turkey and Bulgaria is referred to as the Central Powers, whereas that principally between France, Great Britain, Russia and Italy is referred to as the Allies.

In order to make a clear distinction in the text between infantry brigades and artillery brigades, the former are expressed using Arabic numerals, as in 94 Brigade, whereas the latter are expressed using Roman numerals, as in CLVIII Brigade. Specific artillery batteries are identified by an abbreviated format: C/LXIV, for example, refers to C Battery of LXIV Brigade.

Ranks are private unless stated otherwise.

Pre-decimal British currency in which there were 12 pence (*d*) in a shilling (*s*), and 20 shillings in a pound (*£*) is used throughout the text.

Distances are expressed in miles (1 mile = 1.61km) and yards (1yd = 0.91m).

Chapter 1

A Determination to Make Good

On 9 November 1912, the Council Chamber of Accrington's Town Hall was filled to capacity as councillors and public alike gathered to witness the election of 65-year-old Captain John Harwood as the new mayor. The outgoing mayor, Alderman Arthur Smith Bury, a Liberal by political inclination and a cotton manufacturer by trade, described Harwood as a thoroughly broad-minded man of great tact in proposing him for the post. Seconding the proposal, Alderman Doctor Counsell Dewhurst, a fellow Conservative, remarked on the well-known popularity of Harwood and, while referring to his poor health during recent months, expressed the hope that his mayorship would be the happiest year of his life. Councillor John Barlow, a Liberal and a director of cotton mills, also spoke in support of the proposal, and commented on the grit and perseverance shown by Harwood throughout his career. The proposal was carried by the Council unanimously and Harwood was led to the mayoral chair while 'the Council rose and applauded heartily'.

While the year that followed may well have been, as Councillor Dewhurst had wished, the happiest of Harwood's life – it included the visit to Accrington of King George V and Queen Mary on 9 July 1913 – his popularity saw him re-elected for a further two years so that the mayorship remained his throughout the first fifteen months of the First World War. Harwood would need to call on all of the qualities ascribed to him by his fellow councillors as he responded to his country's need to build an army capable of fighting a continental war by founding and raising not just a complete infantry battalion, the Accrington Pals, but also an artillery brigade, the Accrington and Burnley Howitzers.

John Harwood had been born into a working class Lancashire family on 14 December 1847 at a dwelling called the Pantry in Blacksnape, a hamlet belonging to the township of Over Darwen. His first association with Accrington seems to have come about through the death from gastro-enteritis of his father, Henry, a 27-year-old textile warper, on 20 April 1853. Henry was survived by his wife, Mary, and at least three of their children, Jane Alice, Edward and 6-year-old John. Twenty months after Henry's death, Mary re-married at the age of 30; her new husband was Edmund Walsh, a 24-year-old widower employed as an engine tenter. Some five years later, the family moved to Accrington.

As his mother, Mary, and step-father, Edmund, began a family of their own, John was sent to work at the age of just 7. On moving to Accrington, John started out as a warehouse boy at Fountain Mill in the Scaitcliffe district of the town, and by the age of 13 was a cotton power-loom weaver. At some point in the 1860s, John left to work in Chorley, where on 4 July 1867 he married Sarah Fisher, a 22-year-old local girl, at the Wesleyan Chapel in Park Road.

The decade of industrialization from 1851 to 1860 had seen Accrington transformed from little more than a village into a sizeable town of some importance; the several watercourses that flowed through the town had favoured the establishment of cotton mills along their banks, the opening of railway lines to Blackburn, Burnley and Manchester in 1848 had given a further stimulus to the town's economy, and the formation of a Local Board in 1853 represented the beginnings of local government. By 1859 the Accrington area offered employment through forty-seven cotton factories, seven calico printing works, ten chemical manufactories, two corn mills, eight machinist and ironfounders' works, as well as four collieries and many other smaller manufactories and places of business.

The period 1862–3 saw great hardship in the Lancashire cotton towns, and it is reasonable to suppose that John left Accrington at about that time to look for work; the determination to 'make good' that would characterize his entire life was already in evidence. By 1860, Britain relied on America to supply 80 per cent of the 620,000 tons of cotton that she needed to feed her textiles industry; a further 15 per cent was sourced from India, but the Lancashire spinners had been loath to use it owing to its inferior length and quality. The efforts of Manchester organizations in preceding years to encourage the cultivation of a better quality of cotton in India had largely come to nothing, and it was the continued dependence on America that would lead to the distress of the Lancashire cotton famine in 1862–3. On the election of Abraham Lincoln as 16th President of the United States in November 1860, seven cotton-growing states – rebelling against Lincoln's opposition to the expansion of slavery – broke away from the Union to form the Confederate States of America. When Civil War broke out in April 1861, the southern states' conviction that Britain's dependence on their cotton would force her into the war on the side of the Confederacy led them to try to force the issue by imposing a ban on exports even before the Union began to attempt a blockade of the southern ports. Shipping of the 1861 crop would normally have begun in September but, despite the looseness of the Union blockade, most of the crop, little short of a million tons, remained on land. In the spring of 1862, half of the land in the southern states that would normally have been used for cotton was turned over to food production. Across the Atlantic, manufacturers in Lancashire were confronted not only with soaring prices for cotton, but also with the threat that a sudden end to the war in America could release vast quantities of cheap cotton onto the market, thereby inflicting potentially ruinous losses on those who were sitting on large stocks of goods made from expensive cotton. The threat was enough to lead manufacturers to introduce short-term working, or even shut down their mills. In May 1862 there were 11,000 operatives out of work in Preston alone, and 8,429 in Blackburn; the distress increased as the year wore on, to the extent that during the winter of 1862–3 36,000 in Blackburn were on charitable relief; the suffering in Accrington could have been no less. Despite the damage being inflicted on Britain's cotton industry – not to mention the terrible hardship being imposed on its workforce – the British government took the decision that Britain's interests in the longer term were better served by keeping out of the war. The distress in Lancashire saw some relief through a dramatic increase in imports of Indian cotton – a change that ironically would eventually have dire consequences for the Lancashire industry – but continued into 1865 when the war finally came to end with the surrender of the Confederate army.

By 1871, John and Sarah had returned to Accrington, where they were living in a terraced house in Maudsley Street with their 2-year-old son, Thomas Edward. John, employed as a cotton mill labourer, would have struggled to support his young family adequately; Lancashire mill owners had cut wages by 10 per cent in 1869 and, given John's undoubted strength of character, it is not surprising that he joined thousands of other Lancashire spinners and weavers who had been encouraged by their unions to emigrate to the United States.

Economic migration from Lancashire to the textile manufacturing centres of New England was hardly a new phenomenon by the 1870s; as early as the 1850s it was said of the Massachusetts towns of New Bedford and Fall River that Lancashire immigrants 'abounded as nowhere else'. By the mid-1870s, English immigrants made up 34 per cent of the workforce in Fall River, where the cotton textile workforce had quadrupled in the ten years following the end of the war to satisfy a massive increase in demand for inexpensive cotton clothing.

John and Sarah's second child, Henry (Harry), was born in April 1872, and it seems that later that year John set out alone for America in order to establish himself before sending for his family to join him; Sarah, Thomas and Harry followed early in the next year, reaching New York on the SS *Egypt* on 11 February 1873. The Harwoods' time in America brought advancement for John as he rose to become foreman of the winding, warping and slashing department of a Fall River mill. It also brought joy in the birth of the couple's only daughter, Lily, in December 1874; yet tragedy too had already touched the family with the death of Harry in November 1873. Despite the opportunities afforded by life in America at a time of great industrial expansion, John remained there for no more than four years. At this distance, we can only guess at John's decision to transplant his family for a second time. While it is certainly true that a fresh opportunity presented itself elsewhere, John may well have lost his motivation to further his career in Fall River because of the business practices prevalent there at the time. The business model of the Fall River mill owners in the 1870s was to dominate the market by producing high volumes of cotton fabrics at the lowest possible cost, a strategy that depended for its success on the mill owners' ability to crush what they regarded as the 'chronic insubordination' of their English workers; in turn, the workers held their masters in contempt for producing textiles that relied on the cloth printing process to disguise their poor quality. Matters came to a head in 1875; although the Fall River mill owners were forced to back down from their first attempt to cut wages, they eventually prevailed when a strike of nearly 15,000 workers in 34 mills crumbled. It was about this time that the Harwoods left America in order for John to take up an offer of work at a Bombay cotton mill. John left his wife, son and daughter in the care of his mother and her family in Accrington while he went on to India. Although Sarah would join him a short time later, Thomas and Lily remained in England for their education.

Imports into Britain of Indian cotton had fallen away again as the cotton-growing states of the American south resumed exports when the civil war ended in 1865. At a time when Manchester's lobbying for a better quality of Indian cotton was finally being acted upon, the sudden surplus of home-grown cotton acted as a stimulus for the development of India's own textile industry. For the industry to grow at a rapid rate, however, it would need experienced technicians of the likes of John Harwood.

Whereas the Indian textile industry had its beginnings in and around the port city of Bombay (present-day Mumbai), associations were soon created to build mills in cotton-growing centres deep inside the Indian subcontinent. Located 700 miles to the north-east of Bombay, the city of Cawnpore (Kanpur) is naturally favoured by its central location in the fertile Gangeatic plain, and to the extensive area of black cotton soil to its south. Its growth however was established only in the early nineteenth century after the East India Company recognized the strategic importance of its location on the banks of the Ganges River and developed it into a military base. The completion of a direct rail connection to Allahabad in 1859 aided the development of Cawnpore, and by the 1860s the city had become an important industrial and commercial centre; one author writes that 'carts laden with cotton crowded into [Cawnpore] until roads became blocked and bales were stacked higher than the roofs of the houses'. It was not long before the Cawnpore Cotton Committee saw an opportunity to produce cotton goods close to the source of the raw material, instead of shipping its cotton elsewhere to be converted; on 8 December 1864, the foundation stone was laid for the first mill building of the Elgin Cotton Spinning and Weaving Company on the banks of the Ganges.

It was to take up the position of weaving master at the Elgin Mills – and thereby to take a further step forward in his career – that induced John

Harwood to leave Bombay for Cawnpore in 1880. This was the move that would take John's ambitions to 'make good' to an altogether higher level. After spending only two years at Elgin, John somehow arranged sufficient funds to enable him to leave his employment there in 1882 in order to found the Cawnpore Cotton Mills; on 4 July 1885, the Harwoods' eighteenth wedding anniversary, Sarah started up the first engine of the new mill.

John was later to recall how he had started with a floor shed containing 100 looms, and as he became successful added another storey above, and started another 100 looms. When his competitors attempted to stifle his business by refusing to sell him yarn, he travelled to Allahabad to buy yarn at a 12 per cent premium in order to keep going. From then on, he was able to raise more capital, building a further three spinning mills, each with a greater capacity than the last. John sourced all the carding machinery and ring–spinning for three of the four mills from the Globe Works of Howard and Bullough in Accrington, and only a lack of capacity forced the company to turn down the contract for the fourth mill. By the end of the nineteenth century, the spinning capacity of the four mills was surpassed by only two rivals in the whole of India.

At the time of John's arrival in Cawnpore, less than a quarter of a century had passed since the city had witnessed the most notorious of the atrocities perpetrated during the Indian Mutiny of 1857: the massacre of some 200 British women and children in a building called the Bibighur and the subsequent British reprisals. It is no surprise that John threw himself enthusiastically into the activities of the Cawnpore Volunteer Rifle Corps, a body of British and Anglo–Indian men which had been formed after the Mutiny to provide support to the official forces in the event of another emergency. Indeed, John is credited with having founded the Volunteers' Club: comprising reading and smoking rooms, a music room, a ballroom and a bar, the club quickly established itself as the social centre for the expatriate community of Cawnpore. The club regularly held shooting competitions, and John even organized an annual competition against Accrington riflemen, the competitors' scores being transmitted by post!

Sarah gave birth to three more children during the couple's time in India – Mary, born in 1881, John in 1883 and Jack in 1887 – but none seems to have survived beyond infancy. By 1890, their eldest child, 21-year-old Thomas Edward, had joined them and was employed at the Cawnpore Cotton Mills as an assistant manager; the mills had also found employment for John's elder brother, Edward (mill master), and their nephew, Richard (spinning master). Another nephew, Henry, had also come out to India as an engineer and, on 21 October 1890, a double wedding took place at Bowen Methodist Episcopal Church in Bombay as Thomas and Henry married two Lancashire girls, Margaret Ingham and Mary Hannah Mills.

By 1895, John was not only managing director of the Cawnpore Cotton Mills – which proudly advertised itself as 'sole manufacturers in India for

Stromeyer's patent porous waterproof cloths' – but vice-chairman of Cawnpore Municipality, and a captain in the Volunteer Rifle Corps. His son, Thomas Edward, had reached the rank of lieutenant in the Rifle Corps, and was employed as mill manager for the Aryodaya Spinning and Weaving Company Limited in Ahmedabad.

The 1890s saw the appearance of a new generation of the Harwood family. Thomas Edward and Margaret had two children born at Cawnpore, Thomas Yates, on 25 November 1891, and John Richard, in 1895. Henry and Mary Hannah had three children, Katherine Evelyn (Katie), born at Cawnpore, Edmund Mills, born at Accrington on 22 September 1894, and Frank, born at Delhi on 14 August 1896.

John continued to run the Cawnpore Cotton Mills until his retirement at the early age of 50 in 1898, at which point he and Sarah returned to Accrington to live at Jesmond House on Hartmann Street. On leaving the Volunteer Rifle Corps, he was given permission to retain the rank of captain, and to wear the uniform of the Corps. Only a short time passed before John was ready to travel once more, and the winter of 1899–1900 saw him embark on a round-the-world trip via India, China and the United States in the company of his close friend, Major Richard Sharples. During their time in India, they spent a whole month in Cawnpore, staying at Thomas Edward's bungalow. Shortly after their departure from India, John wrote with his characteristic dry humour:

> We left Cawnpore on Sunday, the 14th January [1900] at 10am, and a whole crowd of friends came to the station to see us off, and I believe were sorry to part with us, though one Accrington lad did say, when shaking hands with Captain [*sic*] Sharples, that 'he was glad to have the pleasure of seeing us off', which was to say the least of it equivocal.

On his return to Accrington, John found himself unable to enjoy life in retirement. Not only did he successfully seek election to Accrington Town Council as a Conservative in November 1900, but he also acquired fresh business interests by becoming chairman of directors at Lang Bridge Limited of Accrington and a director of Henry Livesey Limited of Blackburn. Local sport commanded his attention too: John took on the presidency of Accrington Stanley Football Club which joined the Lancashire Combination for the 1900–1 season. Each year, John awarded a set of medals to the non-reserve side which finished highest in the league, an honour that the Stanley players were to receive on several occasions. The highlight of his presidency came in the 1902–3 season when Stanley became the first non-reserve side to win the league championship; considering that the Lancashire Combination contained the reserve teams of leading First Division clubs, it was an outstanding achievement.

Chapter 2

On the Verge of War

The divergent fortunes of Turkey and Germany in the late nineteenth century led to a situation in which war, if not inevitable, became considerably easier for the European powers to justify.

The decline of the Ottoman Empire, hastened by an upsurge in Balkan nationalism and Russian aggression, led through the 1878 Treaty of Berlin to the creation of the independent states of Romania, Serbia and Montenegro; Bulgaria gained autonomy while Bosnia and Herzogovina were occupied by Austria-Hungary. In 1908, the Russian Foreign Minister, Alexander Izvolsky, and his Austrian counterpart, Count Alois von Aehrenthal, discussed mutually beneficial amendments to the treaty, including Russian tolerance of an Austrian annexation of Bosnia and Herzogovina in return for Austrian acceptance of the opening of the Bosphorus Strait to the Russian Black Sea Fleet. In the event, Austria succeeded in its aims to annex Bosnia – bringing neighbouring Serbia to the brink of war in the process – while failing to back Russia whose subsequent and lasting sense of betrayal would contribute to the acceleration into war six years later. Serbia, with her own dreams of territorial expansion, posed a constant threat to Austria. It was a threat to which the Chief of the Austrian General Staff, Count Franz Conrad von Hötzendorf, saw preventive war as the only solution; allegedly he demanded war with Serbia twenty-five times in 1913 alone but was restrained by Aehrenthal and the heir presumptive to the Austro-Hungarian throne, Franz Ferdinand.

Germany, in contrast, was a power on the rise: unification of the German states under Kaiser Wilhelm I after Prussia's victory over France in the war of 1870–1 had been followed by consolidation through a Triple Alliance forged in the years 1879–82 with Austria-Hungary and Italy. Entering the twentieth century, Germany's ambition was at a much higher level: to rival Great Britain as a world power. It was an ambition – most blatantly displayed in the massive expansion from 1888 of Germany's Imperial Navy driven by Kaiser Wilhelm II – that led Britain ultimately to form alliances with Japan (1902), France (1904) and Russia (1907). To successive Chiefs of the German General Staff, however, the threat to Germany's ambitions lay in the new armaments programmes of both France and Russia. In the spring of 1914, the German Foreign Minister,

Gottlieb von Jagow, was reportedly told by the Chief of the General Staff, Helmuth von Moltke, that within two or three years the

> military superiority of our enemies would . . . be so great that he did not know how he could overcome them. Today we would still be a match for them. In his opinion there was no alternative to making preventive war in order to defeat the enemy while there was still a chance of victory. The Chief of the General Staff therefore proposed that I should conduct a policy with the aim of provoking a war in the near future.

In short, the summer of 1914 found the European powers trapped in a web of mutual loathing and fear. All that was needed was an excuse to go to war, and on 28 June 'the most famous wrong-turning in history' provided it.

In between articles looking forward to the next season for Haslingden Football Club and 'Personal Gossip', the *Accrington Observer and Times* of 30 June 1914 reported the assassination two days previously of Franz Ferdinand and his morganatic wife, Sophie, in the Bosnian capital of Sarajevo:

> The Archduke had paid no heed to warnings to him not to go to Bosnia on account of the disturbed state of the province. Anti-Austrian demonstrations were made before his arrival at Sarajevo on Saturday. Two attempts were made to kill the Archduke and his wife at Sarajevo on Sunday. The first failed. The second was only too successful. A 21-year-old printer of Serbian nationality, living in Herzogovina, threw a bomb at the Archduke's motor car in the street. The Archduke deflected the bomb with his arm. It fell to the ground and exploded. The heir to the throne and his wife escaped, but eleven other people were injured, six of them seriously. A little while later the Archduke and his wife were driving to see the victims of the bomb explosion when a student, aged nineteen, apparently also of [Serbian] nationality, fired at them with a Browning automatic pistol. Both were wounded and both died shortly afterwards.

The successful assassination was a matter of atrocious luck: the driver of the Archduke's car had taken a wrong turning on the way to the hospital and, while attempting to reverse, came to a halt within a few yards of one of the six members of *Mlada Bosnia* (Young Bosnia) who was armed for an assassination attempt; Gavrilo Princip drew his pistol and fired the two fatal shots.

With the death of Franz Ferdinand at the hands of an organization that undoubtedly had had the support of the pan-Serb society *Crna Ruka* (Black Hand), the Austrian government had the pretext to provoke a war with Serbia which it expected to win decisively and rapidly. Not only was Franz Ferdinand no longer around to argue for restraint, but when Austria sought the support of

Germany on 5 July, Wilhelm II and the German Chancellor, Theobald von Bethmann Hollweg, gave their agreement.

On 23 July, Austria delivered an ultimatum to Serbia which demanded that all anti-Austrian propaganda be condemned and suppressed, that all Serbian officers and officials who had engaged in such propaganda be dismissed, that the Serbian nationalist organization, *Narodna Odbrana* (The People's Defence), be dissolved, and that Austrian officials be allowed to take part in the suppression process and in the prosecution of those involved in the assassination conspiracy of 28 June. The deadline for reply was 6pm on 25 July. Just 10 minutes before the deadline expired, Serbia replied, yielding to practically all of Austria's demands, and rejecting only the involvement of Austrian officials in the investigation into the conspiracy.

Wilhelm now backed away from war, describing Serbia's acquiescence as 'a brilliant achievement in a time-limit of only 48 hours! It is more than one could have expected! A great moral success for Vienna; but with it all reason for war is gone . . .' Wilhelm's hopes of averting war were short-lived: the German Minister of War, Erich von Falkenhayn, told him that 'he no longer had control of the affair in his own hands'.

Austria rejected Serbia's response to its ultimatum and, on 28 July, declared war. Russia, whose Foreign Minister, Sergei Sazonov, had already made it clear that his country would not stand aside in the event that Serbia was threatened, began to mobilize on the following day, just as the Serbian capital of Belgrade began to come under shellfire. On 30 July, Russia moved to full mobilization, finally giving the German military the pretext to mobilize against both Russia and France. The politicians had by now lost all control of events: von Bethmann Hollweg, belatedly realizing the scale of the impending confrontation, frantically tried to reign in the Austrian army; it was to no avail.

At this point in time, Britain was by no means committed to supporting either France or Russia. While the Foreign Secretary, Sir Edward Grey, was in favour of intervention in a European war – seemingly because he was convinced of the threat to Britain from Germany should France be defeated – he was supported only by the First Lord of the Admiralty, Winston Churchill, when the British Cabinet convened on 31 July. Of the other seventeen Cabinet members who met that Friday, at least five argued for an immediate declaration of neutrality.

Reading through the pages of the *Accrington Observer and Times* for July 1914, it is difficult to build a picture of a town overly concerned with the prospect of war in Europe. In fact, the townspeople had more pressing problems to contend with. Accrington's prosperity had been built on the spinning and weaving of cotton, but by 1914 the industry was already in decline. For all too many, pleasurable anticipation of the annual Wakes holiday, brought forward in 1914 to the last week in July, had been ruined not just by the awareness that many cotton mills would stay shut for a further week because of a shortage of orders, but also by the calamitous ongoing lock-out at Howard and Bullough's machine works, the town's major employer. Following the refusal of Howard and Bullough's management to meet the demands of the Amalgamated Society of Engineers (ASE) for trade-union recognition and a minimum wage, up to 600 engineers at the works had gone on strike on 2 July. In response, 6 days later, the management locked out the whole workforce of nearly 5,000 men and boys. Although members of the ASE received £1 per week lock-out pay while on strike and 1,100 members of the Gasworkers and General Labourers Union received 10s a week, some 2,000 non-union workers had been left without any income.

As late as 1 August, the *Accrington Observer and Times* carried a lengthy article under the headline 'On the Verge of War' without alerting the casual reader to the reality that Britain stood on the brink of being drawn in to the European crisis; one small paragraph reported that the War Office had inquired of the Accrington Corps of the St John Ambulance Brigade how many of its members might be willing to serve with a British expeditionary force, while another commented that around 10,000 men of the Special Reserve were being mobilized for service at home.

On that same day, France, Germany and Belgium all mobilized, while Germany declared war on Russia. The Tough family of Accrington would see more than its fair share of tragedy in the coming years, but for now it was a time of great excitement for Margaret (Peg), the oldest of the three daughters of William Robb Tough, a general practitioner. Travelling through France, Peg had reached Dinon when France announced mobilization; in a letter to her father, she wrote: 'The scene outside the Town Hall that evening was one we shall always remember, the crowds cheering and singing the three National Anthems – French, Russian and English. The way the French shook hands with the English visitors, and got so excited was so very foreign to us.' Even if Britain was far from committing herself to war, France was clearly fully expecting her support. Two days later, France and Germany declared war on each other.

Germany's strategy for victory was to concentrate her armies for a rapid thrust through Belgium and north-west France, passing to the west of Paris before turning to crush the French armies; victory within the space of six weeks would allow time to switch the focus of attack to the Eastern Front where the Russian armies posed less of an immediate threat. The strategy has come to be known as the Schlieffen Plan, the name originating from a memorandum written by Alfred von Schlieffen, probably in 1906 shortly after his retirement as Chief of the Imperial German General Staff, though it was subsequently modified by von Moltke. Critical to the success of the Schlieffen Plan was the ability of the German armies to move through Belgium practically without hindrance.

On 2 August, under the pretext that France intended to advance against Germany through Belgium, Germany demanded free passage of her own troops through the country in order to pre-empt the supposed French attack. In fact, while France did have an offensive plan – the so-called Plan XVII – it concentrated on an advance into Alsace and Lorraine, the two regions that had been lost in the war of 1870–1. On 3 August, Belgium rejected Germany's ultimatum. In the end it was Germany's contempt for Belgian neutrality, a status that had been guaranteed by the major European powers in the 1839 Treaty of London, which reversed the mood of the British Cabinet. On the morning of 4 August, the Belgian Legation in London reported that German forces had entered Belgium at Gemmenich. The British government demanded an assurance from Germany before midnight that Belgian neutrality would be respected; as no such assurance had been received by 11pm (Greenwich Mean Time, one hour behind Central European Time), Britain declared war on Germany.

Chapter 3

Why Not Accrington?

If the prospect of Britain's involvement in a European war was not at the forefront of the minds of Accrington folk in the last days of July 1914, that surely changed in the afternoon of Monday, 3 August when Accrington men belonging to the local territorial battalion, 5/East Lancashire, returned home from camp a week earlier than planned. Artillerymen from the 5th (Church) Battery of 1st East Lancashire Brigade, Royal Field Artillery (RFA) Territorial Force, also returned from camp having left town only two days previously. That same evening, more than fifty men of the Accrington Corps of the St John Ambulance Brigade volunteered for service in the event of war. Shortly after 7pm on Tuesday, 4 August, 4 hours before Britain declared war on Germany, the War Office order summoning the Reserves, the Territorials and the Ambulance men to report to their respective depots reached Accrington: within a short time, notices had been posted all round the town. Thousands of people crowded the streets in the vicinity of the depots in the expectation that the men would be leaving town immediately but dispersed once the men were dismissed at around 9pm.

An enthusiastic crowd numbering more than a thousand assembled in the area of Accrington railway station on the following morning to see nearly a hundred ex-Regular Reservists leave town on the 8.49am train for London. The Territorials' turn to leave came shortly after 8am on Thursday when they marched from the Drill Hall at Bull Bridge up Whalley Road, along Queens Road and on to battalion headquarters at Burnley. On Friday, 7 August, crowds again lined the streets of Accrington, this time to watch 100 khaki-clad Ambulance men march from the Drill Hall to the railway station where they left on the 10.35am train for Euston. It was said that:

> there was much waving of arms and hats and handkerchiefs from the carriage windows, and shouting of departing words. There was a hearty response from the crowd, both vocally and by waving of hand-kerchiefs and hats. Then as the train got up speed there was a general cheer. It was a hearty send-off, although there were sorrowful faces among the womenfolk and not a few tears.

Accrington was at war.

In London, meanwhile, the government was trying to come to terms with its role in the developing conflict. The British Army, though highly professional, was in terms of size wholly inadequate for the purpose of fighting a European war: the Regular Army comprising 247,000 men of all ranks, 79,000 of whom were in India, could be reinforced with 416,000 ex-Regular Reservists, Territorials and Special Reserve. By comparison, France and Germany could each put more than 4 million men into battle. On 5 August, the Prime Minister, Herbert Henry Asquith, addressed a particularly thorny yet critical issue by persuading 64-year-old Field Marshal Earl Kitchener of Khartoum to accept the post of Secretary of State for War. Asquith would have preferred Viscount Haldane in the role: Haldane had after all established both the Territorial Force and the British Expeditionary Force (BEF) while holding the post from 1905 to 1912. Haldane, however, was scurrilously accused by the press of pro-German sympathies while Kitchener's status as a national hero ensured public support for the government. At the first War Council meeting on 5 August, Lieutenant General Douglas Haig, at that time commander designate of I Army Corps at the age of 53, argued for immediate action to create a million-strong Army in readiness for a war lasting several years. It took Kitchener, however, to drive through the necessary rapid expansion of the Army.

On the day following the first War Council meeting, the House of Commons granted the Army the power to increase its strength further by no less than 500,000 men of all ranks. Two days later, on Saturday, 8 August, Accrington's newspapers carried Kitchener's emotive appeal: under the heading 'Your King & Country Need You' came the call for an additional hundred thousand men between the ages of 19 and 30 to join the Regular Army for a period of three years or until the war was concluded. By the Wednesday of the following week, a special recruitment office had been opened at the old Labour Exchange on Accrington's Union Street; between sixty and seventy men enlisted before the weekend.

Although the strike and lock-out at Howard and Bullough's had been displaced in the newspaper headlines by the latest developments in the war, the distress throughout Accrington occasioned by the long-running dispute had in no way diminished, and it was with some relief that the *Accrington Gazette* announced that the company intended to re-open its gates on Monday, 17 August for those who wished to return to work. By the time Monday came around, the engineers and plate moulders had decided to remain out on strike; pickets assembled at each entrance to the vast Globe Works, ready to harass non-union workers who were prepared to take the work of those on strike. Crowds of onlookers gathered in anticipation of trouble breaking out; they were not disappointed. Mounted police escorting around half-a-dozen men who left the works at 5.30pm came under attack from missiles thrown by the crowd while stones and bricks were later hurled against the men's houses. The dispute at Howard and

Bullough's would drag on until the engineers voted on Tuesday, 20 October to return to work, fifteen weeks after the lock-out began.

The German strategy of winning a rapid and decisive victory in the West before switching to the offensive in the East unravelled during the month of August. While the German right wing carved a passage of destruction through Belgium, valuable time was lost in overcoming the resistance of the fortresses of Namur and Maubeuge. It was von Moltke's reaction to events on the Eastern Front, however, that arguably completely undermined the Schlieffen Plan: as the pincer-like advance of the Russian First and Second armies into East Prussia threatened to engulf the German Eighth Army, von Moltke weakened his right wing in the West by stripping out two corps and sending them East. To the south of the main German thrust on the Western Front, the French Plan XVII conspicuously failed to meet with success: offensives by the French First and Second armies in Alsace-Lorraine were driven back, as were attacks by the Third and Fourth armies in the Ardennes. Commanded by Field-Marshal Sir John French, the BEF, comprising I Corps (Haig) and II Corps (Smith-Dorrien), had begun to disembark in France on 7 August, and by 20 August had concentrated on the extreme left of the French line where it lay directly in the path of the German First Army (von Kluck). On 23 August the BEF went into action at Mons, blunting the enemy advance before being compelled to withdraw as a gap opened up between it and the French Fifth Army (Lanrezac). At Le Cateau, three days later, the British II Corps again inflicted heavy losses on the enemy in a desperate rearguard action. Any lingering hopes that von Moltke may have harboured of pushing to the west of Paris were ended on 29 August when a counter-attack by Lanrezac against the German Second Army (von Bülow) at Guise induced von Kluck to turn inwards and to the east of the French capital.

On the Eastern Front, the Central Powers were having mixed fortunes: while 66-year-old General Paul von Hindenburg, having taken over command of the German Eighth Army on 22 August, destroyed the Russian Second Army at Tannenberg only a few days later, the early successes of von Hötzendorf's Austro-Hungarian offensive into Russian Poland had been countered by a victory by the Russian Third and Eighth armies at Gnila Lipa. Serbia, meanwhile, had repulsed the Austrian invasion that had begun on 12 August.

While Kitchener's call to arms sufficed to kick-start the recruitment campaign, something more was needed to stimulate voluntary enlistment on the scale that was necessary to provide Britain with an army capable of winning a continental war. The concept of raising whole companies, if not battalions, from a single community was nothing new; it was already commonplace in Territorial battalions such as 5/East Lancashire. The twist that was introduced in August 1914 was the promise – regardless of Kitchener's insistence on recruitment directly into the Regular Army rather than into the Territorials –

that recruits would serve together with their friends and workmates. The first battalion to be formed on such a basis was probably 10/Royal Fusiliers: recruited from London City office workers between 21 and 27 August it was popularly known as the Stockbrokers' Battalion. Yet it was the industrial towns of the north of England that proved to be the most fertile recruitment grounds for 'Pals battalions', a term that seems to have been coined by Lord Derby on 28 August at a public meeting to recruit a battalion from the commercial and shipping houses of Liverpool. By 4 September, Liverpool had provided enough volunteers to fill not one battalion but three; Manchester followed by taking little more than a fortnight to raise four Pals battalions by 16 September.

As the BEF came into action at Mons and Le Cateau, the *Accrington Observer and Times* published an emotive article under the byline of T Clayton which used news of the fighting to bring pressure on the strikers at Howard and Bullough's to return to work:

> Men of Bullough's, what are you doing in this time of stress and trial? Shall I tell you the plain and unvarnished truth? You are daily wasting bright golden hours in registering yourselves at your club house. You are sitting on your heels on the kerbstones twiddling your thumbs. You are propping up the railings of the Ambulance Hall. You are trapesing aimlessly through the already too crowded streets. You are lounging, sitting and standing near the war office in Dutton-street discussing tactics and methods of a warfare in which you will not, either with hammer or gun, play your part for the honour of your country.

The same issue of the newspaper carried a letter to the editor from 'A Patriot' urging Accrington to follow the examples set by Liverpool and Manchester of raising battalions of local men at their own expense: 'We hear of great numbers of men coming forward in different parts of the country, and Manchester is earning itself distinction for the readiness of its men to offer themselves. Why not Accrington?' John Harwood would certainly have read this letter from 'A Patriot' with some interest. Indeed, his mind was probably already working on similar lines and, on 31 August, two days after the letter was published, he telegraphed the War Office with an offer to raise a half-battalion from the Accrington district.

Events now moved rapidly. Harwood's initiative in taking the first steps towards the formation of a local battalion was brought up by Captain Dr Andrew Gordon Watson at a meeting of the North-East Lancashire Squadron of the Legion of Frontiersmen at the Bull Hotel, Burnley on the evening of Thursday, 3 September. Chairing the meeting, Arthur Chambers Robinson, a 52-year-old Territorial officer, suggested that – as the Burnley battalion of the Territorials was essentially complete – Burnley might raise one or more Pals companies which could combine with those from Accrington. In contrast to Harwood, it seems that the mayor of Burnley, Alderman James Sellers Kay, had little enthusiasm for raising a local battalion: Robinson reported that after approaching the mayor with the idea, he had had no further word from him.

On 5 September, the Army Council replied to Harwood, stating that an offer of less than a full battalion could not be accepted. This now left Harwood with a difficult decision. The local recruitment pool had already been severely depleted with more than 500 volunteers from Accrington having been passed for service since the outbreak of war, and he could not have been certain of his ability to raise a full battalion of 1,100 men from Accrington and district alone. It would have been out of character for Harwood to back down, however, and, after conferring with other town officials, he raised his offer on Sunday, 6 September to one of a complete battalion. In doing so, Harwood must have accepted that to be sure of making his offer good, he would have to extend recruitment for the battalion to outside of the Accrington area, and doubtless was quick to make approaches to the officials in neighbouring towns. On Monday, 7 September, Harwood was able to report to Accrington Town Council that he had received word from Harold Baker, Member of Parliament for Accrington, that his offer had been accepted by the Army Council.

Among the conditions imposed by the Army Council, enlistment was to be for three years or for the duration of the war, and generally restricted to men aged between 19 and 35 years; old soldiers could be accepted at up to 45 years of age, while for certain ex-non-commissioned officers (NCOs) an upper age limit of 50 applied. No special privileges or considerations were to be given to the battalion, and Harwood – as raiser of the battalion – was to take full responsibility for clothing, housing and feeding the recruits, and to arrange for their local training. As a consequence, the recruits would have to be trained locally with most being billeted at their homes. The new battalion was initially designated as the 7th (Accrington) Battalion, East Lancashire Regiment.

Harwood was probably greatly relieved when, as early as Monday, 8 September, he received an offer from Captain James Clymo Milton to provide 250 men from Chorley. On the evening of the following day, at a meeting organized by the Legion of Frontiersmen to start a Pals movement at Burnley, it was reported that Harwood was looking to recruit 'about half a battalion' from outside of Accrington: some fifty to sixty of those attending the meeting indicated their intention to join.

Before the week was out, Harwood had motored to Chester to meet with the General Officer Commanding-in-Chief for Western Command, Lieutenant General Sir William Henry Mackinnon. Mackinnon formally approved the arrangements made for recruiting the Accrington battalion, and agreed to the first provisional officer appointments: in command of the battalion would be Richard Sharples, Harwood's closest friend in Accrington and now 64 years of age;

the senior captain and acting adjutant would be 48-year-old George Nicholas Slinger who, like Sharples, was an Accrington solicitor; 38-year-old Accrington general practitioner Dr Andrew Gordon Watson was appointed surgeon captain; and 31-year-old Philip John Broadley, a printer and stationer from Clayton-le-Moors, and James Clymo Milton, a 45-year-old solicitor from Chorley, were each ranked captain. All five officers had previously served with the Territorials. The absence of any officer candidates from Burnley is perhaps explained by the fact that hopes were still being voiced of Burnley raising a Pals battalion of its own.

It was around this time, perhaps even during the meeting with Mackinnon, that Harwood learned the news that Sharples was later to describe as a 'bombshell', the raising of the height standard for recruits to 5ft 6in. Sharples was quoted as being 'rather distressed about [the news], since the people in the Lancashire cotton districts were, perhaps, not quite so sturdy and massive as those in the more agricultural districts'.

Recruitment for the battalion – now being referred to as the Accrington and District Pals Battalion – began on Monday, 14 September when recruiting offices opened at Accrington, Church, Oswaldtwistle, Clayton-le-Moors, Rishton, Great Harwood, Burnley and Blackburn. It was reported that in the 3 hours between 2pm and 5pm, 104 men enlisted while many more failed to meet the minimum physical standards: 52 of those who enlisted were from Accrington, 3 from Church and Oswaldtwistle, 8 from Clayton-le-Moors, 19 from Rishton, 4 from Great Harwood, 14 from Burnley and 4 from Blackburn. That evening Harwood and Sharples travelled to Chorley to address a meeting at the Town Hall to recruit for a Chorley Pals company to form part of the Accrington battalion. Harwood was quoted as saying that he made 'no apology for coming to Chorley' to plead for the Pals' Company: amidst laughter and applause he told of how nearly half a century ago he had robbed the town of the finest girl in the place; he and his wife had been pals together for nearly forty-eight years, and he had always held the town in very high respect. The recruiting office at Chorley opened on the following day.

Each recruit to the battalion was posted to one of four companies which, following normal practice, were designated as A, B, C and D. Less conventionally, each company was also referred to by a geographical label, so that A Company was also known as Accrington Company, B Company as District Company, C Company as Chorley Company (Chorley Pals), and D Company as Burnley Company (Burnley Pals). The labels would create confusion over the geographical make-up of the battalion which continues today. Taking each town as including its surrounding areas, the breakdown given in the regimental history is as accurate as any: two companies came from Accrington, three platoons from Burnley, three from Chorley and two from Blackburn.

At Burnley, 50-year-old Raymond St George Ross, an ex-Territorial officer employed as analytical chemist for the borough, had been appointed temporary recruiting officer for the station which opened at the Drill Hall in Bank Parade. It was as evident at Burnley as it was elsewhere that the higher physical standards were preventing large numbers of men from enlisting, and Harwood was quick to telegraph the War Office to request that an exception be made for his battalion so as not to delay its completion. On Thursday, 17 September, Harwood was able to announce that the War Office would allow him to recruit under the previous minimum standards: a height of 5ft 3in, and a chest measurement of 34in.

Harwood's other major problem was one that bedevilled all the battalions of Kitchener's New Armies: a lack of officers and NCOs with military experience. Harwood's only recourse was to recruit his junior officers from prominent local families, and on the Thursday evening he forwarded recommendations for twelve young local men to be granted commissions in the battalion. While most had little or no experience of the Army, they were for the most part professional men, respected and liked by those who knew them: Harry Bury, a 22-year-old commercial traveller, Walter Henry Cheney, a 38-year-old of independent means, Thomas Yates Harwood, a grandson of John Harwood and, at 22 years old, a bank cashier, Sydney Haywood, a 23-year-old marine engineer, Anton Peltzer, an 18-year-old commercial traveller, James Ramsbottom, a 28-year-old builder and contractor, Arnold Bannatyne Tough, a 24-year-old dentist (all the above resident in Accrington), Harry Livesey, a 32-year-old director at a company making cotton weaving machines (Blackburn), Walter Roughley Roberts, a 27-year-old business proprietor (Blackburn), Frederick Arnold Heys, a 26-year-old solicitor (Oswaldtwistle), John Victor Kershaw, a 27-year-old architect and surveyor (Hapton), and Thomas Welburn Rawcliffe, a 20-year-old cotton cloth designer (Clayton-le-Moors).

By Friday evening, half the battalion was complete, with more than 500 men having enlisted. Accrington alone had contributed 250 and, after A Company was completed on the following day, Accrington men began to be posted to B Company. The recruits had already begun their training: at Accrington they assembled at the Ambulance Drill Hall on both Friday morning and afternoon before marching to Ellison's Tenement where they were put through a number of drills and manoeuvres under the interested gaze of a large number of spectators. Training relied greatly on the experience of former NCOs, men such as 52-year-old George Lee, 55-year-old Andrew Muir and 59-year-old Walter Stanton who were gratefully accepted into the battalion despite being over the prescribed age limit.

Born at Widecombe in Devon, George Lee left work as a farm labourer aged 16 to volunteer for Army service, and was with the 24th Regiment (South Wales Borderers) at Ulundi, the concluding battle of the Anglo-Zulu War, on 4 July

1879. Lee reached the rank of colour sergeant with 1/East Lancashire before being appointed drill instructor to The King's (Liverpool Regiment); after twenty-one years and twenty-three days in the Army, Lee retired to live in Accrington, only to re-join in July 1900 as temporary drill instructor to the local Territorials.

Andrew Brown Muir was a native of Maryhill, Scotland; brought to Clayton-le-Moors as a boy, he was apprenticed as a calico machine printer at Oakenshaw Works. Muir joined the local Volunteers – precursors of the Territorials – at the age of 17, reaching the rank of colour sergeant before his discharge in 1910. Just a few days after he joined Harwood's battalion, his son, 19-year-old Rifleman John Muir of 1/King's Royal Rifle Corps, died of wounds on 23 September 1914.

Walter Stanton was born in Accrington, and went out to America as a youth where it is said that he served with the United States Army. After returning to Britain, Stanton joined the 88th Regiment (Connaught Rangers) in November 1876, and held the rank of sergeant major for twelve and a half years. Stanton was described as a 'man of high principle, industrious and conscientious, a man who was looked up to and admired by all whose privilege it had been to meet him'. Temporarily appointed battalion sergeant major to the Pals, Stanton was replaced shortly after the battalion's completion by Colour Sergeant Shorrock.

The Burnley recruits meanwhile were being drilled daily at the Drill Hall in Bank Parade, and had been able to accompany the local Territorial battalion on a route march. The local newspaper described how the recruits were made up of a great diversity of trades and professions – a cotton manufacturer, underclothing manufacturer, surveyors', solicitors' and stockbrokers' clerks, book-keepers and other clerks, dentists, overlookers, linotype operator, foremen, architects, weavers, clothlookers and colliery employees.

The *Burnley Express* of 19 September carried an advertisement placed by 33-year-old Henry Davison Riley of a meeting to be held to discuss the possibility of raising a half-company for Harwood's battalion from the membership of the Burnley Lads' Club. Outside of his several business interests, Riley devoted much of his time to providing working class youths with opportunities to develop themselves through sport and education. In 1901 – prompted by the success of the Ancoats' Lads' Club in Manchester – Riley founded the Burnley Lads' Club, immediately taking on the post of Honorary Secretary. The Club's first premises amounted to three rooms over a stable in Chaffer Court, Adlington Street. By 1907, the Lads' Club had also taken over the old Foresters' Club in Lindsay Street and had a regular membership of 200; for an entrance fee of 2*d* and a membership fee of 1*d* per week, the Club provided a reading room, a large gymnasium, games rooms, five football teams, a cross-country team, a swimming club, a cricket club, a cycling club and an annual seaside camp. Increasingly pressed for space, the Club acquired the old Keighley

Green Police Station later in the year. From 1911, evening classes were offered in subjects such as English, mathematics and drawing. In addition to his work with the Burnley Lads' Club, Riley took an active interest in the Industrial School movement, and was a member of the Preston and Mid-Lancashire Discharged Prisoners' Aid Society. In August 1912, he was appointed a County Magistrate. His business interests extended beyond the Riley family's fancy cloth manufacturing business in Colne to include a directorship with R J Elliott & Co. Ltd, cigar manufacturers, of Huddersfield and Leicester, and membership of the Manchester Exchange. Riley would ultimately take seventy members of the Lads' Club with him into the battalion.

After two further days of recruiting, a total of 784 men had joined the battalion. D Company was about three-quarters complete, with B Company a little further behind, but C Company was still little more than half-complete. On the evening of the following day, Tuesday 22 September, a public meeting was held at St Paul's School, Brinscall to encourage recruitment into C Company. Chairing the meeting, Alderman William Henry Killick remarked on 'the magnificent progress made elsewhere in regard to recruiting, and said it would not do [for Chorley] to be behind in any respect'. A welcome forty-four recruits joined at Chorley that day, bringing C Company three-quarters the way to completion.

Remarkably, one week into the battalion's recruitment, hopes were still entertained in Burnley of forming a complete battalion from its own recruits. Any remaining thoughts along these lines were finally ended when it was reported that the Army Council had decided not to sanction the formation of any more Pals battalions, and it had to be accepted that the Burnley Pals would form part of Harwood's battalion.

In a letter addressed to Harold Baker on Tuesday 22 September, Harwood wrote that over 900 men had been sworn in by Tuesday night, and that he expected the battalion to be complete by the Wednesday evening or, at the latest, by Thursday morning. He informed Baker that he had recommended to Lieutenant General Mackinnon the appointment to the battalion of Captain Ross 'who is over-age – but as strong and healthy as a man of 40, and he has done splendid work in recruiting and drilling our Burnley detachment'. He also referred to his twelve nominations for first commissions as being 'all very efficient and suitable men for commissions being selected out of 20 or 30 applications'. Harwood would that evening send two further nominations to Mackinnon – Henry Riley and, from Accrington, Francis Geoffrey Macalpine, the 20-year-old youngest son of Sir George Macalpine – and was expecting two more nominations to come from Chorley to fill completely the vacancies for officers: these would prove to be 18-year-old William Geoffrey Morris Rigby, a dental student, and 27-year-old Charles William Gidlow-Jackson, a mechanical engineer. The position of quartermaster, along with the honorary rank of captain, was given to 62-year-old George Lay. Lay had enlisted as a 15-year-old into 59th Foot (2/East Lancashire) and had seen action at Ahmed Khel in 1880 during the Second Afghan War.

In reality, only A and B companies had been completely filled by the end of Thursday, 24 September; C and D companies took until the Saturday to fill their final few vacancies.

Harwood's battalion was finally complete, but what motivated its 1,100 men to volunteer for Army service? A number of factors can be identified.

Anger at Germany

While the British government used the violation of Belgian neutrality as justification for going to war, some historians have questioned its significance in boosting recruitment. Yet there is ample evidence to show that anger against Germany influenced recruitment into Harwood's battalion.

Fred Sayer (D Company) recollected that when as a 17-year-old in Burnley:

> One morning something snapped. I often thought that it was the arrogant move of the Kaiser and his gang, barging their way through Belgium in such a bellicose manner and breaking up the whole country, without so much as declaring a state of belligerency ... I was a jolly sort of peaceful fellow, happy to look after poorly folks and roam the moors at sunrise, but it just happened. I went to the Drill Hall and joined the Pals. I grew two years older, in two minutes, and was carefully examined, not only by the doctors, but also by Mr Ross himself. He gloated over my big hefty figure, prodding my sturdy legs and examined my feet. 'Very important Sayer. Feet!' 'You'll need them if you are to keep up with me! Ha! Ha!' He always finished any remark in this manner. Later on, I respected his joke, he used a horse, I walked!

Writing to his parents in March 1915, Sam Hardman (A Company), a 24-year-old teacher at St Andrew's Mission, Oswaldtwistle, remarked:

> when we, in England first received news of the awful things that were happening in Belgium, I began to think, and [the] more I thought, the more I felt it my duty to offer myself to do my share in fighting against that power which the Germans have craved for, but which is all-together opposite to the power of Jesus Christ which is Love.

The newspapers had certainly not spared their readers any lurid details when it came to describing the German advance through Belgium. The *Accrington*

Observer and Times of 19 September 1914 carried an article with the headline 'German Atrocities. Shocking Stories from Belgium':

> In the towns and villages where they stop they begin by requisition-ing food and drink, which they consume till intoxicated. Sometimes from the interior of deserted houses they let off their rifles at random, and declare that it was the inhabitants who fired. Then the scenes of fire, murder and especially pillage begin, accompanied by acts of deliberate cruelty, without respect to sex or age. Even where they pretend to know the actual person guilty of the acts they allege, they do not content themselves with executing him summarily, but they seize the opportunity to decimate the population, pillage the houses, and then set them on fire. After a preliminary attack and massacre, they shut up the men in the church, and then order the women to return to their houses and to leave their doors open all night.

Financial Hardship

Financial hardship incurred from the ongoing dispute at Accrington's Howard and Bullough's works affected the families of a large proportion of the town's male population, and was certainly a factor that favoured recruitment. On top of the military pay and billeting allowance which amounted to 21*s* per week, an additional incentive came when on 17 September the government announced an increase in the separation allowance payable weekly with effect from 1 October: a wife would receive 12*s* 6*d* each week (previously 11*s* 1*d*), for a wife with one to three children there was an additional allowance of 2*s* 6*d* per child (1*s* 9*d*), while a fourth child brought a further 2*s* (1*s* 2*d*).

The Pals Concept

There is no question that the Pals concept significantly boosted recruitment. Before Harwood took action to form a local battalion it was reported that about fifteen young men from the Accrington area had gone to Manchester to join the Pals battalion that was being organized there; perhaps this news even contributed towards Harwood's actions. On 3 September during the meeting in the Bull Hotel, Burnley, Robinson had remarked that a great number of young men in the town would offer their service but did not want to be separated.

Female Pressure

The story was told of a young lad being asked what his mother thought of him joining the Pals. 'Oh,' came the reply, 'she's quite proud of him. In fact, it was [mother] who acted as recruiting sergeant in my case!' Although this tale is apocryphal, there can be little doubt that women at both local and national level put pressure on men to join up. The *Accrington Observer and Times* of 8 September reported that, in the course of approaching over 500 male spectators at a football match at Ewood Park, Blackburn, a group of young women recruiters were subjected to 'much bustle and not a little insult' and were repeatedly told to 'go home and mend the stockings'.

The newspaper had earlier published an impassioned appeal by Lady Louise Selina Maxwell for Englishmen to take up arms for their country. Although her words make bizarre reading to later generations, the tone was not un-characteristic of the time:

> Must we feel ashamed to be Englishmen when we see you skulking at home, watching football or cricket matches, lying on the grass in the sun safe and secure – as you fondly delude yourselves while the manhood of Europe is shedding its blood on the battlefield. Awake!
>
> If you will not answer to the bugle call, at least let the women's voices call you out to fight for us and for our children. I am a woman, alas! and I cannot go. But my man has gone, and had I sons I would send every one forth to fight for England's sake!
>
> England needs you to save her liberty and to protect her shores. Oh, men, need one say more? Wives, give up your husbands. Mothers send forth your sons. It is time the women rose and bid you go, or they must hang their heads for very shame before the brave women of other countries, who have given their all for their country's sake. Awake! Awake! England needs her sons.

Chance of Adventure

It is inconceivable that the hundreds of thousands who flocked to join the colours in the first few weeks and months of the war would have done so had they known of the horrors of trench warfare that lay ahead.

In the early days of September, news of the fighting on the Western Front remained bleak. The BEF had fallen back across the Aisne by 30 August and four days later crossed the Marne, destroying the bridges behind them. On 3 September, German cavalry patrols pushed forward to within 8 miles of Paris. Yet on Tuesday, 8 September – alongside the news that an Accrington battalion was to be raised – the *Observer and Times* reported of Franco-British successes that had compelled the Germans to fall back. The inward turn of von Kluck's First Army to the east of Paris had left its right flank open to a counter-attack: on 5 September, the French Sixth Army (Maunoury) struck at the rear of the German First Army, forcing von Kluck to divert one corps after another to face Maunoury. The French Fifth Army and the BEF then struck at the gap that von Kluck's diversion had opened up between the German First and Second armies. By 10 September, the German right wing was in full retreat. On 15 September – the day after recruiting for Harwood's battalion opened – the *Observer and Times* reported:

> News of the German defeat [in what became known as the first Battle of the Marne] is said to be now filtering through to the great German cities, and is causing profound despair. Mobs are said to have assembled in many towns clamouring for accurate news. At Munich the newspaper offices have been closed through fear of riots. In Hamburg there is said to be something like a food famine. All works are stopped, and 1,600 ships are lying idle in harbour.

There was every reason to think that the war would be over rapidly. Even as late as 22 September, Captain Milton, addressing the recruitment meeting at Brinscall, remarked that 'Berlin was "on the spree" and if they were in the spree at the finish, say sometime next spring, they would not be in for a very bad time'.

By the time Harwood's battalion was complete any chance of a rapid and decisive victory on the Western Front had already been lost. Having re-crossed the Aisne, Haig's I Corps fought its way onto the dominating Chemin des Dames Ridge on 14 September. Had Haig been able to reach the ridge a couple of hours earlier, German resistance on the Aisne might have collapsed; as it was, the German VII Reserve Corps arrived in the nick of time to hold the ridge. Both sides dug-in to hold their hard-won positions.

The deadlock that was reached on the Chemin des Dames Ridge on 14 September marked the start of trench warfare that was to characterize the Western Front for the next three-and-a-half years.

Chapter 4

Very Badly Shaken

As the first Battle of the Marne drew to a close, the ailing von Moltke was replaced as Chief of the German General Staff by 53-year-old General Erich von Falkenhayn. There followed a phase of the war on the Western Front in which each side attempted to outflank the other: the so-called 'Race to the Sea' merely extended the line of trenches towards the English Channel. On 1 October the BEF was transferred north, shortening its lines of communication with the Channel ports.

The first Battle of Ypres that began on 19 October formed the last phase of the 'Race to the Sea' and saw Germany's final attempt of 1914 to break through the Allied front come desperately close to achieving success. The battle reached its critical point on Saturday, 31 October in the fight for the village of Gheluvelt which guarded the approach to Ypres along the Menin Road. Hubert Conway Rees, an officer who would later play a key role in the story of the Accrington Pals, was on this day a 32-year-old captain with 2/Welsh which held the line at Gheluvelt; B Company of the Welsh (Lieutenant Marshall) held 150yd of trench north of the Menin Road and on a forward slope 400yd east of the village, two platoons of D Company (Lieutenant Charles Alan Blackman Young) echeloned back along a hedge to their left, C Company (Captain Waldo Alington Gwennap Moore), less one platoon which was south of the road, held a small copse on the extreme left, battalion headquarters (47-year-old Lieutenant Colonel Charles Bernard Morland) along with one platoon of D Company (Rees) was in a sunken lane behind the trenches but in front of the village, with the last platoon of D Company kept as reserve along with two platoons of A Company. To the left of 2/Welsh, 1/South Wales Borderers held Gheluvelt Chateau while 1/Queens was to the right. In his memoirs, Rees gave a vivid account of the day's fighting:

> As soon as it became light [just after 6am], the storm broke. The trenches, the [sunken] lane and the village were deluged with shells of all calibres. It was impossible to move in the lane and many men were hit. After this bombardment had been going on for some considerable time, a few slightly wounded men from B Company

came in to say that Lieutenant Marshall had been killed and that practically the whole Company had been destroyed.

With the sunken lane being indefensible, Morland decided to pull the defensive line back to the front edge of the village at about 9.30am. After Young came in very badly wounded by a rifle bullet, Rees went forward to try to get back some of his men who by this time were in a hopeless position. After seeing a number of his men killed while attempting to cover around 50yd of open ground to reach the sunken lane, he realized the futility of his efforts, collected the more-or-less intact platoon of D Company from the village and tried to locate Morland:

> The shellfire around the barricade was very violent. Two shells burst in the house behind which I was sheltered, one cut the sign post neatly in half at the corner, another came through a wall about ten yards away and killed a man who was passing. Eventually I got away with about a dozen men, four of whom were carrying Young in a mackintosh sheet, and one man had a machine gun, of which the tripod had been blown to pieces and for which we had no ammunition.

Concluding that Morland had been forced to move further back, Rees led his men through the northern outskirts of Gheluvelt and finally arrived at the battery position of 54th Battery RFA (Major Edward John Russell Peel): 'I confess to being very badly shaken, the stock of my rifle had been shot through in two places and the strap of my water bottle cut . . . I remained with the guns for some time, collecting stragglers until I had about forty or fifty men.' At about 11.30am the enemy broke into Gheluvelt, overwhelming the Welsh. In a last, desperate attempt to recover the situation, Brigadier General Charles FitzClarence VC ordered 2/Worcestershire under 39-year-old Major Edward Barnard Hankey to 'advance without delay and deliver a counter-attack with the utmost vigour against the enemy'. Rees watched the Worcestershires advancing in line of companies through a heavy and accurate shrapnel fire before following them forward, eventually finding Morland who had been engaged in a desperate fight on the north side of Gheluvelt. Rees and Morland led the survivors of the Welsh back to the guns and into a trench near the battery. Rees was soon left in command of the few survivors of his battalion when a shell exploded immediately ahead of the trench killing instantly Captain Moore on his left and mortally wounding Morland on his right. Rees deployed the twenty-five men that remained in a thin firing line to protect the guns. Then 24-year-old Lieutenant Ralph Blewitt came forward from the guns with a request:

> Lieutenant Blewhitt [*sic*] of this battery came to say that the Germans appeared to be bringing up a gun to the barricade in the middle of

Gheluvelt and asked permission to take an 18-pounder on to the road and have a duel with it. Having got permission, he man-handled the gun out on to the road. The German gun fired first and missed and Blewhitt [*sic*] did not give them a second chance.

Blewitt was awarded the Distinguished Service Order (DSO) for this action.

In the meantime, 2/Worcestershire had succeeded in filling the gap between the northern edge of the village and 1/South Wales Borderers. The counter-attack had unbelievably proved sufficient to deter the enemy from renewing their attempts to capture the village. Rees remarked that 'If the Germans had pushed home their attack during the afternoon, there was nothing to stop them', while Haig three years later recalled how 'A German officer prisoner was very astonished and excited at seeing on his way to the rear no reserves at all! While he told us that the German reserves were standing in masses in the rear of the German front.'

The counter-attack by 2/Worcestershire at Gheluvelt was to have far-reaching consequences: Haig was never to forget that it would have taken the enemy just one more determined attack to force a breakthrough.

Rees relinquished command of 2/Welsh in January 1915 and returned to Britain, where he eventually joined the General Staff of 43rd (later 38th) Welsh Division. The division moved to France in November, where it took over the line first at Neuve-Chapelle and later at Festubert and Ginchy. On 13 June 1916, Rees returned from leave to find himself promoted to the rank of brigadier and, on the following day, he left for the Somme to take over command temporarily of 94 Infantry Brigade, just two weeks before the brigade was due to assault the fortress village of Serre.

Chapter 5

We Want to be There

In the early days of Harwood's battalion, its public drills evidently provided much amusement for idle spectators; a letter to the editor of the *Accrington Observer and Times* complained:

> Raw recruits want drilling, and even the elementary evolutions cannot be learned all at once. It has been very trying, therefore, for those who have assembled for drill on Ellison's Tenement to have heard the giggles of idle women and frivolous girls, mixed with the sneers of the supercilious men at the slightest misapprehension and mistake of a man or two.

On the afternoon of Saturday, 26 September, the battalion assembled on Ellison's Tenement in Accrington. While many of the men had already been provided with new boots, they were in civilian clothes, and would have to remain so for many weeks to come. Although one newspaper report implied that the entire battalion of 1,100 men was present, it has also been said that C Company, along with the Blackburn detachment, had, with Harwood's agreement, remained at home. At 4pm, led by the Accrington Old Band, the battalion set out on a march through the town's streets, the pavements of which were crowded with onlookers. On reaching the Town Hall the band stopped and played as the men marched past the mayor and other civic dignitaries. It is easy to imagine Harwood's pride at seeing so successful an outcome to an undertaking which he had begun less than four weeks previously with a telegram to the War Office, and perhaps we can forgive him a touch of smugness at raising a battalion ahead of the larger neighbouring towns of Blackburn and Burnley.

For as long as Harwood's battalion remained in east Lancashire, its companies trained separately in their home towns of Accrington, Burnley and Chorley, coming together only on rare occasions. In the absence of rifles, training activities in the early weeks of the battalion's life were limited to physical exercise, drill and marching. Although around 200 rifles were delivered to the battalion on 2 October, they were found to be outdated Lee-Metfords and useful only for drill purposes.

With the battalion complete, Harwood indicated his willingness to continue as mayor for a third term, perhaps a little surprisingly in view of the fact that twelve months previously he had agreed only with reluctance to remain in office for a second year. In the intervening time, the pressure of work had increased considerably: the dispute at Howard and Bullough's which had contributed greatly to the distress in Accrington had only just been resolved and, with the additional responsibilities brought on by the war, Harwood had been working at the Town Hall from 8.30am until 9.30pm day after day. While Harwood's readiness to continue as mayor may well have been 'received with the utmost pleasure by the vast majority of Accringtonians', as one local newspaper had it, he was not without his critics: the committee of the local Amalgamated Society of Tailors expressed their anger at Harwood's handling of the clothing contract for the battalion in a letter published in the *Accrington Observer and Times* of 3 October. The local Master Tailors had been under the impression that Harwood would order the battalion's clothing locally as long as the tendered price was within government guidelines. In the event, Harwood divided the orders for greatcoats between three suppliers, one a Leeds company with a local shop, the other two both local employers who had selectively been given the opportunity to revise their tenders downwards to meet the lower price offered by their Yorkshire competitors. Nevertheless, Harwood was unanimously re-elected as mayor on Monday, 9 November.

Clothing issues would rumble on for months to come. The uniforms were first expected to be ready on 15 November, yet it was a week later before a large number of men could be said to have been supplied with greatcoats, while a smaller number had received suits and kits. It was December before the men were 'practically all fully equipped'. Even then the uniforms were not khaki but temporary blue serge outfits which became known as 'Kitchener blue'.

Replying to an open letter from a Chorley Territorial which complained of the special attention being paid to the Pals – a theme that would run and run – one Pal vented his anger at the recompense for his services:

> Does [he] know we have been training now for about ten weeks without uniform, while [he] has [a] uniform [in which] to do his training? Again, is he aware that the East Lancashire 'Pals' Battalion is one of the worst paid battalions in the country? How is it that the married men of the Salford 'Pals' get 3s 11d per day, and how is it that the Manchester City Battalions got 7s 6d for taking their own overcoats? Also I am informed that the men of Kitchener's Army in the South of England are also being compensated for wear and tear of their own clothes, while we, up to the present, have not received anything for the wear and tear of our clothing. How would [he] like

to pay his own railway fare to go to his military training like a few of the 'Pals' have to do?

Within a short time, Harwood had issued the men 3s 11d per day with back pay; it is not clear why he had been slow to issue a clothing allowance, for as early as 8 September the War Office had sanctioned an allowance of 8s 6d – raised two days later to 10s – to be paid to each recruit who had to provide his own suit, boots and overcoat.

The Blackburn men, about ninety in number, who trained with the two Accrington companies also had a grievance concerning their transport to and from training. For three days in early December, they had been marching the 5 miles between Blackburn and Accrington in protest at the decision of Blackburn Tramways Committee to withdraw the Corporation's offer of free passage by tram because of the overcrowding and inconvenience to regular passengers that had occurred through the Pals – not unnaturally – all preferring to travel on the latest possible service. The issue was resolved when the authorities agreed to operate a special free service for the Pals leaving Blackburn at 8am and returning at 6pm.

The battalion's first appraisal by an outsider came on the morning of 5 November when it was inspected by Colonel Robert John Tudway commanding No. 3 District at Preston. It is said that Tudway poked one Pal in the ribs while asking him how long it would be before he was ready for the front; 'I am ready now, sir, and we want to be there' came the reply.

By early November, exercises in open warfare had been introduced into the training programme, with some predictably comical results. Fred Sayer recalled how all too many men of D Company were content to play dead during an exercise at Towneley Hall in Burnley:

> Tactical exercises planned that two sections should represent a defensive force while rest of company should attack. In a rather vague way, a certain number of casualties were to be inflicted by the defenders in the woods surrounding the Hall. Ground was dry, grass green and soft. Approach was to be made in short rushes, cover to be taken whilst on the ground. After the first rush, it was remarkable to see what good marksmen the Towneley defenders really were. Half of the troops attacking, evidently tired by their long walk from the barracks, died peacefully and were fast asleep – at a rifle distance of around a half mile – ere the shouts of the more gallant attackers echoed through the woodlands.

Towards the end of the month the *Accrington Observer and Times* reported that, despite snow drifts and strong winds, the Pals had been engaged on outpost, picket, patrol and reconnoitring exercises around Hambledon, Dunnockshaw

Close and Moleside Commons. It was noted that 'Wandering inhabitants were captured in trying to get through the lines, and in one case a friend or relative in charge of a small hot-pot for one of the men was seized, but was subsequently allowed liberty, and it was to be hoped the savoury and welcome dish reached its legitimate owner.'

The battalion's first fatality came when 27-year-old Robert McGregor, a paper mill labourer from Rishton, drowned in the Leeds and Liverpool Canal. McGregor had suffered a nervous breakdown about one week after joining the Pals, and had been missing for almost two weeks before his body was found in the canal on the morning of 19 November. The inquest that followed resulted in an open verdict of 'found drowned' at the insistence of the jury – at least several of whom had known McGregor personally – even though the Coroner had directed that all the evidence pointed to suicide.

By mid-November there were twenty-two officers gazetted to the battalion: Colonel Sharples was in command with Major Slinger as second-in-command; Broadley, Cheney, Livesey, Milton, Ross and Watson were ranked captain; Gidlow-Jackson, Peltzer, Riley, Roberts and Tough were ranked lieutenant; Bury, Harwood, Haywood, Heys, Kershaw, Macalpine, Ramsbottom, Rawcliffe and Rigby were ranked second lieutenant. Captain Watson had by this time resigned his position as a medical officer under the Royal Army Medical Corps (RAMC) in order to apply for a combatant commission, and was in temporary command of a company. On 4 December, Frank Bailey, a 27-year-old yarn agent from Blackburn, was also gazetted to the battalion with the rank of second lieutenant.

Between 1,600 and 1,700 men from Accrington alone had enlisted into the armed forces in the first 14 weeks of the war. Taken together with Harwood's earlier readiness to accept help from Chorley and Burnley towards raising the 1,100 men needed for his Pals battalion, it is quite surprising that when the War Office asked him to raise a reserve company of 250 men he was confident that he could do so without going outside of the Accrington district. Recruitment for the reserve (E Company) began on Wednesday, 8 December; by the weekend, thirty or forty men had enlisted.

With the recruitment of a reserve company, there was a need to add to the number of officers, a requirement that was met by promotions from within the battalion's ranks. Before the year was out, four new promotions were announced: Sergeant George Gabriel Williams, a 28-year-old draper from Accrington, Lance Sergeant Thomas J Kenny who had joined the Pals while performing in Accrington with Daly's theatre company, Acting Corporal John Henry (Jack) Ruttle, a 32-year-old textile engineer who had returned to Accrington from Japan at the outbreak of war, and Private William Slinger, the 20-year-old elder son of Major Slinger and a clerk by profession. Another vacancy arose when

Lieutenant Haywood left the battalion on 8 January at only a few hours' notice in order to join the Royal Flying Corps (RFC) as an observer.

Early in December it was announced that the battalion had been re-designated the 11th (Service) Battalion, East Lancashire Regiment, a title it would retain for the remainder of its existence. The battalion now formed part of 112 Infantry Brigade, 37th Division. An invitation to become honorary colonel of the battalion was extended to Harwood, and the offer was gratefully accepted.

Route marching had become an established part of the training programme, and on 17 December the Accrington companies marched 22½ miles through Huncoat to Simonstone – where they were joined by the Burnley company – then through Sabden and over the Nick of Pendle to Clitheroe before return-ing. Evidently one or two consignments of more serviceable rifles had by now arrived, as the men were able to have some shooting practice. In addition, seven horses had been delivered for use by the officers.

A break in training for Christmas was marked by a concert at Accrington Town Hall on the evening of 23 December in which all but one of the entertainers were members of the battalion. After the concert had come to a close, each man came forward to collect a parcelled gift of two pairs of socks from the officers' wives and other ladies; then, to the surprise of the officers, they too were called forward, each to receive a boxed silk handkerchief from Elizabeth Ann Sharples, the wife of the battalion's commanding officer.

The activities of Harwood's battalion just over three months into its exist-ence were well summarized by a local newspaper:

> Following the Christmas break, the battalion resumed duties at the usual hour on Monday morning, and have been busy during the week in entrenching exercises and company drill. On Monday night Captain Broadley gave a lecture at the Drill Hall, taking as his subject 'Advanced and flank guards', his remarks being illustrated by means of a large cartoon. On Tuesday Lieutenant Rawcliffe gave a very interesting lecture on the history of the British Army, which, naturally, was much appreciated by the men. On Wednesday there was bathing, as usual, and on Thursday company and entrenching drills. Yesterday (New Year's Day) duties were suspended. This (Saturday) morning drills will be resumed, and in the afternoon there will be a route march. To-morrow (Sunday) the members of the battalion attend St James' Church, whilst the Roman Catholics in the battalion will attend Altham Chapel.

Evening lectures from the officers (at least one NCO, Shorrock, also contri-buted) had become an established feature of the Pals' training programme. While it is likely that many of the officers dreaded being called upon to speak with authority on a subject which in all probability was as alien to them as it was to their audience, the lectures seemed to have been more popular with the men: Major Slinger's lecture on 'The Netherlands' early in the new year even attracted a number of wounded soldiers from Baxenden Military Hospital.

Although recruitment of E Company was progressing satisfactorily, with around 200 men having enlisted by mid-January, the company was slow to complete, perhaps because of the news that Harwood had agreed to raise a local artillery brigade. Regardless of competition from the artillery, the reserve company was complete by the end of the month.

At this time, the battalion make-up approximated to three companies raised from Accrington (60 per cent), three platoons from Burnley (15 per cent), three from Chorley (15 per cent) and two from Blackburn (10 per cent). (Of the 170 men – excluding officers – from these five companies who would be recorded as having lost their lives in the period from 1 to 5 July 1916, 112 (66 per cent) had enlisted at Accrington, 25 at Burnley (15 per cent), 30 at Chorley (18 per cent) and 3 at Rishton (2 per cent).)

The atrocious weather of January 1915 in east Lancashire inevitably disrupted the battalion's training, even though at Accrington it became possible to use the new tram shed for drill. The weather no doubt also contributed to the deaths of two Pals from pneumonia: 21-year-old George Milton of Chorley on 1 February and, on the following day, 27-year-old John Brierley of Blackburn.

On 13 February it was reported that eight more officers had been appointed; all had been promoted from the battalion's ranks and, with the exception of Charles Douglas Haywood, a 20-year-old clerk from Accrington who was stepping into the boots of his elder brother, Sydney, all were from the Blackburn/ Langho area: Herbert Ashworth, a 28-year-old yarn agent, Frank Birtwistle, a 30-year-old cloth salesman, Edward Jones, a 26-year-old coal merchant, Henry Harrison Mitchell, a 28-year-old insurance inspector, Leonard Ryden, a 23-year-old cotton spinner, John Charles Shorrock, a 23-year-old cotton-cloth salesman, and Charles Stonehouse, a 32-year-old architect. A week earlier three promotions had been announced: Ross and Milton to major, and Peltzer to captain. Harold Edgar Whittaker, a 24-year-old cotton salesman from Wilpshire, also joined the battalion as a subaltern at about this time.

It was now time for the five companies to be brought together, not at Accrington, but at the Welsh town of Caernarvon, the move to take place on 23 February. On the same day that official instructions were received to leave for Caernarvon, Tuesday, 16 February, the Chorley Company was treated to a farewell dinner hosted by Mr James Sumner at Chorley Town Hall. While Sumner can hardly have been surprised when his invitation to Kitchener to join the dinner was declined, he must have been genuinely saddened on being turned down by both Richard Sharples and John Harwood. In the course of replying to a toast to the health of the Chorley Pals, Major Milton claimed that every single item of clothing for the company had been bought and paid for locally; perhaps Milton had learned from the ill-will generated from Harwood's negotiations with the Accrington tailors. He also spoke of being 'exceedingly sorry' to be losing Lieutenant Gidlow-Jackson to the Royal Engineers.

Sunday, 21 February witnessed farewell church services for both Anglican and Roman Catholic members of the battalion at Accrington, Burnley and Chorley. The largest – at which some 700 officers and men of the battalion were said to be present – was held at St John's Church in Accrington: it was reported that a very large congregation was even crowded into the aisles, with many more unable to gain admission.

When the time came for the battalion to leave its home towns for Caernarvon, the public interest in 'their' battalion or company was immense. In Accrington it was noted that the Pals had become 'part and parcel of the life of the town, and the inhabitants had become accustomed to the spectacle of groups of blue clad soldierly young fellows in the streets'. Their departure would be a real occasion, very different from the subdued manner in which many hundreds of Accrington men had already departed town for service with their Regular or Territorial regiments. Many of the mill and workshop owners closed their factories in order to give their employees the chance to witness the send-off, while other less-charitable employers found that their workers were leaving work regardless.

In Accrington, 18,000 people lined the streets on a morning that was bright but cold. Shortly before 9am, Major Slinger led A, B and E companies on the short march from Ellison's Tenement to the railway station, mounted police going on ahead to force a passage through the enthusiastic crowds. The Pals were in good heart, smiling and waving as the crowd called out greetings and waved handkerchiefs. Trotting behind was their mascot, a fox terrier clothed in a Union flag. At the station, John Harwood, along with fellow members of the Town Council, mixed among the Pals, wishing them 'God-speed'. Two companies boarded the first train, each man searching for an open carriage window through which he could catch a glimpse of a loved one or just soak up more of the atmosphere. At 9.15am the train moved slowly away from the platform accompanied by a cacophony of scores of fog signals while the crowd cheered and waved their hats. As the train passed through the station at Church more fog signals were fired, while schoolchildren on the crowded platform waved Union flags. The second train carrying the last of the three companies left an hour later to similar scenes.

Shortly before the second train left from Accrington, crowds lining the streets in Burnley were watching Major Ross lead D Company from the Barracks on Accrington Road to the Town Hall. Marching ahead of the Pals, the bugle band of the Territorial Depot companies added greatly to the sense of occasion. Owing to the absence of the mayor (Alderman Sellers Kay was said to have been unavoidably prevented from being present), it was left to the deputy mayor, Alderman E Keighley, to make a brief address before the Pals marched on amid cheers to Bank Top station where a large crowd had gathered. Their train left shortly after 11am, the 'deafening cheers' of the crowd being 'as heartily and lustily returned' by the Pals.

The last departure was from Chorley, where the mayor, Alderman R Hindle, addressed C Company at the Barracks shortly after 10.30am. After Mr Richard Edward Stanton had presented the company with a dog for a mascot (named 'Ned' by Major Milton after its donor), Milton called for three cheers for the mayor and Corporation, followed by three for the mascot, all of which were 'heartily given'. At 11.20am, Lieutenant Rigby and Ned, followed by the North Lancashire (Chorley) Band and the mayor and other dignitaries, led the company to the station in wintry conditions. As at Accrington and Burnley, cheering crowds lined the streets and it was said that when the train carrying the Burnley company steamed into the station, 'the cheering was almost as loud as when it left at 11.55 bearing the Chorley Pals'.

Although heavy showers of snow and sleet had fallen on Caernarvon earlier in the day, the weather was fine when the first train carrying 19 officers and 604 men from Accrington arrived 15 minutes ahead of schedule at 2.30pm. Following behind were the second train carrying 6 officers with the remainder of the Accrington and Blackburn men – also ahead of schedule – and the third train carrying 412 officers and men from Burnley and Chorley. Caernarvon had determined to give the Pals a warm welcome and the mayor (Councillor John Pritchard), the town clerk and members of the Town Council were prominent among a large number of townspeople who had gathered at the station. The detraining was efficiently carried out, so that by 4.30pm all the men had been led to their billets – where hot meals should have been waiting for them – the baggage had been removed and the horses had been taken from their boxes and stabled. In what remained of the day, the men were allowed to wander about the streets of the town and begin to familiarize themselves with their new surroundings.

Despite Major Slinger's immediate observation that 'the billets were excellent', it is evident that some of the accommodation provided was less than adequate: Fred Hacking, a young cotton weaver from Oswaldtwistle, wrote to his aunt: 'I am sending a photo on blue as I don't know when we get our khaki. We got in bad digs at first. There were forty-eight of us in an empty house but now we got very good digs and we are having a time of our lives.' The language barrier also presented difficulties, as Sam Hardman explained in a letter to his parents and sisters:

> By the way, all the people in Carnarvon speak Welsh . . . You should here [*sic*] the old maids at our place, you would laugh your sides sore.

One minute they will be speaking to us in English then the next they will jabber away to-gether like, well I don't like to say monkeys, but, oh dear me, here they are at it again, laughing and talking to-gether, and me by my-self and I can hardly keep from laughing, and you know, they might be talking about me for what I know.

Sam was sharing the home of the Ensor sisters at 33 Bangor Street from where the four spinsters – Mary (aged 72 or 73), Jane (65), Margaret (54) and Hephzibah (49) – ran a boarding house and confectionery business.

An amusing example of a misunderstanding between a Pal and a Welsh housemaid was quoted in the *Accrington Observer and Times*: 'I had stained my tunic, and I asked the servant of the house where I am billeted if she had some ammonia. "No" she replied, "but there's a piano in the front room"!'

On the Saturday after the battalion's arrival in Caernarvon, Major Slinger hurriedly returned home with his son after learning that his wife, Ellen, was critically ill: she died the following day, at the early age of 49.

Although Caernarvon Town Council and the local Young Men's Christian Association (YMCA) did everything possible to provide amenities and entertainment for the Pals, not everyone was satisfied. A letter of complaint from a Pal who signed himself 'Whalley Nab' was published in the *Accrington Observer and Times*:

> Rot! The place is so dead it will soon be responsible for a certain amount of insanity. We are at a loss to know what to do with ourselves. If we go for a walk there is nothing to see . . . We all sit around the fire, asleep – oh, no, not drunk, for we have to drink wasser here on the Sabbath, as all the pubs, cigarette shops, and rest of cemetery are closed. As for the 200 yards sail across the Straits to Anglesey, we have even to beg for a pass to go, through someone who, being troubled with solitary confinement or insanity, got loose and crossed the Straits to Anglesey and pinched a few mussels off the sands, so now we stop indoors and play patience or drink wasser.

The author of the letter was strongly criticized by the newspaper editor, and also found himself attacked by a fellow Pal in a letter that was published a week later:

> We have been here over a fortnight now, and I am sure the Carnarvon people have tried their best to make us comfortable in every way. I admit it is quiet here on Sundays and that all the public houses are shut . . . He cannot [in Lancashire] see anything to compare with what he can see on the drill ground here, with the sun shining, the air clear, snow on the mountains and a good sea view . . . no pass is

required [to go over the river], but the mussels, as he calls them, were oysters, and who wants a lot of folk 'pinching' oysters when they are put there at great expense by the owners?

'Whalley Nab' seems to have been in a small minority. Writing home shortly after arriving at Caernarvon, 16-year-old Charles Owens from Clayton-le-Moors gave a rousing endorsement of the Welsh countryside:

> We have a grand field for drilling in, right facing the open sea . . . and the breezes that blow while we are drilling fairly buck us up. All our drilling is done in the morning, and we march every afternoon. The country lanes here beat anything I have yet seen . . . This place suits me and we are all like turkey cocks for colour.

Occasional grumbles persisted: one Pal wrote to the local newspaper to complain that some Caernarvon people had warned their girls not to be seen talking to a soldier. The issue was quickly smoothed over when Mr Isaac Edwards, chairman of the Caernarvon YMCA, took the opportunity while addressing the Pals at a sacred concert on the following Sunday evening to ask the leaders of the local Young Women's Christian Association 'to discourage any deprecating of the association of our girls with the soldiers'.

A step-up in the battalion's professionalism took place on 1 March when 40-year-old Lieutenant Colonel Arthur Wilmot Rickman took over command from Colonel Sharples. Rickman was the sixth of eight children born to Major General William Rickman and his wife, Mary. After obtaining a commission at the age of 22, he served with 2/Northumberland Fusiliers in the Anglo–Boer War of 1899–1902, gaining the Queen's Medal with four clasps (Transvaal, Laing's Nek, Orange Free State and Defence of Ladysmith) and the King's Medal with two clasps (South Africa 1901 and South Africa 1902). On 19 March 1903, Rickman married Florence Maud Mildred Cammell at All Saint's, Knightsbridge. Mildred was a grand-daughter of Charles Cammell whose steel-foundry business had turned into Cammell Laird shipbuilders; known as 'Mouse' to her family and friends, Mildred is said to have had a lively personality if not to have been a great beauty. It is hard to see Rickman as having other than a very amiable personality: called 'Sunny' by Mildred, he had the knack of getting along with practically anyone, a necessary skill when it came to dealing with farmers' grievances in his role as Honorary Secretary of the Percy Hunt. He was a proficient horseman and was regularly highly placed in point-to-point races. The couple lived at Alnwick and had three children before the marriage broke down, a decree having been served on Rickman immediately before he arrived at Caernarvon.

At 8am on Monday, 1 March, Rickman made his first inspection of the battalion before dismissing the men for the day. He made an instant and favourable impression, judging by a letter written by Robert Bullen, a 24-year-old house painter from Padiham: 'We have got a new Colonel this week, not a bad sport, he played pop over the suits we were wearing. So we expect the khaki shortly, then I will have my photo taken.' Rickman also insisted on an immediate change: the five companies of the battalion were to be re-designated as W, X, Y, Z and R.

Straightaway Rickman implemented a more exacting training programme. A typical day began with parade and physical drill at 7am, after which the men would return to their billets for breakfast. After re-assembling in Castle Square at 9.15, the Pals would march over the Aber swing bridge to the drill ground for rifle practice, field training and tactical exercises. A similar programme was followed in the afternoons. Route marches and kit inspections also featured prominently in the battalion's activities.

Rickman's ability to conciliate seems not to have extended to Second Lieutenant Edward Jones, who was accused of being 'under the influence of Liquor' at the Royal Hotel on the evening of 17 March. Although Rickman clearly wanted Jones removed from the battalion, he was eventually forced by Lieutenant General Mackinnon, as General Officer Commanding (GOC) Western Command, to give Jones 'an opportunity of redeeming his fault'. In general, the conduct of the Pals at Caernarvon seems to have been excellent: an ex-mayor of Caernarvon spoke of the Pals as 'a splendid lot of fellows, and their behaviour is excellent', while Caernarvon Alderman Robert Parry was reported as saying that the people of Caernarvon greatly appreciated the excellent conduct of the men.

Not surprisingly, sport occupied much of the battalion's leisure time, with officers as keen as the men to take part: in a well-attended football match held on Saturday, 13 March, the battalion's officers scored 8 goals against the sergeants, apparently without reply, leading one observer to comment that 'the sergeants are better at drill than football'. Evidence that the battalion might have a football team of some strength came on Good Friday, 2 April when an XI drawn entirely from Z Company beat Caernarvon United by 2 goals to nil.

The battalion also enjoyed success over the locals at games of roller-skating hockey played on the rink in the Caernarvon Pavilion: after a narrow defeat in the first encounter, a battalion team registered wins of 3–2 and 3–0 over a Caernarvon Pavilion team on the evenings of 9 and 16 March respectively. At billiards, the battalion seems to have been less successful, judging from a report of a 6–1 defeat at the hands of a YMCA team. The Pavilion also hosted boxing matches in which 17-year-old Harry 'Kid' Nutter from Rishton topped the bill. Nutter, who had worked in a cotton bleaching works before the war, was a promising flyweight who had won about half his fights before joining the Pals.

Aside from sports, the Pals were entertained by nightly sing-songs at the YMCA and weekly concerts arranged by their own Tom Coady, a 33-year-old from Oswaldtwistle who was well known locally for his impressions of George Formby Snr, a famous music-hall comedian of the day. Coady also worked together with Isaac Edwards to put on at least two concerts for the enjoyment of patients at the King Edward Tuberculosis Sanatorium.

Training was gradually stepped up in the weeks that followed Rickman's arrival. Daytime exercises in manoeuvring and skirmishing were soon supplemented by mock night-time attacks against entrenched positions, suggesting that Rickman had a realistic and imaginative outlook of what would be needed to break into the enemy lines on the Western Front. As further evidence of his foresight, Rickman approached Harwood early in April with a shopping list of field instruments: four mekometers (range finders), one set of armourer's tools, one electric camp and signalling 'buzzer', eight trench periscopes, one field telephone, sixteen pairs of binoculars for scouts, ten Morris tubes (which when inserted into the barrel enabled the rifle to fire a smaller calibre round), sixty-four Metropolitan Police whistles and other small items. Whereas the government would provide the instruments at the time when the battalion went overseas, Rickman wanted to have them earlier in order to prepare the battalion fully before it was ordered to the front; Harwood duly raised the £125 required through public donations.

While the countryside around Caernarvon provided ample opportunities for extending the battalion's training in signalling, it also presented some unexpected dangers, as one Pal reported:

> We have had the use of all land near Carnarvon, so we have had moving station work, viz. so many men in a fixed station, and the others go to a mile and a half out, and get into communication with headquarters. After every message we move on and call them up elsewhere ... On Thursday my pal and myself were on the same job and he tried to 'tice a 'cow'. Anyway she came for him before he saw what was the matter, and all he could do was to grab hold of her horns. She swung him clean off his feet, and he was dangling about three feet in the air. He had to let go before long, and dropped into a bog two or three feet away.

Training in and around Caernarvon was broken by the occasional 9-mile route march to Penrhyn Park, Bangor where the various battalions comprising 112 Brigade came together to be inspected by Brigadier General Gerald Mackay MacKenzie. Following the inspection at Bangor on Easter Monday, 5 April, Brigade Orders included the remark: 'The Brigade Commander desires officers commanding Battalions to inform all ranks under their command that he was much pleased with the smart appearance in Penrhyn Park, Bangor. He is also much gratified to hear the good reports from all sources of the soldierlike behaviour of the battalions in North Wales.' The smart appearance was no doubt in part enhanced by many of the Pals having finally received their khaki uniforms. Reports of the good relationship between the Pals and the people of Caernarvon continued to abound: in the course of a concert provided for the Pals by the Caernarvon Choral Society on the evening of Easter Sunday, Councillor Pritchard spoke in front of an audience said to number more than 5,000 of the privilege that it had been for the people of Caernarvon to host the battalion in their town. Rickman, given a rousing reception when he stood up to reply, said that he could trust the men of his battalion anywhere. Amid much laughter and cheering, Rickman went on to say that while they might expect to hear singing from the Germans when in the trenches, there could be no comparison to what they had heard at Caernarvon. The close relationship that had quickly developed between the battalion and the people of Caernarvon was further demonstrated when four Pals acted as pall bearers at the funeral of a young woman in whose house they were billeted.

By mid-April, Richard Ormerod, a 22-year-old cotton weaver from Blackburn, was able to tell his sister, Polly:

> We are making rapid progress with our training and are hoping to give a good account of ourselves should we get the chance. By the end of June we (at least I think so) will be moved to the firing line then I should be able to give a good blow with the machine gun I have been appointed in charge of.

At about the same time, another Pal was overheard to remark: '[we have had] more work these last three weeks than we have had for three months'. The firing line, however, was still some distance away. There had been an expectation that the battalion would move on from Caernarvon as early as 7 April, in order to go into camp at Belton Park, Grantham with the other battalions of 112 Brigade, while the reserve company would go to Heaton Park, Manchester. In readiness for the separation of the reserve company, a number of men had been transferred into and out of it in the days immediately preceding the anticipated move. In the event, the move to Grantham was first postponed because of the poor condition of the huts, and later cancelled completely.

On Monday, 26 April, the whole battalion was able to parade in khaki for inspection by Major General Edward Thompson Dickson, the Chief Inspector of Infantry. It was reported that not only was Dickson fully satisfied with the bearing of the battalion, but that he had remarked on the neat way in which the men's packs were fixed, and on the exceptionally clean and polished appearance of their packs and tunics.

Over the weekend of 8/9 May news was received that the battalion would move, not to Grantham, but to Penkridge Bank on Cannock Chase where it would form part of a brigade alongside battalions of the York and Lancaster Regiment; the reserve company was to go to Chadderton Camp in Oldham under the command of Major Slinger. For the following Tuesday and Wednesday, Rickman granted his men an extra hour until 11pm to enjoy the hospitality of Caernarvon: reports that 'there was a sound of revelry by night' suggest that the gesture was appreciatively taken up.

By the time of the battalion's departure from Caernarvon, several more subalterns had been posted to it: Ernest Ashwell, a 27-year-old construction engineer from Walsall, George Joseph Beaumont, a 22-year-old clerk from Kitchener, Ontario, Herbert Brabin, a 23-year-old teacher from Oldham, William Faulkner, a 28-year-old chemist's assistant from London, George Helson, a 19-year-old architect from Plymouth, Wilfred Arthur Kohn, a 21-year-old from Kensington, Walter Affroville Lewino, a 27-year-old from Paris, and Noël Cameron Robinson, an 18-year-old from Emsworth, Hampshire. Faulkner, Helson and Robinson were posted to the reserve company: it seems a strange decision on Rickman's part to send Faulkner to Oldham, as he alone of the officers had had recent experience of trench warfare, having spent eight weeks in France with 9/London.

The battalion may well have secured a new medical officer by this time. 34-year-old John William Nelson (Jack) Roberts had been educated at Shrewsbury School where he was a contemporary with Henry Riley, and had been serving as a ship's doctor in the Merchant Navy. It was perhaps a chance encounter with Riley at Caernarvon, close to Roberts' home at Criccieth, which led to his appointment as medical officer.

At 7.20am on Thursday, 13 May, the officers and men of W, X and Y companies paraded in Castle Square from where they marched to the railway station, led by Lieutenant Colonel Rickman and Battalion Sergeant Major Shorrock. Of the hundreds of people who turned up to watch the battalion's departure, most were said to be women, either landladies of the houses in which the Pals had been billeted or girlfriends. Despite the sadness of the occasion for many, there was also jollity: flags and handkerchiefs were waved from balconies and windows, the Pals sang and the spectators were much amused when one Pal yelled out 'Da bo chi' (goodbye). In a slightly shocked tone, the *Accrington Observer and Times* reported that at the station 'one young lady could not restrain her feelings, for she grasped one of the men in her arms and kissed him in full view of the crowd'. The train carrying the first three companies steamed out of the station at 8.30am; the crowds grew still further as Z Company left the Square at 8.30am followed by R Company at 9.30am. At 10.30am, the train carrying the last of the Pals left Caernarvon.

Chapter 6

Not Enough Men Born

Allied strategy on the Western Front in 1915 was of necessity dictated by that of France, and for 63-year-old General Joseph Jacques Césaire Joffre, commander-in-chief of the French armies, this amounted to driving attacks into the flanks of the Noyon salient occupied by the enemy. In principle, the strategy was a sound one – the Germans were after all occupying the industrial heartland of France – but in execution it was fatally flawed. A series of French offensives launched in the Champagne region between 20 December 1914 and 17 March 1915 gained no appreciable ground at a cost of 90,000 casualties.

Britain's first material contribution to the strategy stemmed from a proposal for a tactical operation to take out the salient formed by the German line around the village of Neuve-Chapelle. Haig, now in command of the British First Army, extended the scope of the operation to include an assault on the Aubers Ridge which lay 1½ miles beyond the village. A number of tactical innovations were made for the attack including the use of aerial photography and observation to map the enemy lines and spot artillery, the provision of telephone communications as far forward as battalion headquarters, and the use of shrapnel shells to cut the enemy barbed wire. Had the scope of the attack been limited to its original objectives, the outcome of the battle would have been regarded as a clear success.

At 7.30am on 10 March a 35-minute hurricane bombardment of the German positions at Neuve-Chapelle began; it was a concentration of artillery fire that would not be surpassed even in 1917. With the crucial exception of a 400yd stretch of line that had been allocated to batteries that had come into position as late as the previous night, the artillery largely accomplished its destructive work well: 18-pounder guns firing shrapnel tore gaps through the wire, 4.5in and 6in howitzers obliterated the German front line and communication trenches, while 9.2in howitzers steadily reduced the village of Neuve-Chapelle to rubble. Less successful were the 4.7in and 6in guns which had been charged with eliminating the enemy artillery batteries. At 8.05am, the infantry attack began. On the right of the attack made by IV Corps (Lieutenant General Henry Seymour Rawlinson), 25 Brigade had broken through the German front line by 8.20am and was fighting its way into Neuve-Chapelle at about 8.50am. To the left of 25 Brigade, where the artillery preparation had been inadequate, heavy machine-gun and rifle fire had largely prevented 23 Brigade from getting forward; nevertheless, bombing parties were eventually able to work northwards along the German front line from the right of the brigade front and by about 11.30am 23 Brigade was able to move across no-man's-land. By 1pm the first objectives of IV Corps had been gained but when the infantry advance was finally resumed in gathering darkness at 5.30pm by 24 and 21 brigades it was done without an adequate artillery preparation: less than 500yd were gained before nightfall.

The second day of the battle opened with attacks made by 21, 20 and 24 brigades at 7am following a 15-minute artillery bombardment that had failed to hit the new German trench line which had been dug overnight; the attacks were driven off by heavy machine-gun and rifle fire. A further attack planned for 24 Brigade at 2.15pm descended into chaos.

The third day of the battle saw another attack thrown in without the necessary artillery preparation but on this occasion it was a German counter-attack made at dawn that failed. Following up the retreating enemy, 2/East Lancashire from 24 Brigade occupied part of the German trench only to be blown out of its position by friendly artillery fire. IV Corps returned to the offensive at 12.30pm after a 30-minute artillery bombardment but achieved only limited success.

After being wounded in the hand by a bullet at Neuve-Chapelle, 18-year-old Owen Broadley from Accrington wrote home to his parents:

> Perhaps you will have read about the East Lancashires at Neuve-Chapelle. Well, I went through that, and I never want to see a sight like it again. You talk about dead Germans – there were trenches full of them. Of course, we lost a lot of men, but the enemy lost ten times as many as us [British losses were at least as great as those of the enemy]. I tell you, I had given myself up of ever coming out of it alive. You don't know what it is to be as near death as I have been, but thank God I was lucky enough to come out with nothing but a reminder of what an advance really is.

On 13 March, the day on which Haig called off the battle, Gerald Thomas (Gerry) Gorst, a 19-year-old subaltern in the East Lancashire Regiment, wrote to his sister Betty from 4th Infantry Base Depot at Rouen:

> Isn't it good news that we've got Neuve-Chapelle back at last; I'm afraid our losses must have been very heavy. (I expect the [Censor] will scratch this out: however I'll have a run for my money!) The Middlesex and the Scottish Rifles lost a thousand men between them: and the S.R.s had every officer killed except two, who arrived at the hospital here last night.

Four days later, after being posted to 1/East Lancashire at Ploegsteert Wood, Gorst wrote again: 'I think the 2nd battalion must have had a bit of a doing at Neuve-Chapelle; we hear that their casualties were 8 officers and 392 men.' After only one day in the trenches with 1/East Lancashire, Gorst was posted to A Company of 2/East Lancashire at Neuve-Chapelle which he described as 'the last place I expected or wanted to be in'; his elder brother, Eric William Gorst, had been killed in action on 26 October 1914 during an attempt by 4/Royal Fusiliers to recapture trenches west of Neuve-Chapelle in a night attack. In another letter to his sister, Gorst wrote of his friends who had lost their lives with 2/East Lancashire:

> We've lost nearly five hundred men; poor Billy Wolseley was killed
> by a shell [29-year-old Second Lieutenant William Joseph Wolseley],
> and I've just heard that Hodgson has died in hospital [28-year-old
> Second Lieutenant Philip Ormiston Hodgson]. He was shot in the
> head during the charge. The colonel is wounded, and many others
> you didn't know are gone. It has been frightful: so many were killed
> by our own artillery. If it costs all this to clear that bit of ground,
> there aren't enough men born to clear Belgium.

On 9 May 1915, IV Corps formed the northern arm of a converging assault which was intended to take the Aubers Ridge while supporting a new French offensive in the Artois. The experience of 2/East Lancashire serves to illustrate the complete failure of the attack. On the night of 8/9 May, the battalion took up position led by one platoon from each of B and C companies in an advanced trench on the Pétillon–Fromelles road. At 5am on the 9th, the British artillery began a bombardment of the enemy trenches: estimated to have had only 20 per cent of the intensity per length of trench of the bombardment at Neuve-Chapelle, the artillery fire was largely ineffectual. At 5.20am, the remaining platoons of B and C companies began to move up towards the advanced trench in readiness for the attack, followed closely by D and A companies. As soon as the infantry began to move across the open ground, they were exposed to a murderous hail of rifle and machine-gun bullets. On the right of the battalion's front, B Company advanced across no-man's-land until almost all were either killed or wounded; on the left, a few men of C Company managed to break into the enemy line alongside 2/Rifle Brigade. Behind them, D and A companies both suffered heavy casualties before even reaching the advanced trench. Orders were issued for the battalion to renew the attack after a second bombardment of the enemy lines at 1pm; in the event, the artillery fire fell short, and the further casualties inflicted on the battalion effectively ended it as a fighting force. By the end of the day, 2/East Lancashire had lost 449 officers and men killed, wounded or missing. No ground was taken in the battle, at a cost of just over

11,000 casualties. The French offensive in the Artois was called off in June after losses had mounted to 100,000 men.

The East Lancashires' attack on 9 May left Gerry Gorst with a bullet wound through his left arm. A Medical Board assembled at Cambridge four days later noted that he was suffering from partial paralysis of the extensor muscles in his forearm with some loss of sensation of his thumb and outer fingers. Five months later, he was assessed to be once more fit for military duty. Gorst, by now promoted to lieutenant, left Britain again on 25 May 1916, this time to find himself posted to the Accrington Pals whom he joined at Courcelles-au-Bois in the afternoon of the 28th.

Chapter 7

Men of the Mechanic Class

Entering the new year of 1915, John Harwood had every reason to be proud of his successful recruitment of a Pals battalion for Kitchener's New Armies. Still, he had found it necessary to recruit two of the four original companies from outside of the town, and recruitment of the reserve company was less than half complete after nearly a month. It is rather surprising then that, on receiving an invitation from the War Office on Friday, 15 January to raise one or more artillery or engineer units, it took him little more than the weekend to respond with an offer to raise a howitzer artillery brigade. It has to be supposed that Harwood's pride made it impossible for him not to accept the challenge.

Within two weeks, Harwood received a reply from the War Office asking if an ammunition column was included in his offer to raise an artillery brigade. Harwood immediately wired through his confirmation and late in the afternoon of that same day, Friday, 29 January, a telegram was delivered to Harwood confirming the Army Council's 'grateful acceptance' of his offer.

It was reported at the time that, when looking to raise artillery and engineer units for his New Armies, Kitchener targeted those individuals and communities who had already raised a local infantry battalion. Harwood was not alone in responding: in the first week of February alone the Earl of Derby raised three field artillery brigades, a howitzer brigade, a divisional ammunition column and a heavy artillery battery complete with ammunition column, Glasgow raised a field artillery brigade and a company of engineers, Leeds raised two companies of engineers, Manchester raised four companies of engineers, the West Yorkshire Coal Owners' Association raised a field artillery brigade and Hull raised a divisional ammunition column.

Harwood immediately threw all his energies into raising the new brigade, for which 700 men would be needed in the first instance. As early as Monday, 1 February he was so deeply absorbed in matters connected with the raising of the brigade that he was unable to find the time to attend the monthly meeting of the Town Council. Although the brigade would have its headquarters in Accrington, Harwood determined from the outset that it would be recruited from the whole of east Lancashire, an area taking in Greater Accrington, Burnley, Colne, Nelson, the Rossendale Valley and Haslingden; for this he needed, and readily received, the full support of the mayor of Burnley, Alderman Sellers Kay.

The following Friday, Harwood motored to Chester to meet once more with Lieutenant General Mackinnon to obtain formal permission to begin recruiting. In fact, Harwood had already made a number of provisional appointments. In command of the brigade with the temporary rank of lieutenant colonel would be Major Thomas Purvis Ritzema, a 39-year-old newspaper director from Blackburn. Ritzema had received his first commission in January 1897 with 3rd East Lancashire Volunteer Artillery. During the Boer War, he had been acting adjutant with 1st East Lancashire Brigade RFA, and was promoted to the rank of major in November 1909. He had transferred to the Reserve in April 1913 and, on the outbreak of war, had offered his services to the War Office in any capacity. Also provisionally appointed to senior posts within the brigade were Lieutenant Harry Renham, a recruiting officer in his mid-40s from Accrington who had risen from the ranks and was to be adjutant with the temporary rank of captain, and Captain Harold Gray, the 39-year-old head of Accrington's Electrical Staff, who was to command one of the brigade's four gun batteries. Mackinnon did insist that he would only consider applications for appointment to commissions from men having had previous military training, a stipulation that would at least help Harwood to deal more easily with the overwhelming number of applications that he had received.

Harwood by this time had already also appointed four battery sergeant majors and a number of other NCOs; Church Artillery Barracks had been taken over for use by the new brigade and it was anticipated that Burnley Barracks would become available as soon as the Pals departed for Caernarvon.

Recruitment for the brigade began in Accrington on Saturday, 6 February, and elsewhere in east Lancashire two days later. Recruits were to be between the ages of 19 and 38, though ex-NCOs would be accepted up to the age of 50; prospective gunners were to be between 5ft 7in and 5ft 10in in height, whereas drivers were accepted between 5ft 3in and 5ft 7in; the minimum chest measurement was 35in. It was well known that more generous separation allowances were likely to be introduced shortly, and would no doubt aid recruitment. Poor dental health had resulted in an early discharge from Army service for many men who had volunteered to take up arms in the early weeks of the war and it is worthy of note that recruits to the new brigade who required dental treatment would be put on Army pay at once, yet would remain at home until treatment was completed by their own dentist.

On the first day of recruitment 26 men enlisted at Accrington, with a further 32 on the following Monday; after the first 6 days, the total at Accrington had reached 114, and the first battery, designated A, was almost complete. At Burnley, 64 men had enlisted during the first week, 8 of them coming from Nelson and Colne. Although 'men of the mechanic class' were particularly sought after for the brigade, its first service number, L/1, was allocated to 19-year-old George Nicholas Slinger Jnr, a solicitor's articled clerk and son of George Nicholas Slinger, adjutant and second-in-command of the Pals. Within a week the Artillery Barracks at Church was 'a scene of extraordinary activity' as the recruits of A Battery began training: one squad drilled in the Hall, another did physical exercises in the riding school while the third drilled in the open air. There were three names put forward for commissions: Haslingden-born 24-year-old David Rostron Worsley, a cotton manufacturing agent who had joined up on 4 September 1914 and had been serving in the ranks of the 12th Reserve Cavalry Regiment, 20-year-old Lawrence Kershaw Whittaker, an Accrington engineer, and, from the ranks of the Pals, 25-year-old Harold Bancroft, another Accrington engineer and son of James Bancroft, manager of Howard and Bullough's.

On the second day of recruitment, the younger grandson of John Harwood, 19-year-old John Richard Harwood, a mechanical draughtsman, enlisted into the ranks of the brigade and was posted to A Battery as a gunner with the number L/99. With his grandfather's influence, it would surely have been easy for him to have secured a commission, yet he remained in the ranks throughout the five years of his Army service.

By the end of the second week, nearly 350 men had joined the brigade, bringing 3 of the 4 batteries close to completion. It was suggested that the men might take delivery of their khaki uniforms over the weekend of 20/21 February and that, if this proved to be the case, they should line the streets for the Pals' departure for Caernarvon. Whether through fortune or design on Harwood's part, the uniforms were delivered late: the sight of the newly formed artillery brigade already in khaki would certainly have infuriated the Pals, as they were still resentfully clad in blue. Within a day or two of the Pals' departure, the Accrington artillerymen had been issued with new khaki overcoats and caps; they were said to have created an excellent impression on the following Thursday as they marched up Burnley Road for exercises on the Coppice. The delivery of khaki uniforms was not far behind and Harwood, probably still smarting from the criticism meted out to him by Accrington tailors less than five months previously, had ensured that the orders for all the uniforms and suits had been distributed among local tradesmen.

Recruitment continued at a steady rate, so that by 26 February the fourth battery was nearing completion with 490 men having joined the brigade. Gradually the vacancies for officers were also being filled. Appointed respectively to command B and C batteries were 32-year-old Thomas Wilde Rice, a farmer and native of Euxton near Chorley who had previously held the rank of captain with a Lancashire artillery brigade, and 31-year-old Thomas Riley of Burnley, who had been a major with 1st East Lancashire Brigade RFA before retiring in 1912 to become a missionary in British Columbia. Three new commissions were to be awarded to men who had been serving in the ranks of the 12th Reserve Cavalry Regiment: 23-year-old William Chambers, a cotton manufacturer from Rishton, 27-year-old William Slater, a solicitor, also from Rishton, and 25-year-old Nicholas Tomlinson, a manager of a cotton mill from Haslingden. Also to be newly appointed to a commission were Robert Mercer, a 32-year-old architect from Great Harwood who had been serving with the Duke of Lancaster's Yeomanry, and, plucked from the Officer Training Corps at Clifton College in Bristol, 18-year-old Frank Harwood, a great-nephew of John Harwood. Two additional officer appointments were yet to be completed, including that of 19-year-old Harold Aubrey Pearson, an apprentice learning the cotton trade at Manchester who, like Worsley, Chambers, Slater and Tomlinson, was joining from the ranks of the 12th Reserve Cavalry.

Even with the brigade nearing completion, Harwood refused to rest: during the previous week he had addressed audiences at both the Peel Street Picture Palace in Accrington and the Queen's Hall in Church with the intention of pushing recruitment. His drive and determination contrasts sharply with that of Burnley's leaders, a point driven home in an anonymous quote published in the *Accrington Observer and Times*:

> Burnley men responded with alacrity to the call for recruits for the Howitzer Brigade, and we believe that the whole brigade could have been raised in the town. Two of the four batteries are wholly composed of local men, and there were quite a number of others diverted over to Accrington or into the Welsh and other artillery brigades. Burnley has so far done its work nobly in raising the strength of the army, but it has not a battalion or brigade of its own. This is surprising. Accrington has the credit for raising an infantry battalion and an artillery brigade, and yet the outside assistance it has received has been very great. There must be more public-spirited leaders in Accrington than Burnley, or an old military centre like this would not be outdone, as it has been on two occasions. It is to be hoped that something will be done to remedy this.

Even at this time there was argument as to whether Burnley or Accrington had supplied the greater number of men for the brigade. While Burnley spoke of diverting men to the Accrington batteries, Accrington claimed to have supplied the ammunition column of 150 men and officers. Harwood was later to remark that 1,300 of the 2,000 men that formed the Pals and the Howitzer brigade came from Accrington, though this is surely an exaggeration, even taking Accrington to include its districts.

While the substantial coverage given to the Howitzer Brigade and the Pals in the newspapers of east Lancashire was predictable given their local identity, it continued to be resented by men who were serving elsewhere, as can be seen from a letter published in the *Accrington Observer and Times*:

> I am writing a few lines to you for my comrades and I. We get your paper sent to us every week, and have done ever since we enlisted in September, [and] we are quite happy when the [postman brings it] to see the local news but we notice every week a lot about the 'Pals'. My comrades and I would like to know if they [are the] only lot thought about in Accrington [as it] seems so the way Captain Harwood makes his stirring speeches about them. We should like the Mayor to know that our hearts were in the same place as theirs when we answered our King and Country's call before the 'Pals' were formed.

Just five weeks after recruitment had begun, the four batteries and ammunition column of the brigade were complete, save for a few specialists. Riding practice had not yet been possible owing to the lack of horses, and the training routine had been focused on drill and physical fitness. It was an exhausting regime, judging by the words of one artilleryman: 'You should try running up the breast of Moleside for all you are worth and then playing a hard game of football on the top, besides plenty of exercises and drill, and then next day turning out for about fifteen miles of a route march.'

With the exception of two majors, the brigade's officers were completed with new commissions for five more men promoted from the ranks: John Albert Bower, a 19-year-old student of law from Barrowford, Gilbert Grimshaw, a 19-year-old apprentice architect from Fence, Reginald Jackson from Nelson, George Nicholas Slinger Jnr and Thomas Crowther Turner, a 22-year-old who had been working with his father, a licensed victualler at the Crown Hotel in Colne. By the end of March, orders were issued for the recruitment of the first reinforcements for the brigade, though as extra drivers had already been recruited, only an additional officer and some fifty gunners and artisans were required. The brigade, officially known as CLVIII (Accrington and Burnley) Brigade, Royal Field Artillery, was known locally simply as the Howitzers.

The first occasion on which the entire brigade, including its ammunition column, came together was the route march to Whalley on Wednesday, 31 March. Indeed, it was the first time that the Accrington and Burnley batteries had come together. A and B batteries, each comprising around 133 men, together with the 150 men of the ammunition column, left Accrington shortly after 9am, reaching Whalley at 11.30am. After the arrival from Burnley of C and D batteries 1½ hours later, the occasion was marked by a keenly contested football match from which the Burnley batteries emerged victorious by the odd goal. On the return march, the Accrington batteries drew up where the roads forked and exchanged cheers with the Burnley men as the latter marched off towards Read and Padiham.

Accrington Stanley FC team photograph, 1905. (*Author's collection*)

The family of William Robb Tough, 1906. Standing, left to right: Margaret (Peg), William Alexander, John James, Christina (Chris); seated, left to right: Gertrude Hay (Gert), William Robb, Annabel Mary, Jessie, Arnold Bannatyne. (*Marjorie Lloyd-Jones*)

Burnley Lads' Club football team, photograph taken in or shortly before 1914. William Ingham (back row, far left), James Sullivan (back row, second from left), Harry Routh (front row, far left) and Samuel Wilson (front row, fourth from left) would later join the Accrington Pals. (*Mike Townend and Towneley Hall Art Gallery & Museum, Burnley*)

The Welsh Regiment bobsleigh team winning the 1908 Kaiser's Cup. Lieutenant (later Lieutenant General) Hubert Conway Rees is second from right.
(*Diana Stockford*)

Accrington Pals on parade at Ellison's Tenement in Accrington, 1914. Photograph taken by Sam Harrison.
(*Author's collection*)

No. 1 Platoon, B (District) Company, photographed in 1914 on land adjoining Hyndburn Park School, Accrington. Behind the figure lying down on the right is 15997 Arthur Robinson (with hands resting on his shoulders).
(*Robert and Tony Robinson*)

Accrington Pals in Kitchener blue uniforms on Avenue Parade, Accrington. (*David Bent*)

Officers of the Accrington Pals in the Drill Hall, Accrington, February 1915. (*Author's collection*)

Officers and sergeants of C (Chorley) Company, February 1915. Back row, left to right: CQSM Joseph Swift, Sergeant Edward Sharpe, Sergeant William Heaton; centre row, left to right: Sergeant Austin Lang, Sergeant Stephen Loveless, CSM James Donnelly, Sergeant Thomas Grimshaw, Sergeant Walter Gent; front row, left to right: Second Lieutenant John Charles Shorrock, Second Lieutenant Frank Birtwistle, Captain James Clymo Milton and Second Lieutenant William Geoffrey Morris Rigby. (*John Garwood*)

D (Burnley) Company officers of the Accrington Pals, 1914. Left to right: Raymond St George Ross, John Victor Kershaw, Frederick Arnold Heys and Henry Davison Riley. (*Nelly and Jacquie Ainslie*)

1 and 2 Platoons, A (Accrington) Company in the Drill Hall, Accrington, February 1915. (*Author's collection*)

C (Chorley) Company marching along Chapel Street in Chorley on the way to the railway station, 23 February 1915. (*John Garwood*)

Lieutenant Colonel Arthur Wilmot Rickman, officer commanding 11/East Lancashire, 1915. (*Bindy Wollen*)

W Company, Accrington Pals on parade in Castle Square, Caernarvon, probably on 24 February 1915. (*Malcolm Bury*)

Accrington Pals group at Caernarvon, 1915. 15981 William Ashworth is seated in the centre. (*David Bent*)

W Company, Accrington Pals on parade in Castle Square, Caernarvon, 1915. (*Frances Morris*)

B Company, 2/East Lancashire, winners of the Lambert's Cup, 1907. (*Barry McAleenan*)

The Ritzema family, photographed most likely in 1915. Lieutenant Colonel Thomas Purvis Ritzema is standing at the far left of the back row. (*Mike Ritzema*)

Inspection of CLVIII Brigade RFA (Accrington & Burnley Howitzers) on Ellison's Tenement, Accrington by Major General Sir Thomas Perrott KCB, 15 April 1915. (*Jane Ramagge*)

Accrington Howitzers marching to Accrington railway station, 5 June 1915. (*Jane Ramagge*)

Although the brigade's activities were relaxed over the Easter weekend that immediately followed the march to Whalley, training soon stepped up a gear with signalling work added to the routine of drill and route marching. In Accrington, A Battery trained at Church, B Battery at the Argyle Street Drill Hall and the Ammunition Column at Accrington Tram Shed. Competition was encouraged, and there were football games played 'with about fifty a side' on the Stanley ground, and swimming contests held at the baths.

The brigade's officers – like those of the Pals – were expected to give the occasional evening lecture to the men. The officers too had to learn their trade and there were regular departures to training courses in gunnery at Shoeburyness and in field telephony at Dunstable.

The increased workload that Harwood had taken on to raise the Howitzers had finally taken its toll on his health. Not long after visiting the Pals at Caernarvon over the weekend of 20/21 March, Harwood suffered a severe bronchial attack and was confined to his home over Easter.

The two Burnley batteries marched to Accrington on Thursday, 15 April in order to take part in an inspection of the brigade on Ellison's Tenement by Major General Sir Thomas Perrott KCB. Perrott was reportedly well pleased with the 'very smart brigade', later taking the salute alongside John Harwood, happily recovered from his illness, as the brigade marched past the Town Hall.

Despite the growing number of British casualties on the Western Front, most recently from the Battle of Neuve-Chapelle, there was little evidence of public disillusionment with the war when the brigade made a route march to Sabden on Wednesday, 21 April. It was said that 'neither child nor elder escaped the contagion, and school was deserted and mill left to enable them the better to share in the proceedings'. There was again a football match played between teams formed from Accrington and Burnley, but the result on this occasion seems not to have been recorded.

On the following day, 22 April, the German Fourth Army at Ypres tried a new approach to breaking the deadlock on the Western Front by releasing clouds of poisonous chlorine gas against the French 45th (Algerian) and 87th (Territorial) divisions. The French formations broke, creating a 4-mile wide breach in the Allied lines which the Germans were fortunately slow to exploit, enabling the 1st Canadian Division to plug the gap.

Early in May, the Howitzers took delivery of their first horses followed a week later by four or five 15-pounder quick-firing field guns; two of the guns went to Burnley Barracks with the remainder going to Accrington. Now, at last, it was possible for the brigade to have riding practice and gun drill.

The number of members of the Harwood family in the brigade increased to three with the appointment of Frank's elder brother, 20-year-old Edmund Mills Harwood; Edmund had returned to England from Bombay where he had been serving with the Royal Engineers. All of John Harwood's close relatives who were of age were now employed in the Army.

Over the weekend of 8/9 May, John Harwood received news that the Howitzers as well as the Pals were to go into camp for further training. While the Pals would leave Caernarvon for Penkridge Bank, the Howitzers were to go to Weeton Camp near Blackpool. By the time the brigade was ready to depart, each gun battery had increased its complement to about 148 men: a captain, 3 subalterns, a battery sergeant major, a battery quartermaster sergeant, 2 sergeants, 5 corporals, 13 bombardiers, 65 gunners, 52 drivers, a fitter, a shoe-smith, a saddler, a wheeler and a trumpeter.

Not surprisingly, there were local events organized to mark the imminent departure of the brigade. Most notably, the members of Church and Oswald-twistle councils provided a potato-pie supper for about 130 men of the brigade who had been recruited from the 2 townships, as well as for some 20 wounded soldiers who were convalescing at Paddock House in Oswaldtwistle. With the meal over, the artillerymen formed up outside Oswaldtwistle Town Hall and, led by the Church and Oswaldtwistle Subscription Band, delighted the watching crowds by marching down Union Road and back again. The evening concluded in a concert, the star attraction from the Howitzers being Gunner Clegg who 'rendered three or four songs in the most approved music hall style'.

Saturday, 29 May saw the advance party comprising 147 men of the ammuni-tion column, led by Lieutenants Mercer, Turner and Edmund Harwood, leave Accrington to prepare for the brigade's arrival at Weeton Camp a week later. Despite newspaper reports of large crowds having assembled to watch the departure, it seems to have been a relatively low-key affair. The column paraded at the tram shed at 9.30am, listened to a short, rousing speech from the mayor to which they responded with three cheers, then marched along a circuitous route to the railway station. Harwood, it seems, had been unable on this occasion to arrange for a band to accompany the column owing to most of the local bandsmen being absent on munitions work. Amid 'hearty cheers' the column's train steamed away from the platform at 10.35am.

On the following Saturday, A and B batteries followed the ammunition column out of Accrington, having heard Harwood promise that 'I shall come to see you at Weeton and as I told the "Pals" you must not be surprised if you see me tumbling off an ammunition wagon when you are at the front'. Despite the rain, large crowds were again said to have gathered to witness the departure.

At Burnley too, the gloomy weather failed to prevent large numbers of well-wishers from lining the streets as C and D batteries marched from the barracks to the railway station led by the bugle and drum band of 3/5th East Lancashire.

Harwood was quick to keep his promise to visit the brigade in camp. On the first full Saturday of the brigade's stay at Weeton, Harwood arrived by motor car shortly before lunchtime, accompanied by Accrington's chief constable

(George Sinclair) and deputy town clerk (James Kenyon). The visit was marked by photographs being taken, first of Harwood with the brigade's officers posing alongside an artillery piece, then of the whole brigade. Probably to the relief of all, the visit was concluded shortly after lunch without any speeches being made, leaving those men granted weekend leave the chance to catch a train back home or to go into Blackpool.

With the departure from the town of the Howitzers, it seems clear that Harwood justifiably felt that it was time to draw a line under his extraordinary duties on behalf of King and Country. There is a sense of this in the address that he made to the next meeting of the Town Council once its ordinary business had been concluded, as reported in the *Accrington Gazette*:

> Though little had been said whilst the work was in progress in appreciation of generous concessions granted by the Corporation, he wished now to say how greatly it had all been valued. He wished to tender the Corporation and all the Committees his heartfelt thanks for the help they had given. He had great pleasure now in handing over to the Tramways Committee the tramshed, to the Baths Committee the baths, to the Town Hall Committee the Town Hall. (Laughter and applause.) Concluding, the Mayor said he had in his possession certain printed official documents relating to and authorizing the formation of the Pals Battalion and Howitzer Brigade, which he suggested should be framed and preserved as a memento of what Accrington had accomplished, and he gave the Finance Committee notice that he intended to bring such a proposal before them. (Applause.)

A month later, Harwood relieved himself of another of his responsibilities when he resigned the presidency of Accrington Stanley Football Club because his conviction that it was wrong to continue to play football while the country was at war was not shared by the club's directors. The directors accepted his resignation with regret, and expressed the hope that he would agree to resume the presidency once the war was at an end.

In August, the War Office again came to Harwood with a request, this time for his assistance in raising a pioneer battalion: Harwood declined.

The daily routine of the brigade at Weeton was well described in a letter written to relatives in Accrington by Robert Higgin, a 20-year-old who had been working in Bristol for the Civil Service prior to enlistment:

> The 'reveille' goes at 5.30am, and at six o'clock there is the first parade. In the intervening half hour we are expected to turn out and get our tent cleared out, beds, blankets, and greatcoats arranged neatly

and clean in a straight line, with our pots on top. From 6–7 there is physical training and foot drill for gunners, stables and work in connection with the horses for the drivers, and flag drill for all signallers. We are then dismissed on to the lines for completion of straightening up, breakfast, and getting ourselves properly dressed and cleaned for the second parade, which is the important parade of the day, at 8.45am. Gun drill, physical training, and riding are the general rule for the batteries, and we signallers get out into the unoccupied fields for signalling practice till 11 (11.30 for the battery). The time from 11.45 to 12.45 is mostly spent in lectures for all except drivers, who are more or less occupied all day on the horses. Dinner, and then the afternoon parade at 1.45 to 4.30, spent in a route march and, for us, more signalling, when we finish for the day. Tea comes along at about five o'clock, and the evenings are spent as best we can spend them. First post goes at 9.30, last post at 10, and lights out at a quarter past. Saturday afternoon is a half-holiday, and on Sunday there is the roll call at 6.30 (reveille at 6), and field service for about 3,000 men and officers at about 9.45, parade being at 9.15. When the service is over there is a camp inspection by the Colonel. After this we are dismissed.

Mealtimes were keenly awaited, and the tents were emptied of men as soon as the mess orderly was seen coming up to the brigade's lines. Along with half a loaf of bread per day and pots of strong tea, each man could expect three meals: breakfast might be bacon and egg, salmon, sardines, or herring in tomato sauce; lunch – the main meal of the day, known as dinner to the Lancashire men – was boiled meat with potatoes and vegetables; tea was typically jam and tinned fruit.

The brigade's development now visibly accelerated, though its equipment was slow to come through. During the first week in camp, one battery was able to practise with all four guns for the first time, but about six weeks would elapse before the gunners caught sight of an example of the 4.5in howitzer that they were supposed to be firing. The drivers had to wait until a week or more into July for the chance to test their newly acquired skills with a team of horses hitched up to an ammunition wagon; it was no easy task, for the horses, used to moving freely, jibbed, reared and kicked. At the same time, the brigade's signallers earned a following of spectators as they were introduced to signalling by lamp after dark; before long, messages were being clearly transmitted by Morse code over distances of ½ mile.

After the day's work was done, the men were able to take part in all the usual sporting activities. Games of cricket began immediately after tea and went on until dusk. Boxing contests were popular and were enlivened by rivalries such as Accrington versus Burnley. The brigade football team had its successes without matching the reputation of the Pals' team: wins against Kirkham (3–0) and a team from the RAMC (4–3) were balanced with defeats by teams from the Army Service Corps (2–5) and 2/West Lancashire (1–2).

The hot and sunny weather that the brigade had enjoyed from the time of its arrival in camp broke on the night of 22/23 June, creating an uncomfortable dampness in the tents into each of which eight men were tightly packed; at least, by this time, most of the tents had been equipped with boards for flooring. With the weekend of 3/4 July being a part of Burnley holidays, large numbers of friends and relatives were expected to visit the camp, but a heavy downpour on the Saturday was enough to discourage many from travelling. The following week brought the worst weather yet; from Tuesday evening until late afternoon on Wednesday, a strong, gusting wind drove rain through the tents soaking everything in its path. The inclement weather ruined an eagerly anticipated half-day holiday that the artillerymen had been granted in order to watch a charity cricket match between teams from the brigade and from Accrington Police.

Amid anticipation that the brigade would be leaving Weeton imminently, Wednesday, 14 July saw Harold Baker fulfil a promise to visit the brigade in camp. Accompanied by Harwood, and Sir George Watson Macalpine, owner of substantial collieries and brickworks in the Accrington area and father of Lieutenant Francis Macalpine of the Pals, he arrived at Weeton where the whole brigade was paraded in full dress on the camp square. The inspection lasted barely an hour before Baker left for Blackpool.

The brigade, which had been expecting orders to move camp since the first full week in July, was still at Weeton when Accrington holidays began. The weather was evidently more favourable than that of Burnley's holiday week, for it was reported that there were a great number of visitors to the camp on Sunday and Monday (25 and 26 July). Only days later, the brigade received orders to move on 4 August to Masham in Yorkshire where, alongside CLVII, CLIX and CLXIII brigades, it would form the divisional artillery of 35th Division. The division was notable for its infantry comprising bantam battalions into which recruitment at below the Army minimum height of 5ft 3in had been allowed.

An advance party of about forty men, taken on this occasion from the gun batteries and led by Lieutenant Mercer, left Kirkham railway station at about 11am on Saturday, 31 July. The 11½-hour journey by train to Masham was followed by a 2½-mile march to the camp on Roomer Common, and it was practically midnight before five tents had been erected and the men were able to rest. Despite rain on each of the following days, including a downpour on the Wednesday which inundated the camp ground, everything was ready for the main body of the brigade when it began to arrive on the Thursday afternoon.

The second of the two special trains carrying the brigade from Kirkham passed through Accrington on the Thursday morning; although no stop could be made, the artillerymen cheered lustily and a bugle 'rang out a clarion note' as the train steamed through the brigade's home town.

The artillerymen's early impressions of Masham were not wholly favourable, though the rain that began to fall shortly after work was completed on the first Saturday in camp hardly helped: by evening the streets and lanes in and around the village had turned to mud. The public houses in the village were closed to soldiers after 7pm and, in any case, it was remarked that 'soon after darkness has come, the streets, or street, [of Masham] is quickly cleared, and everybody makes his way home. This state of things is not entirely in accord with East Lancashire at night, for night in a Lancashire town is the busiest part of the day.' Adding to the grumbles was the absence of a Sunday train service at Masham, making it impractical to exchange visits with the Pals who had followed the Howitzers across the Pennines and were now at Ripon. Masham did at least boast a single fish and chip shop which 'did a roaring trade, for where chips are East Lancashire fellows will find their way'. As the weather improved, the men were better able to appreciate the beauty of the landscape surrounding Masham and there were reports of the brigade revelling in glorious sunshine and of the pleasure of exercising horses on the moors adjoining the camp.

The brigade's stay at Masham was a short one for, as early as 17 August, an advance party was preparing to leave for Salisbury Plain. For a few days, the four artillery brigades had Roomer Common to themselves after the divisional infantry left for Tidworth but on Wednesday, 25 August orders were received to move out of Masham that same day. Gun drill and horse work were immediately stopped, as every man was needed for transport work. By 2am on Thursday the brigade was entrained and on its slow journey south. Short stops at York and Leicester were followed by the welcome sight of Red Cross nurses waiting on the station platform at Banbury to dispense hot drinks. A further stop at Basingstoke brought the Howitzers a step closer to the realities of war as the artillerymen wandered over to an ambulance train to chat with men who had returned wounded from the ill-starred Gallipoli campaign. After the discomforts of a 12-hour journey during which the men with their kits had been packed eight to a compartment, the march up to the brigade's tented camp on Bulford Field may not have been unwelcome and would certainly have been enlivened by the sight of aeroplanes in the sky, a novelty to most of the Howitzers.

In the leisure time granted to them on Salisbury Plain, the Howitzers were allowed to roam within a 5-mile radius of Bulford Field without a pass, a greater degree of freedom than had been available to them at either Weeton or Masham. Writing to a friend back home, John Clough, a 34-year-old house painter from Accrington, described the possibilities for exploration and entertainment:

The small villages around about are almost what you could call picture postcard villages, you know the real old country thatched roof style, and all a different shape. We are within easy distance of Stonehenge, Amesbury, Fickledeane [*sic*], Netheravon, and Durrington, not forgetting what we call 'tin town' [Bulford Camp], a place about a mile away and composed of huts for troops ... also a theatre, a variety palace, and a picture palace. So you see it is not bad.

The brigade's gun batteries were said to have made a good impression when, a few days after their arrival on Salisbury Plain, they were inspected by Brigadier General William Cathcart Staveley who had just taken over command of the divisional artillery, having previously commanded XXX Brigade in France. Training was far from complete, however, and it seems to have been the end of September before horses and men were sent into manoeuvres in full battle kit, the horses encumbered with head-ropes, canteens, nose-bags, greatcoats, waterproof sheets and blankets, while each man carried a bandolier, water bottle and haversack.

Within about 5 minutes' walk from Bulford Field there was Nine Mile River, a welcome refuge from the hot and sunny weather that prevailed until well into September. The evenings, however, were soon turning chilly and by the end of September with the first day of really bad weather upon them, the Howitzers could hardly have been pleased to be the only brigade in the division still under canvas. A week into October, the Howitzers were finally able to move into the relative luxury of huts in the section of Bulford Camp known as Sling. Each hut housed a sub-section of about thirty-five men, and was equipped with beds with blankets and pillows, a stove, tables and bookshelves; the camp had a proper cookhouse and a mess, and the washhouses were a great improvement over the facilities available in Bulford Field.

Training courses continued for the officers, though for Captain Rice a gunnery course at Larkhill was to end his association with CLVIII Brigade: while lifting a gun trail on 30 September he severely damaged his right knee, and it would be May 1916 before he was again fit for active service. On 16 November, Rice was replaced by 32-year-old Captain Charles Pomeroy Hughes-Gibb, a Regular Army officer from Blandford in Dorset. On leave in India when war broke out, Hughes-Gibb had returned to Britain where he joined a battery of heavy artillery, subsequently seeing action in the battles of the Marne, Aisne and Ypres.

Although the Pals had followed the Howitzers to Salisbury Plain, they were camped 20 miles away at Hurdcott; until the Pals moved to Larkhill for the last two weeks in November, opportunities to come together were limited to the weekends when it was possible to meet half-way at Salisbury.

A radical change for the brigade took place on 2 December when each of its four batteries was allocated four 18-pounder quick-firing field guns in place of its howitzers. At the same time, CLXIII Brigade, which had been raised by the mayor and corporation of West Ham as a field gun brigade, was converted to howitzers. The reason for the switch is unclear.

Speculation had been rife concerning the division's destination overseas with India, Egypt and Gallipoli having been suggested at various times but on 26 January 1916 CLVIII Brigade received orders to embark for France. Lieutenant Colonel Ritzema had by this time left the brigade. Although Lieutenant Colonel Hope-Johnstone was appointed in place of Ritzema, he was almost immediately re-assigned to command CLIX Brigade. On 27 January, Lieutenant Colonel Percy Harrison Fawcett took over command of CLVIII Brigade, and four days later the brigade embarked at Southampton.

The brigade's officers at embarkation on 31 January were as follows:

Headquarters Staff: Lieutenant Colonel P H Fawcett, Captain H Renham, Second Lieutenant J R I Scambler, Lieutenant G M Jackson, Lieutenant W Walker.

A Battery: Captain H Gray, Second Lieutenant H Bancroft, Second Lieutenant R Jackson, Second Lieutenant M P Benton.

B Battery: Captain C P Hughes-Gibb, Second Lieutenant F Harwood, Second Lieutenant E M Harwood, Second Lieutenant G Grimshaw.

C Battery: Captain T Riley, Second Lieutenant R Mercer, Second Lieutenant H A Pearson, Second Lieutenant G N Slinger.

D Battery: Captain J C Crocker, Lieutenant D R Worsley, Second Lieutenant W Chambers, Second Lieutenant J A Bower.

Ammunition Column: Captain J F M Wilkinson, Second Lieutenant N Tomlinson, Second Lieutenant G Webster, Second Lieutenant T C Turner.

Chapter 8

A Most Colourful Personality

Percy Harrison Fawcett, born on 31 August 1867 at Torquay, was the younger son of Edward Boyd Fawcett, a militia officer and Fellow of the Royal Geographical Society (RGS). Although Fawcett was to claim that his childhood had been 'devoid of parental affection', his father surely had a strong influence over his chosen careers as Army officer and later as South American explorer. Nor were Fawcett's memories of his childhood entirely unhappy ones, for he wrote of the 'grand times' shared with his brother, Douglas, and sisters, Myra and Blanche.

Fawcett passed through Woolwich as a cadet before being granted a commission in the Royal Artillery in 1886. His first overseas posting was to Ceylon (present-day Sri Lanka), where he met his future wife, Nina. By the time of his marriage on 31 January 1901, he had returned to England and was well on his way to completing the RGS course in surveying that would change his life.

Although the surveying course led directly to a secret-service assignment in Morocco, it seems that Fawcett resumed a conventional Army career after returning from North Africa in 1902; following postings to Malta, Hong Kong and Ceylon, Fawcett was stationed at Spike Island in County Cork, Ireland when early in 1906 he was called back to the RGS in London. The Society had been commissioned by the government of Bolivia to find an experienced army officer to survey the disputed border where Bolivia, Brazil and Peru met: it was to Fawcett that the Society turned. Fawcett, who 'loathed army life', surely needed little persuading and, with the permission of the War Office, left for South America in May 1906. This first expedition was evidently judged a success for, after Fawcett returned to La Paz in October 1907, 'a bearded ruffian, burned almost black by the hot sun of the tropics and the glare of the snows', he was offered survey work on the border of Bolivia with Brazil. Fawcett was again able to accept the work while retaining his Army commission, and it is to this second expedition to South America of 1908–9 that the start of the obsession that was to haunt Fawcett's later life can be traced: the quest for the remains of civilizations more ancient than the Incas. The political outcome of the expedition was that about 1,200 square miles of border territory were secured for Bolivia, a result that helped Fawcett to secure the offer of yet more work from the Bolivian government, this time on the border with Peru. As the patience of the War Office could not be stretched further, Fawcett, disgruntled at having served twenty years 'for a wage less than that of most curates', decided to retire from the Army. His dissatisfaction with his former employers increased further on learning that his Army pension was to be reduced on the grounds that he had been in the service of a foreign government.

Fawcett's work on behalf of the Bolivian government ended in January 1912 when a dispute over the border with Peru had escalated to the point where the two countries were almost at war. Although Fawcett now found himself unemployed, he was at least free to undertake the private exploration that he had been 'itching to make'. Since 1910, Fawcett had been accompanied on his expeditions by an ex–NCO from the Rifle Brigade, Henry John Costin. Early in September 1914, Fawcett and Costin were in the Bolivian town of San Ignacio when they learned that war had broken out; anxious to play their part, they started on the long journey back to Britain by covering 231 miles by foot over two weeks in order to reach the city of Santa Cruz de la Sierra. Fawcett recalled the jubilation of the German population of Santa Cruz: 'After an orgy of beer-drinking, they tore down the bulletins on the British Vice-Consul's door and paraded the streets singing patriotic songs.'

Fawcett and Costin arrived back in Britain early in December. Whereas Costin is recorded as having gone to France with 4/Rifle Brigade on 20 December 1914, Fawcett had the chance to spend Christmas with Nina and their three children, 11-year-old Jack, 8-year-old Brian and 4-year-old Joan before re-joining the Army in January 1915. Fawcett was eventually given command of a field gun battery in the newly formed 25th Division before it went overseas in September 1915. The battery had been temporarily under the command of 22-year-old Second Lieutenant Cecil Eric Lewis Lyne, who had already been out to the Western Front where he had been caught in a chlorine gas attack at Ypres. Lyne regarded Fawcett as 'a most colourful personality, a man of magnificent physique and great technical ability, from whom I learned much'. Writing home on 22 October 1915, Lyne described how Fawcett had been quick to make himself as comfortable as possible on the Western Front: 'the Major has built himself a superb villa sunk 4ft 6in below the ground and banked up with earth and sandbags; the walls and floor are of wood, tapestried with canvas; a real proper door with real wooden steps and the whole painted green and finished in quite the latest style!!'

While Fawcett undoubtedly had his admirers, there were others who took a very different view after making his acquaintance. Henry Harold Hemming met Fawcett when, at the age of 24 and already recognized as an expert in counter-battery intelligence, he was appointed staff captain to VI Corps early in 1917. He regarded Fawcett, then counter-battery colonel at VI Corps, as 'probably the nastiest man I have ever met in this world'. Hemming also recalled that Fawcett's decisions on counter-battery fire were not necessarily based on science:

> Colonel Fawcett, however, had an entirely personal source of information. He owned a Ouija Board. So after a location had come in from say the sound rangers, he and his intelligence officer, who was a nice but down-trodden little waif, would retire to a darkened room and put their four hands, but not their elbows, on the board. Fawcett would then ask the Ouija Board in a loud voice if this was a confirmed location, and if the miserable board skidded over in the right direction, not merely would he include it in his list of confirmed locations, but often order twenty rounds of 9.2 howitzer to be fired at the place regardless of expense.

While home on leave at the beginning of January 1916, Fawcett was led to understand by the War Office that the strong recommendations for promotion from his commanding officer had appeared to fall on stony ground only because of an oversight that had seen his name deleted from the Army List! Before the month was out, the War Office wired Fawcett to take over command of CLVIII Brigade with the rank of lieutenant colonel.

Chapter 9

'Some' Colonel

A letter from an Accrington Pal published in the *Accrington Gazette* of 15 May 1915 vividly described the battalion's arrival at Penkridge Bank Camp two days earlier:

> We have arrived here safe, sound and in good time. But what a change! When we left Carnarvon this morning, at 8.20am, it was awfully hot, but when we got here at 1 o'clock it was pouring down, and cold enough to freeze you to death. It has been raining here for days, and I have never seen so much mud on a road in all my life, as it came over your ankles on the main road. We had to march 4½ miles to the camp in the rain, and all uphill. I think we are on the top of the Pennine Range, but the mud on the road was nothing to what it was in camp. You absolutely sunk into it about six or seven inches deep. We are in huts, which are quite new, as we are the first troops to be here. Nothing was ready when our men came on Tuesday; no roofs on most of the huts; no water within half a mile, and no lights. They must have buckled to, for they were quite ready for us, and had stoves going for us in all the huts. And for tea we had corned beef and bread and butter and tea. The stuff was very good, and we had a good tea. It was real butter, and the tea we had was without sugar and milk. There are about fifty in a hut. They are not exactly flock beds, but straw mattresses and pillows, with three blankets, though I guess they will be warm. We wash in the open air. Where we shall be able to buy anything I don't know ... There were crowds to see us off at Carnarvon, and everybody is sorry that we were leaving, us included ...

Three other Pals battalions also arrived at Penkridge Bank Camp on 13 May: 12/York and Lancaster (Sheffield City Battalion), 13/York and Lancaster (1st Barnsley Pals) and 14/York and Lancaster (2nd Barnsley Pals). Along with 11/East Lancashire, the four battalions now formed 94 Infantry Brigade, 31st Division.

Plaudits for the Pals continued to come in from the people of Caernarvon, and Rickman was proud to pass them on when he addressed the battalion at morning parade on the first Wednesday at Penkridge. By this time the Officer Commanding (OC) 94 Brigade, Brigadier General H Bowles, had already inspected the battalion and 'expressed his appreciation of the smartness of the men in every respect'. On Monday, 31 May, almost nine months after the Army Council sanctioned Harwood to raise a battalion, a ceremonial parade was held on the drill ground at Penkridge to mark the formal takeover of 11/East Lancashire by the War Office.

After Caernarvon, Penkridge had little to recommend it: the heather that thickly covered the moors around the camp made for harder field training, and the hot, dry weather of late May and early June not only added to the men's discomfort, but contributed to moorland fires that on occasion threatened to engulf the camp. In the late afternoon of Whit Sunday, 23 May, the entire brigade of 4,000 men turned out to fight fires on two sides of the camp; working with picks, shovels and entrenching tools, the men hastily created fire breaks to prevent the flames from reaching the huts. Writing to his sister on 21 June, Richard Ormerod made no attempt to hide his dismay:

> It is a terrible place up here, no-one has a good name for it. It is terribly dusty. If you are marching your eyes, mouth and clothes are filled with dust. The moors for miles around continually keep smouldering and setting on fire. The smoke from these fires is terrible especially when we are called out to act as fire brigade when the fire reaches the vicinity of the wood huts. Were it not for being able to get away at weekends it would be miserable.

Each man had at least enjoyed 4 days leave with a free railway pass after arriving at Penkridge, and the first batch of about 120 men were back in their home towns for Whitsuntide. Football as usual provided a welcome diversion from training, and a 7–0 drubbing of W Company by Z Company on 18 May emphasized the superior playing skills of the Burnley men. Six days later, on the morning of the Whit Monday holiday, a battalion team containing as many as 7 players from Burnley inflicted a 2–1 defeat on a team from the Barnsley Pals in a game watched by 500 spectators. Further victories for the battalion over teams picked from the rest of the brigade (7–1) and from the 2nd Barnsley Pals (2–0) were followed by a rare loss in which Sheffield's Pals emerged as 2–1 winners. The battalion failed to shine at athletics during the Brigade Sports held on 10 July, but defeated the Sheffield men by an innings and 6 runs in a cricket match which concluded on 12 July.

Although Rickman had quickly established himself as a commanding officer who expected the highest standards of the men under his charge, he had also won their respect: one Pal was quoted as saying 'We would follow our Colonel anywhere'. As a means of keeping up the men's morale, Rickman was keen for the battalion to have its own band, and soon had twenty volunteer bandsmen under the tutorage of a 44-year-old Chorley man transferred across from 4/Loyal North Lancashire, Sergeant Joseph Henry Whitworth. By 9 June, the band had become a reality, its instruments having been provided by an anonymous donor. Within a short space of time, the battalion acquired a second band after a group of men from X Company had the idea to ask Accrington's Lang Bridge Ltd for the loan of instruments that had been used by the works' comic jazz band; the works' officials approved the loan, and the 'Village Pirate Band' came into being. James Edward Birch, a 28-year-old cotton weaver from Accrington, described the arrival of the instruments at Penkridge:

> On Monday, June 21st, some of our boys carried the instruments three miles from the station to the camp. The first night these merry 'Pals' marched up in fours, playing 'Bluebells of Scotland'. Soon all the men came out from their huts quite surprised, and also from the other lines, in fact, the officers all turned out with a smile on their faces, and contributed to the collection.

Rickman's care for the welfare of his men is also evident from his allowing field training to be done without jackets; the extension in June of mock battles to the wooded estate on Penkridge Bank may well also have been instigated by Rickman to shield his men from the worst of the heat. The trench periscopes that Rickman had requested of Harwood early in April were delivered to the battalion in mid-June, and training for each man in their use began immediately.

Whereas W, X, Y and Z companies had entrained at Caernarvon for Rugeley, the 180 men of R Company were destined for Oldham where they formed a depot for 11/East Lancashire at Chadderton Camp. No explanation has survived as to why the Accrington Pals had the unique privilege in the regiment of maintaining a depot of their own, albeit for the short duration of less than four months. A recruitment drive during June in Accrington and its neighbourhood to bring the strength of the depot up to two full companies progressed only slowly despite the best week-long efforts of about fifty R Company men aided by the band of the Lancashire Fusiliers. At the same time, the battalion's ranks were being depleted with 150 men being required for munitions work and about a further 150 from the depot being transferred to 3/East Lancashire for home defence having been judged unfit for General Service (GS). Towards the end of June, seventeen NCOs and three officers – Lieutenants W Roberts, Kershaw and Ramsbottom – were transferred from Penkridge to the depot at Chadderton. In order to build up the number of officers in the reserve companies, four men were recommended for commissions: 27-year-old George Watson from Accrington, a sergeant in the Accrington and Burnley Howitzer Brigade; 26-year-old John Charles Palmer from Church, a corporal serving with 9/East Surrey, and the son of Superintendent James Thomas Palmer of the Church Police Division; 18-year-old Accrington-born Barton Walmsley Sims; and 29-year-old Ernest Edgar Ritchie from Bradford, a private serving with Inns of Court Officer Training Corps and a friend of the Harwood family. All four commissions were subsequently confirmed.

The markedly cooler weather of July came as a relief at Penkridge, and the showers and rain that developed later in the month put an end to the moorland fires. Some men were diverted to take part in a bombing course at Tynemouth, while others were assigned to the divisional cycling company. Brigade exercises were added to the training programme, each battalion taking its turn at staging a mock attack against entrenched positions held by the other three: the battalion took pride in receiving a commendation from Brigadier General Bowles for the manner in which 'its discipline when severely tested was fully maintained'. Six officers were recommended for promotion to full lieutenant: Bury, Harwood, Kenny, Rawcliffe, Stonehouse and Williams.

Few tears were shed when news came through that the brigade was to move to Ripon. An advance party of twenty-three NCOs and men under Captain Livesey left Penkridge on 27 July to prepare for the battalion's arrival at their new camp. About 200 men were to stay behind to clean up at Penkridge before entraining directly for Ripon, while the remaining 800 or so men would take part in a recruiting march through east Lancashire out of which better results were expected than those achieved by the reserve company.

The battalion began its recruiting march in glorious weather on the morning of Friday, 30 July, detraining at Chorley to find the town brightly decorated for its arrival with flags of all the Allied nations and bunting. After being shown to their billets by special constables, the men re-assembled on the Cattle Market before marching along streets lined with large crowds of spectators to the Coronation Pleasure Ground where a civic welcome from the mayor, Alderman R Hindle, awaited. Hindle pulled no punches, being quoted as saying 'There are a number of men without any ties who could and should enlist, and I should be glad if you would take those young shirkers with you. We don't want them; we can do without them.' While it is doubtful that Rickman would have had any time either for shirkers, he diplomatically replied with the words 'Chorley has given us one company. I hope she will give us another company for the reserve battalion.' The recruitment drive then carried on its way with a parade of the battalion through the town led by its band.

On the following morning, the people of Chorley again turned out in numbers to give the battalion a rousing send-off as it marched off to Blackburn to give a military display at the Lancashire Agricultural Show. If the Blackburn men in the battalion were disappointed at the absence of a civic welcome from their mayor, they would have been cheered by the crowds that gathered on the Sunday for the march on to Accrington. While there is no doubt that the road into Accrington was lined with spectators, and that a huge crowd had gathered to celebrate the battalion's return to its home town, there are contradictory versions of the vocal welcome: one account speaks of the dense crowd in the area of the Town Hall and Market Ground being almost silent while another describes how 'cheer upon cheer broke from the crowd as the men marched past led on horseback by Rickman, followed by Peltzer and Watson'. In any event, Rickman pronounced himself to be 'absolutely stunned' at the sight of the large crowd. John Harwood, as mayor, took the salute 'looking as fit and cheery as ever, and beaming with pride'.

The battalion's efforts to encourage recruits to come forward took the form of route marches through the area on each of the following two days, and a display of bayonet exercise and rifle drill in Accrington's Oak Hill Park on the Monday evening. On the Tuesday evening, Harwood hosted a dinner for Rickman and the other officers of the battalion at the Commercial Hotel. Aware that his speech would be well reported in the local newspapers and scrutinized by Accrington men at the front, Harwood took the opportunity once more 'to correct an impression that was abroad amongst some of the Accrington boys who were fighting for their country, and who were not in the "Pals" ... He wished to inform them through the Press that they were not forgotten by any means.'

Turning to Rickman, Harwood was quoted as saying:

> When any of the men of the battalion came to Accrington they generally called in at the mayor's parlour, and said they thought they would just give him a call, and all of them had the same story to tell – they were proud of their commanding officer, he was strict and saw that they did their duty, but at the same time he looked after them and cared for them.

In response, Rickman admitted to sometimes being known as 'a bit ratty or hot-tempered' but emphasized the trust that he had felt able to place in his men on their return home:

> Surely it was a pretty good test to put 800 men loose amongst their pals and find them turn up in the manner they had done ... There was the spirit of trust between the whole lot of them, and it was a very great pleasure to hear from outside sources that they were such a happy family, because it was the ground work from A to Z of a good battalion. If the men were happy they could be sure they would be doing good work.

It was a happy battalion, of that there can be no doubt. More than sixty years later, Thomas Rawcliffe recalled how the Pals were 'the happiest lot that ever existed' and that 'they were so happy – that was the tragedy of it'.

On the Wednesday morning, the battalion started on the final leg of its march through east Lancashire with Burnley's Major Ross taking the place of Captain Watson to join Rickman and Captain Peltzer at the head of the column. The battalion reached Burnley to find the Market Square 'packed from end to side with a shouting, cheering crowd' and, on this occasion, the mayor, Alderman Kay, was on hand to extend a warm welcome. As the battalion stood to attention in the square, Rickman pinned a Distinguished Conduct Medal (DCM) on to Lance Corporal Harry Watson of 2/East Lancashire who had won his decoration for rescuing a man who had been trapped in barbed wire during the Battle of Neuve-Chapelle. Although each man in the battalion was promised free admission to one of Burnley's theatres in the evening, many of the Accrington men understandably returned home for the night. The battalion left Burnley by train for Ripon on the following morning, and went into huts at South Camp.

It is doubtful that the recruitment march reached expectations. Nationwide, the number of volunteers for Army service had dipped below 100,000 in each of the months of July and August, and fell further to below 72,000 in September. The first step towards conscription came when the National Registration Act was passed on 15 July, its purpose being to give the government transparency on the manpower available for both military service and munitions work. Accordingly, on 15 August, the country's 2,000 local authorities gathered the details of every person between the ages of 15 and 65. The immense task was carried out by civilian volunteers: in Accrington, the work was accomplished mostly by teachers, and resulted in 29,001 inhabitants being included in the National Register. The local authorities were then instructed to transfer the details of every man aged between 18 and 41 to a pink form, to mark the forms of men engaged in essential war industries with a black star and to forward the completed forms to the local recruiting authorities. With the military now having the details of every man in the country eligible for service in the next twelve months, the road to conscription was open.

With the diversion of the recruiting march, 11/East Lancashire was the last battalion of 94 Brigade to reach Ripon. With its arrival, 31st Division – the quintessential Pals division – came together for the first time; alongside 94 Brigade were 92 Brigade comprising 10, 11, 12 and 13/East Yorkshire (1st, 2nd, 3rd and 4th Hull Pals, known as the Commercials, Tradesmen, Sportsmen and T'Others), 93 Brigade comprising 15/West Yorkshire (Leeds Pals), 16 and 18/West Yorkshire (1st and 2nd Bradford Pals) and 18/Durham Light Infantry (Durham Pals), and the divisional pioneers, 12/King's Own (Yorkshire Light Infantry) (KOYLI).

The Pals had arrived at South Camp to find their huts – only some 5 minutes' walk from Ripon – surrounded by fruit-filled apple, pear and cherry trees; it was a welcome change from the remote moorland of Penkridge as George Stubbins, a clerk from the Turkey Red Dye Works at Church, expressed in a letter home:

> The camp itself is quite a garden city, compared with Penkridge. It is built on meadow land, and the huts have been carefully and well put up. In fact, they can keep me here until the war is over, if they like. But at last I am thoroughly convinced that we shall see active service. Since we came here we have been provided with mules, ammunition wagons, and four travelling field kitchens, which of course would not be used for home defence ... We have been told we have finished with drill now, and that our time will be spent firing, bayonet fighting, entrenching, and route marching.

A little over a week after the battalion's arrival at Ripon, it was inspected by Major General Sir Archibald James Murray, Deputy Chief of the Imperial General Staff. Murray, who was accompanied by Brigadier General Bowles, Brigade Major Francis Stewart Gilderoy Piggott and Staff Captain Bernard Robert Dickinson, was said to have reported that 'he had so far never inspected so smart a body of men as the 11th Battalion East Lancashire Regiment'.

The purpose of the battalion's short stay at Ripon was to take a firing course at the rifle range outside the nearby village of Bishop Monkton. The range, which incorporated elaborate and realistic trenches, was still being completed when the battalion arrived, and the honour of christening the range when it opened on Thursday, 19 August fell to the officers and NCOs representing Accrington. The range was able to accommodate 192 men at any one time when it opened, but would eventually allow up to 240 men to fire at once. W and X companies underwent the course first, finishing within twelve days with highly satisfactory results; Richard Ormerod was one of those who took part:

> There is no doubt that we are now progressing with our training. We are now busy, firing our course on a large new range about four miles from Ripon. We are on parade at 5.30am and then walk to the range on a beautiful road which runs amongst some splendid cultivated land which is now undergoing harvest. When on the range you get some kind of an idea what it must be like at the front especially when you are in the trench immediately in front of the targets and butts. You hear the bullets whistle and then kick up the earth in the butts.

Y and Z companies must have finished their course just as quickly for, by 15 September, the entire battalion had either completed or embarked upon four days of special leave (excluding travelling time) prior to moving to Salisbury Plain. Immediately before the first two companies left for leave on 8 September, the entire battalion was inspected by the newly appointed GOC 31st Division, Major General Robert Wanless O'Gowan, who had served as lieutenant colonel of 1/East Lancashire for four years from 1909 to 1913; O'Gowan reportedly said that what he had seen 'exceeded all his expectations'.

On 10 September, as the Accrington men were enjoying their home leave, the town looking 'all the brighter for their promise', Harwood finally closed the door on accepting the mayoralty for a fourth successive year; the stress and strain of the past twelve months had taken their toll on his already poor health.

Only at this time was each man in the battalion in receipt of a new khaki overcoat in place of the blue one which had been issued over the previous winter.

Before the departure from Ripon, command of 94 Brigade was transferred from Bowles to Brigadier General George Tupper Campbell Carter-Campbell, a 46-year-old Scot who had been one of only two officers from 2/Cameronians to come unwounded out of the Battle of Neuve-Chapelle.

The Pals left Ripon in pouring rain on the morning of Friday, 24 September, their 11-hour journey south by train echoing that made by the Howitzers a month earlier. On arriving at Wilton station, the battalion had a 5-mile march in darkness to reach its new base at Hurdcott Camp. A further change in the command structure took place with the arrival of Major Edward Leopold Reiss, a 46-year-old Mancunian, as second-in-command of the battalion. It seems probable that Ross had taken on the duties of the second-in-command after Slinger's appointment to the depot company, and might reasonably have expected to retain the position. With Reiss being appointed instead, it appears that Rickman looked to compensate Ross by recommending that he – rather than Slinger – be given command of 12/East Lancashire, the reserve battalion that had been formed out of the depot companies on 3 September. Brigadier General Sitwell, OC 17 Reserve Infantry Brigade, despite having initially supported Rickman's recommendation, was subsequently swayed by Slinger's claims that Ross's attainments were 'by no means above the average' and that Ross had 'frequently appealed to him for assistance in his carrying out his duties'. The dispute escalated, and ended with neither officer being successful: Major R S Weston was appointed to command 12/East Lancashire with effect from 3 February 1916.

As the battalion continued to take part in mock battles and route marches, the weeks spent at Hurdcott were notable for the terrible weather; early in November, the Pals felt they had been given an insight into conditions at the front when at nightfall they were ordered into trenches which were deep in water and mud following the heavy rain of earlier in the day. The on-going need to identify men for munitions work constantly threatened to deplete further the numbers of the original members of the battalion.

The environs of Hurdcott offered fewer opportunities than Ripon for leisure-time activities and tea 'most cheerfully given' for the small sum of 4*d* in Wilton Town Hall on Sunday afternoons would seem poor compensation for the absence of a cinema in the town. The battalion had little success in the divisional cross-country race held on 1 November, in which D, A and C companies of 15/West Yorkshire took the first three prizes, but continued its successful run at football with wins over 13/York and Lancaster and 11/East Yorkshire, and a draw and a win against 12/York and Lancaster.

Meanwhile, the move towards conscription was gathering pace. On 5 October, Asquith appointed Lord Derby as Director-General of Recruiting, tasking him with formulating a scheme to make use of the pink forms generated from the National Register. The resulting Derby Scheme required that, outside of Ireland, every man between the ages of 18 and 41 was to be asked either to join up immediately or to attest his willingness to serve at some later date. Canvassing was again to be organized by local authorities. Each man who attested was to be allocated to one of forty-six groups according to marital status and age. All the single men were to be called up first, starting with those aged 19 (Group 1) and ending with those aged 41 (Group 23); only then would the youngest of the married men be called up. Local tribunals were to be set up to which men could apply for either postponement of their military service or exemption. Harwood, regardless of his poor health and, it can be imagined, to his later regret, again took an active part in the demands placed on the local authorities to complete the canvass; presiding over a meeting on 12 November to recruit canvassers, he expressed his dismay that only 40 had turned up despite about 10,000 circulars having been distributed. Fortunately, the deadline for completing the canvass was later extended from the end of November to 11 December.

Not content with his work on behalf of the council, Harwood began raising funds to buy Christmas comforts for the Pals and the Howitzers, an action that once more attracted criticism for the apparent favouritism towards the two locally raised units. In a letter addressed directly to Harwood, 31-year-old Captain Douglas Hewitt Hacking from Clayton-le-Moors pointed out that C Company of 2/4th East Lancashire comprised practically all Accrington men, most of whom had enlisted before the Pals and Howitzers were formed, and that they 'feel rather keenly the preference given to the "Pals" and Howitzers in the Accrington district'. Harwood replied that if the response was satisfactory, C Company would not be forgotten.

On 16 November, the Accrington Pals left Hurdcott temporarily for Larkhill in order to take a second firing course. Reaching their new quarters after a 15-mile route march enlivened by views of Stonehenge, the Pals found the camp ill-prepared for their arrival; it took the best of Rickman's organizational skills to sort matters out: 'God only knows how we would go on if it was not for our Colonel. I have just seen him (7pm) and he has not taken his full pack off yet. He has been knocking about here, there and everywhere, looking after dinner, coal, beds, etc. He is "some" Colonel.'

During its two weeks at Larkhill, the battalion was issued with new service rifles which were then used to complete the firing course. When not on the rifle range, the Pals were engaged in routine training, including nights spent in trenches while enduring temperatures as low as 20°F. The weekends at Larkhill did at least provide opportunities to exchange visits with the Howitzers, who were at this time less than 3 miles distant at Bulford.

The battalion returned to Hurdcott with the expectation of a weekend leave to come before being sent overseas. Rickman had even organized a special train to depart from Wilton when the divisional order came through that all leave was to be stopped; despite great disappointment at the cancelled leave, there was only one absentee at the weekend roll-call. On 30 November, an advance party from the battalion was sent to Le Havre as part of the preparation for 31st Division to move to the Western Front; it was recalled however on the following day and, when sun helmets were issued a few days later, it was clear that Mesopotamia or Egypt would be its destination.

The battalion's final days at Hurdcott were memorable for the practice departure from camp on 14 December; allegedly because the battalion had already handed back its detailed maps of the area, it managed to lose its way, and what should have been a 3-mile march was extended to one of 9 or 10 miles in length. The battalion, incongruously dressed in sun helmets, were at least captured on film near the start of the practice march.

On Wednesday, 15 December, a dinner was given for Honorary Captain and Quartermaster Lay on his departure for the reserve battalion, 12/East Lancashire. Lay, by this time 63 years old, had hoped to go overseas with the Pals but was prevented from doing so by his age. In the previous month, the battalion had also lost the services of Lieutenant Rigby, who had transferred to the Machine Gun Corps.

After a fortnight on readiness to move at a moment's notice, the battalion finally received orders to embark for Egypt. During the night of 18/19 December, the Accrington Pals marched out of camp and entrained at Salisbury for Devonport.

Chapter 10

Away From All Civilization

The last days of October 1914 saw Turkey enter into the war on the side of the Central Powers of Germany and Austria–Hungary. It was a development that threatened not only the safety of the Anglo–Persian oil fields located close to Basra – precipitating Britain to land an expeditionary force in Mesopotamia – but also the security of the Suez Canal through which passed men and materials from Asia and Australasia which were vital to the Allied war effort. Before the year was out, Winston Churchill, then First Lord of the Admiralty, had put forward the bold idea of seizing control of the Straits of the Dardanelles, the narrow stretch of water that gives access from the Aegean Sea to the Sea of Marmara, Constantinople (present-day Istanbul) and the Black Sea. The potential rewards of a successful operation were considerable: with Constantinople under threat, Turkey could be forced out of the war, the Suez Canal would be protected and a supply route opened up to allow Russia both to receive munitions from its European allies and to export its reserves of wheat. With deadlock having been reached on the Western Front, the idea of seizing the straits became irresistible.

Tragically for the Allies, their piecemeal approach to executing the plan condemned it to failure. Following a naval bombardment of the straits' shore defences on 19 and 25 February 1915, an abortive attempt by British and French warships to force the straits was made on 18 March. The element of surprise had been lost and, by the time troop landings under the command of General Sir Ian Hamilton were attempted on 25 April, the Turkish defences had been strengthened. The main landings, made by the British 29th Division at Cape Helles, the tip of the Gallipoli peninsula, and by the Australian and New Zealand Army Corps (Anzac) on the western coast, succeeded only in establishing footholds on the peninsula. On 4 June, the newly arrived 42nd (East Lancashire) Division joined the 29th Division, the 63rd (Royal Naval) Division and a French division in an attempt to break out from the Cape Helles position but six weeks later Hamilton's front line at Helles was still no further than about 3 miles inland. The last chance for the Allies to take the peninsula began on 6 August with a diversionary attack on the Helles front by 29th Division followed within an hour by an assault from the Anzac positions. Over the following night, 20,000 British troops landed almost without opposition at Suvla Bay, 3 miles north of the Anzac battle, but the short-lived opportunity to push rapidly out of Suvla and provide the decisive force to drive the Turks from the ridges beyond was lost. There was little consolation to be had in the brilliantly conducted Allied withdrawal from the peninsula; the Anzac and Suvla positions were evacuated without loss over 19/20 December, and an equally successful operation was carried out at Helles over 8/9 January 1916. British (including Anzac) casualties over the campaign totalled 213,930, of which 145,154 resulted from sickness; adding in French losses of 47,000 brought the number of Allied casualties to more than 260,000. Turkish losses have been estimated at up to 350,000.

Of the men who lost their lives through the Gallipoli campaign, at least thirty-three are listed on Accrington's war memorial in Oak Hill Park. A disproportionately high number were officers: 29-year-old Harry Hargreaves Bolton and his brother, 26-year-old John Bolton, both of whom held responsible positions in the local colliery industry, John Bury, the 21-year-old son of Alderman A S Bury and a cotton manufacturer, Gilbert Edwin Sprake, a 28-year-old solicitor, and Sam Harold Walmsley, a 29-year-old engineer.

Once the decision to evacuate Gallipoli had been taken, there remained the question of how Turkey might redeploy its forces after the Allied withdrawal. In order to guard against the possibilities of a Turkish move against Mesopotamia or Egypt, a strategic reserve was assembled in Egypt under the command of Lieutenant General Sir Archibald Murray. Turkey had already attempted one invasion of Egypt: the Ottoman Fourth Army led by General Ahmed Cemal and a German officer, Colonel Franz Kress von Kressenstein, had reached the Suez Canal on the night of 3 February 1915 after marching across the Sinai desert. On the following morning the Turks attempted to cross the canal with the aid of pontoons which had been pre-fabricated in Germany, but were driven off by Indian troops supported by gunfire from Royal Navy warships and an armoured train. It was in order to reinforce Murray's strategic reserve that 31st Division was moved to Egypt where it joined one division redeployed from France, the 46th (albeit briefly), and ten divisions moved from Gallipoli, the 11th, 13th, 29th, 42nd, 52nd, 53rd, 54th, 1st and 2nd Australian, and Anzac divisions.

The Accrington Pals embarked onto troopships at Devonport on 19 December 1915 and left harbour for Egypt that same day. Whereas the battalion transport was accompanied by 2 officers and 47 other ranks on board the SS *Huanchaco*, the bulk of the battalion – 29 officers and 956 other ranks – were transported on the SS *Ionic*. It was shortly after dusk when the *Ionic* pulled away from the dockside with musical accompaniment being provided by the battalion band. For the battalion's officers, it was to be a most comfortable journey as the *Ionic* offered them splendid quarters with well-furnished large lounge, library and smoking room. In contrast, many of the men found it more comfortable throughout the voyage to sleep on deck in the open air than down below in crowded hammocks. Early in the first morning at sea, the single destroyer that had been provided as an escort turned back. Each man was issued with a lifebelt and lifeboat drill was established as a daily routine. The men were kept entertained by the band playing daily on deck, concert parties, deck billiards and quoits, and competitions of boxing and tug-of-war.

After the briefest of stops at Gibraltar in the late evening of 23 December to send off mail and to collect orders, the *Ionic* left for Malta with two destroyers as escort for the part of the voyage during which the troop carrier was thought to be at most risk from submarine attack. In the event, Malta was reached without incident on the morning of 27 December; no sooner had the *Ionic* come to anchor than it was assailed by local traders in 'dozens of small boats laden with tobacco, postcards, fruit, sweets, chocolate, etc.'. Although the *Ionic* was anchored at Malta for two days, only the officers were allowed ashore, leaving the aggrieved men on board to find amusement as best they could. Much entertainment was derived from watching native boys dive in after coins thrown into the water: supposedly not a coin was lost.

Although the *Ionic* left Malta at 8.20am on 29 December without a destroyer escort, the threat from enemy submarines was recognized by a War Office instruction that lifebelts were to be worn at all times. During the day the sun continued to shine with a fierce intensity, and it is hardly surprising that there were cases of sunstroke among the East Lancashire men: an extreme case was that of 24–year-old James Clarence Wixted, an iron-moulder from Accrington, who died after a short illness in the evening. Wixted was buried at sea with full military honours at 6.30am on 30 December.

Less than 24 hours ahead of the *Ionic*, the P&O steamship *Persia* was some 70 miles south of the east end of Crete when it was torpedoed by the German submarine *U-38* shortly after 1pm on 30 December. Within 5 minutes the *Persia* had sunk with the loss of 334 lives.

As the *Ionic* steamed eastwards 60 miles south of Crete on the following day, her master and crew, forewarned by the fate of the *Persia*, were on the lookout for any evidence of submarine activity. At 9.40am an enemy submarine – possibly again *U-38* – broke the surface about 500yd off the port side of the *Ionic*: 'suddenly the ship canted over to an angle of 45 degrees and at the same time the deck trembled as the vibrations came from the engines jumping to "full speed" and the alarm sounded. ... Every man jumped to it and dashed to his post. Rifle shots rang out for the attacker's periscope was visible.' A single torpedo fired by the submarine missed the stern of the troopship by only 100ft, but the *Ionic* was then able to leave the danger behind by steaming ahead at full speed. In response, three extra guards each comprising an officer and twenty other ranks were posted around the sides of the ship, but an hour later the danger was reckoned to have passed.

The torpedo attack against the *Ionic* on the last day of 1915 would later form the basis of an unsuccessful campaign by Harwood and Rickman to see the Pals awarded the 1914–15 Star. The award was important not so much for indicating that the owner had entered a war zone before the end of 1915, but for confirming him as a volunteer for Army service; without it, there was no service medal to distinguish the volunteers of 1914 and 1915 from the conscripts of 1916 and later.

With news of the sinking of the *Persia* having reached east Lancashire, there was 'widespread relief' throughout Accrington when a cablegram was received to report the battalion's safe arrival at Alexandria on the morning of New Year's Day 1916. Three days later, the *Ionic* left for Port Said; the 16-hour final leg of the voyage witnessed a sharp change in the weather: the calm that had prevailed throughout the voyage from Devonport was exchanged for rough and stormy seas, and most of the Pals suffered from seasickness. After docking at Port Said in the midst of a violent thunderstorm at 7.30am on 5 January, the Pals disembarked during the afternoon and went under canvas at No. 5 Camp.

The battalion remained at No. 5 Camp for almost three weeks, during which time the battalion war diary recorded little apart from the provision of parties to act as guards, most usually for neutral ships passing along the Suez Canal. Although the battalion's duties while at Port Said were comparatively light, and the men were able to enjoy the freedom to go into the town between the 2pm parade and 8pm, there was still cause for dissatisfaction:

> The town near which we are stationed (we are only camped half a mile outside) is a very lively place. There are any number of cafes, with plenty of fun going on every night, Sundays included. There are very few English people here. The [locals] are not friendly disposed towards us. Their quarter of the town is 'out of bounds' and we have strict injunctions not on any account to visit their domain ... we are nearly all stony broke. We have had no pay for three weeks ... Since arriving here we have found out that only certain cigarettes are cheap, and they are scarcely worth smoking. English cigarettes are no cheaper than at home. However we are now receiving a weekly allowance (being on active service) of either four packets of cigarettes or two ounces of tobacco ... Since arriving here we have found that our rations are considerably cut down ... All our spare money goes on buying eatables.

On 13 January, Richard Ormerod noted that his tea that day had consisted of dry bread and five dates; a week later he enjoyed his 'best dinner since arrival' of stew, boiled rice and stewed dates.

By the time the battalion moved 40 miles southward along the Suez Canal to El Ferdan (present-day Al Firdan) on 25 January the men had had only one pay day since arriving in Egypt. Nor was the weather during the journey conducive to high spirits as the Pals, travelling in open rail wagons, were exposed to alternating bouts of torrential rain and hailstorms; Richard Ormerod thought it to be the 'hardest day since enlistment'.

On the day after its arrival at El Ferdan, the battalion took over all garrison guard and picquet duties but was mostly occupied over the next days with transporting stores across to the east bank of the canal. It was a time that was to be chiefly remembered for the heavy flat-bottomed ferry which, until the Royal Engineers constructed a pontoon bridge, was the only means of crossing the water and needed considerable manpower for its operation:

> The chief reminder of ancient Egypt was the slavery, for if ever the East Lancs felt the shackles, it was at El Ferdan. Who will forget the varied fatigues – the hauling of those two massive chains which were the primitive means of propelling the giant punt across the canal, carrying men, horses and stores to the Arabian side where the Turks had been, but were to be no more. Ships came alongside to be unloaded, and out of the holds long single files of Lancashire lads brought massive quantities of timber, compressed horse and camel fodder, sacks of dates, raisins, immense quantities of bully beef and biscuits, ammunition and various other stores. NCOs were posted every ten yards or so and apart from the fact that they had no whips, the feeling from the Tommies' point of view, was exactly as those of the slaves of old.

Rather than relying on the canal as a line of defence, Sir Archibald Murray followed a policy of pushing troops well forward into the desert to defend the canal. Accordingly, on 9 February, W and Z companies moved about 6 miles forward to Bir Abu Aruk where for the following nine days they dug trenches to form an outpost line. The march out into the desert was particularly exhausting:

> On the 9th February Z Company left the Battalion and struck out into the desert for a long dreary march, with full pack, and any extras from under the sand that one cared to carry. [Tins of food 'liberated' from the unloaded stores were hidden under sand until they could be safely retrieved.] The start was at sunrise and by 4 o'clock the Company must have been a mile long. Most of the fellows were exhausted and when the halt was called, everybody flopped down on their tummies, and some were too tired to slip off their packs, for some time. The desert proved to be very hilly and the

sand soft and difficult to the tread. Boots sank ankle deep in many places, especially when on rising ground, and seemed to drag one's sinews until they stretched like elastic bands. Abu Aruk was the spot chosen for the defence works Z Coy were to construct. It was on high ground and in the wilderness, away from all civilization.

Under a hot sun, it was exhausting work to dig a defensive line in the soft, shifting sand using only small GS shovels. An initial excavation to a width of 24ft was necessary in order to create a trench 5ft in width at the top; the trench then had to be lined with hurdle fences covered by grass matting or canvas in order to prevent the sand from sifting through. Water was short, such that even the briefest of rain showers came as welcome relief:

> A small black cloud appeared, to be followed by a shower of rain. Instantaneously, as if by command, every man was stark naked, standing there, awaiting nature's bath, with his face turned upwards and mouth wide open, hoping that a few drops would cool his parched tongue. On the 19th the trenches were handed over to another division and Z Company had a tough march back to El Ferdan.

While W and Z companies were working on the outpost line, Y Company and battalion headquarters had left for the railhead on 10 February to take over the distribution of supplies and water to the advanced posts. X Company remained on fatigue duties at El Ferdan. The battalion regrouped at El Ferdan on 19 February, and marched the following day 14 miles north along the canal to Kantara (present-day Al Qantarah). On arriving, there was neither a meal nor a camp to be found, and it was midnight before tents were pitched.

The first fatality among the battalion's officers was that of Lieutenant Mitchell, variously described as 'a great favourite with the whole of the battalion' and 'an officer who had won the hearts of his men by his quiet gentle manner and kindly helpful nature'. Mitchell had been acting as Water Supply Officer at El Ferdan when on 20 February he suffered a compound fracture of his right tibia and fibula when hit by a railway truck; it was two days later before he was admitted to 31st General Hospital at Ismailia where his right leg was amputated, too late to prevent his dying of gas gangrene on 23 February.

News of Mitchell's death reached the battalion at Hill 108, the defensive system some 8 miles south-east of Kantara which the Pals had taken over from 18/Durham Light Infantry on 22 February. The march to Hill 108 had been made on soft sand under a burning sun, and many men had fallen exhausted by the wayside.

During the month of February it had become clear that the threat to the Suez Canal had receded, not least because Turkish attention had been diverted by the defeat inflicted on the Ottoman Third Army by the Russians in the East, and the fall of Erzurum on 16 February. It was therefore possible to reduce the strategic reserve in Egypt to the bare minimum: 13th Division went to Mesopotamia in February, while 31st, 46th, 29th and 1st and 2nd Australian were the first of nine divisions to be transferred to the Western Front before the end of June.

Orders came through on 26 February for 31st Division to embark for France. The following day saw Z Company withdrawn from an outpost where it had been digging trenches, and a platoon of W Company under Lieutenant Ashworth brought back from guard duty at brigade headquarters; in the meantime, the men at Hill 108 were busily packing up to leave. First to depart on the return journey to Port Said were thirty-five NCOs and men of the battalion's transport under Lieutenant Bury who entrained at Kantara in the early hours of 28 February; on the same day the remainder of the battalion made the long and tiring march from Hill 108 back to Kantara but then spent two days waiting for troopships to be arranged before leaving for Port Said by train at midday on 2 March. With the exception of sixty-seven men of Y Company under Second Lieutenant Kohn who travelled on another ship, practically the whole battalion embarked on the SS *Llandovery Castle* on arrival at Port Said and left for France at 10pm.

The liking and respect that the men had for their commanding officer was mutual, as Rickman expressed in a letter he wrote to John Harwood during the voyage to France: 'They are a happy lot of lads and one gets awfully fond of them. They are so willing, and they have had a roughish time but they like the rough with the smooth, and are cheery, singing, and laughing.'

On 8 March 1916, the *Llandovery Castle* reached Marseilles. The Accrington Pals were at last in France.

Chapter 11

No Time for Anything

By the time the Accrington Pals disembarked from the *Llandovery Castle* at Marseilles on 8 March, the Howitzers, as they remained known despite the conversion to a field-gun brigade, had been training in France for more than a month.

The Howitzers had disembarked at Le Havre on the morning of 1 February, news of their safe arrival coming as welcome relief to their relatives and friends at home after 'alarming rumours' had spread regarding their passage across to France. After one night in camp the brigade entrained for Saint-Omer on the night of 2 February, marching on arrival to billets in three villages some 5½ to 7½ miles south of the town: Herbelle, Cléty and Inghem. After six days of training, all units of 35th Division, which now formed a part of XI Corps, moved forward, with the Howitzers going into billets at Witternesse, 6½ to 8½ miles nearer the lines and within the sound of the guns. Witternesse was described as a prettily situated village where 'wines and beer are very cheap – a penny a glass – but they would never make anyone intoxicated, however much they were to drink'. The brigade had by now celebrated the first anniversary of its formation, an occasion marked by its officers sending a message of greetings and best wishes to John Harwood.

On 11 February the entire division was inspected by Kitchener and GOC XI Corps, Lieutenant General Richard Cyril Byrne Haking; despite incessant rain, the parade was judged to be a great success. Training then continued in dreadful weather which alternated between snow and rain. The brigade moved a further 7 miles nearer to the lines on 19 February; on the evening of its arrival at Saint-Venant, south of the Nieppe Forest, Second Lieutenants A C Hopkins, Eric Francis Balderson and Charles Carey Morgan joined from training camp in England and were posted to B, C and D batteries respectively. A fine and clear night followed, during which warnings of a Zeppelin raid were received, and the engines of one were heard; on the following night a Zeppelin dropped fifteen bombs near the adjacent town of Isbergues, while warnings were received of an impending gas attack which fortunately failed to materialize.

Training now intensified with detachments being sent for instruction to units in the line, the brigade sending on 22 February 8 officers, 120 other ranks and

4 headquarters telephonists by motor transport to a position on the La Bassée Canal, 4,000yd distant from the German front line.

As 35th Division took over the line between Laventie and Festubert on 7 March, CLVIII Brigade – with the exception of the men of D Battery who were sent to act as the wagon line for another brigade which was in action – moved into billets on the north side of the Lys River between Haverskerque and Merville two days later. Second Lieutenants Henry Frederick Reginald Adams and George Darby joined the brigade here and were posted to A and B batteries respectively. Shortly afterwards the Howitzers lost one of their officers who had been with them since enlisting into the ranks more than a year earlier: Second Lieutenant Gilbert Grimshaw had been diagnosed on 20 February by the brigade's medical officer, Lieutenant Jackson, as suffering from myopia in both eyes; Grimshaw was subsequently forced to resign his commission by the War Office, and the appeal against the decision that he made on returning home to Fence was rejected.

By this time Fawcett had good reasons to feel content: not only had he heard from the RGS that he was to be awarded the Founder's Medal for his work in South America but he had also brought his brigade to a standard that he regarded as 'quite efficient', whereas only a month ago he had regarded the Howitzers as 'impossibly backward'. In a letter dated 11 March, Nina Fawcett quoted her husband as saying 'I have now no fear about taking them into the firing line and I think they will shape well, they are all content and keen.' The brigade was soon to be tested, for detachments moved temporarily into the line between 13 and 24 March. Although the divisional history states that CLVIII Brigade helped to provide artillery support to a raid made by 17/Lancashire Fusiliers on 24 March – the first raid undertaken by the division – there is no mention of this in the brigade war diary.

As 35th Division made a side-slip to the north-east on 25 March, the three brigades of the divisional artillery were formed into two groups, with the Right Group of seven batteries (the four from CLVIII Brigade together with A/CLVII and two howitzer batteries, B and C/CLXIII) being placed under Fawcett's command. The Right Group moved up through sleet and snow driven by a bitterly cold wind into the line at Laventie, 3,000 to 3,500yd from the German front line. Unlike the early days of the war, in which guns were deployed in forward positions from which the gunners could see their targets but were in turn exposed to direct fire from enemy infantry, now the divisional artillery fired from concealed positions up to 4 miles behind the lines against targets that generally were out of sight; in 1916, a battery would 'register' on a target by adjusting the direction and elevation of its guns according to information fed back by observers, either in the front-line trenches or in an aeroplane, about the fall of ranging shots fired by one of its guns. On 27 March, all the batteries of the Right Group began registration work, a process that continued into 1 April.

Shortly after 8am on 28 March, the brigade suffered its first fatality in action when Second Lieutenant Balderson, a 26-year-old artist born in Melbourne, Australia, was killed as C Battery came under heavy shellfire. The remaining days of March saw the arrival of two new subalterns, Stanley Knocker and Claude Reginald Harper, posted to D and B batteries respectively, and the departure of one of the brigade's original officers: Captain Harold Gray was recalled to Britain and posted to the Ministry of Munitions where he worked until he was allowed to resign his commission in August 1918 after failing in his application to be attached to the Tank Corps.

Stanley Knocker, born in the Essex market town of Great Dunmow, had been three months short of his fortieth birthday when he enlisted into the ranks of the Royal Horse Artillery in December 1915 having returned from South Africa where he had worked as a colonial farmer. Granted a commission in February 1916, CLVIII Brigade was his first posting as an officer.

A letter published in the *Accrington Gazette* gives some idea of the conditions under which the Howitzers lived:

> When I think of the first six weeks we had in France ... rain, snow, and frost, and all our horses in the open, and the boys with fingers swollen and torn, having to untie the head ropes, standing the while up to the knees in slime and mud, chilled to the bone, after sleeping in a too-well-ventilated barn, with their boots under the blankets so as to keep them from being frozen in the morning – chilblains on their feet like over-ripe tomatoes – and yet cheerful in spite of all!

On 2 April, a fine and clear day, Fawcett's Right Group, supported by trench-mortar fire, retaliated to frequent shelling of the British front lines in the Fauquissart section by firing forty shrapnel rounds and sixty high-explosive (HE) shells over the Wick salient in the space of just 2 minutes starting from 6.45am. As the artillery fire died away, the enemy parapet was swept by machine-gun fire, the effectiveness of which could not be determined because of the heavy pall of smoke left by the artillery fire. A retaliatory enemy barrage some 17 minutes later seems to have caused no casualties. On the following day, Second Lieutenant George Henry Lewis Marcus Samuel joined from B/CLXIII and was posted to B Battery.

A 'minor strafe' in the evening of 10 April saw Fawcett's group fire sixty-four HE and forty shrapnel rounds in a hurricane bombardment of the trenches opposite Fauquissart. Smoke bombs thrown out during the bombardment had the intended effect of leading the enemy to man their trenches in expectation of an infantry attack; the enemy parapets were promptly swept by machine-gun fire. A retaliatory barrage was again reported to have been ineffective whereas

Fawcett noted that his fire had been reported as accurate and destructive, causing a good many casualties.

35th Division began to move southwards to the Neuve-Chapelle and Ferme du Bois sectors on 13 April at which point Fawcett was given command of the Left Group of the divisional artillery comprising the four batteries of CLVIII Brigade plus A and B batteries of CLVII Brigade and one howitzer battery, C/CLXIII. The Left Group went into the line at Croix-Barbée in the Neuve-Chapelle sector on 15 April, taking over from the artillery of 19th Division, and began registration on the following day. Even when the batteries were in the firing line, there were opportunities for recreation: C Battery created a garden in the courtyard of a nearby farm, and erected goalposts in the field behind where the artillerymen played football every evening.

Minor strafes were carried out by Fawcett's group on 21 April, 2 May and 7 May, each serving both to destroy enemy material and to keep up morale within the division; the last operation had the further objective of distracting the attention of the enemy away from a trench raid which was planned to be undertaken by 23/Manchester in the late evening of 8 May. The raiding party of one officer and sixteen men started out at 10.39pm and was supported by a barrage from all batteries of the Left Group; the party reached the enemy wire before being broken up by the nearby burst of an enemy shell which killed two and wounded several more of the Manchesters. Retaliation from the enemy's artillery was severe, causing some thirty to forty casualties among the infantry.

By this time, the Howitzers had begun to receive 'comforts' paid for by their home towns. These included a gramophone and 80 records, 1½ gross safety razors, 6 sets of cricket and football gear, 200 woollen shirts, 800 pairs of socks and 100 woollen undershirts. In writing to Harwood to express the brigade's appreciation for the gifts, Fawcett took the opportunity to compliment the men under his command:

> I have delayed writing to thank yourself and the good people of Accrington, who subscribed for the comforts of the brigade, until the last of the cases should arrive, which, consequent upon the enormous demands upon the Military Forwarding Department, have been somewhat slow in transit. The batteries now have everything, and are, I may say, extremely grateful. They have been in the line now some time, as you know, and have all had their baptism of fire, having done and doing all the time extremely well to the efficiency of the brigade and the undoing of the Boche.

The divisional artillery underwent two major reorganizations towards the end of May. In the first, the brigade ammunition columns were absorbed into the divisional ammunition column, a change that was calculated to save 265 personnel, 310 animals and 44 GS wagons; accordingly, on 26 May, the

Howitzers' ammunition column became No. 2 Section, 35th Division Ammunition Column. The second reorganization saw the division's howitzer brigade exchange three of its batteries for 18-pounder batteries, so that each brigade in the division was armed alike with three 18-pounder batteries and one 4.5in howitzer battery. As a consequence, D/CLVIII, one of the two Burnley batteries, was exchanged on 27 May for B/CLXIII whose officers were Captain Frederick Charles Stevens, Lieutenant Vernon William Goss, Lieutenant Geoffrey Arthur Douglas Youl and Second Lieutenants H King, Arthur Cecil Shakerley and R M Forster.

The brigade's C Battery lost Second Lieutenant Harold Pearson when he transferred to the RFC as an observer with effect from 25 May. Pearson went on to win both the Military Cross (MC) and the Distinguished Flying Cross (DFC), ending the war with the rank of captain.

At 7.20pm on 30 May the enemy commenced a 2-hour bombardment against the fire and support trenches held by 15/Sherwood Foresters, causing about seventy casualties and practically obliterating the front line over a length of 200yd. The 35th divisional artillery opened a counter-barrage at 7.26pm, firing more than 3,000 rounds, of which about 1,700 were fired by the Left Group. After the enemy bombardment had ceased, it was found that the enemy had broken into the lines, with discarded shovels and unexploded bombs providing evidence that something more than a raid had been planned. In a letter to John Harwood, Captain Riley enclosed a message sent out on 31 May by GOC 35th Division, Major General Reginald John Pinney: 'The infantry at all points attacked last night all stated that the prompt support and straight shooting of the artillery saved the situation. The General is quite of this opinion and congratulates all ranks of the divisional artillery on the way they stopped the German attack.'

35-year-old Corporal Walter Edwin Bulley, in 1911 a shopkeeper and auxiliary postman in Fleetwood, and 41-year-old William Rucastle, a bricklayer from Accrington, both of B Battery, were recommended for gallantry in repairing wires under heavy fire during the evening of 30 May; both were later awarded the Military Medal (MM). Second Lieutenants Edmund Harwood – one of John Harwood's great-nephews – and George Slinger were also recommended for devotion to duty at the observation post, and for the information they periodically sent back under difficult conditions.

On 8 June, 35th divisional artillery supported a successful raid carried out by 14/Gloucester against trenches opposite the Pope's Nose, south of Neuve-Chapelle. The operation opened at 9pm with a 'box barrage' of 20 minutes duration in which a space about 200yd square around the point of entry was sealed off by artillery fire. The infantry of the raiding party moved forwards while the barrage continued on three sides and, despite encountering rifle and machine-gun fire, forced their way into the enemy trenches where they bombed dugouts, captured two machine guns – one of which had to be abandoned in no-man's-land – and destroyed a third. The raiding party, having lost two officers and four men killed, and twelve men wounded, was back in its own lines by 10pm. The only casualty from enemy fire among the artillery was Second Lieutenant William Chambers, formerly of D Battery but now with CLXIII Brigade, who suffered several superficial HE shell wounds and was returned to Britain.

Evidence that the high standard attained by the brigade under Fawcett's command had been recognized at a higher level came when C Battery was temporarily transferred to stiffen the 61st divisional artillery at Laventie, a move that was completed on 11 June and followed the attachment to the Left Group of five officers and forty-eight NCOs of 61st divisional artillery for instruction. C Battery returned to the Left Group on 16 June.

Shortly before the trench raid of 8 June took place, Charles William Scorah, a 23-year-old ironworker from Burnley, was killed in an accident that was described by a Lieutenant Tunney in a letter to Scorah's widow:

> He was standing round the fire in company with about seven of his comrades about 8.15 in the evening. It was a dull evening and very nearly dark, when a rifle was fired in another part of the workshop, and the bullet passed through your husband and wounded a man who was standing near him. Bombardier Scorah fell to the ground and lost consciousness at once. He was immediately attended to, placed on a stretcher, and sent up to the hospital at once, arriving there within twelve minutes of the accident. He never recovered consciousness, however, and died on the way to the hospital.

Second Lieutenant Percy James Deane Flecknoe, a 28-year-old of British birth from Johannesburg, joined the brigade on 9 June and was posted to B Battery. Two days later, 39th Division began to take over from 35th Division. A, B and D batteries of CLVIII Brigade were gradually moved out of the line between 17 and 20 June, moving first into billets at Busnes and then, on 28 June, into billets at La Thieuloye, 5 miles north-east of Saint-Pol-sur-Ternoise.

C/CLVIII was unfortunate to be the only one of the four batteries of the brigade not to be relieved. Instead it was left in line to support a local attack made on 30 June by 39th Division and designed to divert the enemy's attention from the imminent offensive on the Somme.

The year 1915 had left the Allies with little cause for satisfaction. In Poland, a new German army, the Eleventh (General August von Mackensen), formed from divisions taken from the Western Front, had opened an offensive against the Russians on 2 May, and had advanced an astonishing 95 miles in a fortnight. By the end of May the Eleventh Army had captured 153,000 prisoners and 128 guns; at the extreme point of the offensive, Austro-German forces had advanced 300 miles, captured 3,000 guns and inflicted as many as 2,000,000 casualties. On the Western Front a new British Third Army had been created in July and had relieved the French Second Army on the Somme. Joffre's insistence on a renewed British offensive in the autumn led to the Battle of Loos being fought from 25 September, an operation that resulted in 60,000 British casualties and ultimately the replacement of Sir John French as Commander-in-Chief of the BEF by General Sir Douglas Haig on 19 December; simultaneous French assaults to the south had won little ground for the loss of 145,000 casualties in Champagne and nearly 50,000 more in Artois while German losses in the offensive have been estimated at over 200,000. Bulgaria's entry into the war on the side of Germany and Austria-Hungary on 6 September had finally sealed the fate of Serbia and drawn a British-French force into Salonika, often quoted as being the 'greatest Allied internment camp' of the war. The Mesopotamian expeditionary force led by Major General Charles Townshend had advanced up the Tigris River only to be compelled to retreat through exhaustion to Kut-al-Amara where it was surrounded by the enemy from 7 December.

It was against this depressing background that the Inter-Allied Military Conference took place at Chantilly on 6–8 December 1915. The conclusions from the conference were that a decisive result in the war would require Britain, France, Italy – who had abandoned her neutrality to enter the war in May 1915 – and Russia to deliver simultaneous attacks with maximum force, and that the general action should be launched as soon as possible after the end of March. It was also proposed that the Austro-German forces should be worn down by local offensives, particularly by those Powers still having manpower reserves; this latter proposal was to be strongly resisted by Haig and was finally dropped by Joffre on 14 February. Almost by default, the decision was adopted that the attack on the Western Front would be a joint British-French offensive at the point where the two armies met near the Somme River. There was little to be said in favour of the choice of battlefield: whereas Haig had clearly preferred to attack in the area of Ypres which offered the enticing prospect of destroying enemy forces to the north before turning south to roll up the German line, there was no evident strategic objective on the Somme; furthermore, the German lines threaded through fortified villages and took advantage of the chalky terrain to conceal deep defensive dugouts.

As events turned out, it was the Central Powers who took the initiative in 1916, first in the German offensive that was launched against the French fortress town of Verdun on 21 February and would rage until attacks were called off on 11 July, and then by an Austrian assault on the Italian front launched on 15 May by von Hötzendorf. By the time von Hötzendorf's offensive was halted on 10 June, it had penetrated to a maximum depth of 12 miles; at a cost of about 80,000 casualties, the Austrians had captured 45,000 prisoners and 300 guns and had inflicted a further 100,000 casualties on the Italians.

The French contribution to the offensive on the Somme had originally been planned by 64-year-old General Ferdinand Foch, commanding the *Groupe d'Armées du Nord* (Group of French Armies in the North, generally known as GAN), to involve three armies each of sixteen divisions: the Sixth (General Marie-Émile Fayolle) was to support the breakthrough to the north, the central army (not designated) was to push to and across the Somme and the Tenth Army (General Joseph Alfred Micheler) was to set up a defensive flank to the south. By May, the need to feed divisions into the desperate fight to save Verdun had forced Foch to reduce his plan to a single army attack astride the Somme. The greater responsibility for the offensive would now fall on the British Fourth Army which had been formed on 5 February 1916 under the command of Lieutenant General Henry Rawlinson.

11/East Lancashire was one of the first battalions of 31st Division to reach France, disembarking from the *Llandovery Castle* at Marseilles on the morning of 9 March. A week later, the whole of 31st Division had arrived from Egypt, and was allotted to VIII Corps (Lieutenant General Sir Aylmer Hunter-Weston) which was being reconstituted in the wake of the Gallipoli campaign and would later incorporate the 4th and 29th divisions.

On disembarking from the *Llandovery Castle,* the Accrington Pals immediately entrained for northern France. After a journey of 48 hours, the battalion left the train at Pont Rémy station, 5 miles south-east of Abbeville, and marched 6 miles to billets in the village of Huppy. One Pal wrote home to describe conditions at Huppy and to express an uncompromising attitude towards conscientious objectors:

> At the end of our railway journey the officers and advance guard found us all billets in a pretty little village, though with no comparison to our Carnarvon billets. We are as comfortable as may be in barns, stables, outhouses, etc. Six of us are in a kind of outhouse belonging to a farm. There are plenty of rats knocking about, but we take no notice of them. We had for dinner on Sunday tinned meat, potatoes, carrots, etc., and they make a jolly good meal . . . From the accounts I read in the papers you send me there seems to be a lot of conscientious objectors knocking about. They want a bayonet running through them.

On 16 March, X Company left by bus for Gézaincourt, a village just outside of Doullens, while two NCOs and twenty men from Y Company left for Flesselles, a village 7½ miles north of Amiens. Although the battalion war diary gives no explanation for the detachments, it seems probable that the men were required for fatigue work nearer the lines. It is also likely that a number of officers and men from the battalion were sent into the lines south of Hébuterne in order to gain experience in trench-system organization.

The stifling hot climate of Egypt was soon but a distant memory. In the fourth week of March, temperatures fell below freezing point, with heavy snow to follow.

Huppy may not have stood comparison to Caernarvon, but the villagers would boil eggs, toast bread and even provide coffee laced with rum to the troops in exchange for a few coppers. Rumours of approaching home leave helped to revive spirits further.

At the end of March, 31st Division relieved 36th Division in the line facing the strongpoint of Beaumont-Hamel, close to the northern extremity of the Fourth Army sector on the Somme. When 29th Division took over the southern part of the line on 2 April, 31st Division side-slipped to the north, 94 Brigade taking over the 1,700yd stretch of line that ran north from the point where it crossed the Serre–Amiens road. After climbing for a distance of about 400yd from the road, the line gently descended through a shallow valley passing in front of four copses which were named by the troops after the Evangelists, Matthew, Mark, Luke and John. In front of the copses, the ground rose towards four lines of enemy trenches which protected the fortified hilltop village of Serre. 12 and 14/York and Lancaster took the honours of being the first battalions of 94 Brigade to occupy the front line. 11/East Lancashire, less its detachments, had left Huppy on 26 March and made an arduous march over four days of about 50 miles through Longpré-les-Corps-Saints, Vignacourt and Beauval to reach Bertrancourt on 29 March. The battalion was billeted in wooden huts which lacked floorboards; Richard Ormerod, for one, spent a cold night lying on damp soil. On 3 and 4 April, the battalion moved up through Courcelles-au-Bois into billets of a slightly higher standard at Colincamps where it acted as brigade reserve.

A letter written by an Accrington Pal at Colincamps on or about 9 April described how the battalion had already had its first experience of enemy shellfire:

> We are still in billets. These consist principally of barns, with wire beds permanently erected therein for troops. Our shanty is fairly comfortable, even if it has neither doors nor windows in, and one wall looks as though it had been well bombarded. There are plenty of rats about, but these don't bother us. I dip well under the blankets and sleep soundly. The weather we are having seems to be much the same as yours. Last week was rather warmer and more Spring-like. Furloughs are going on slowly. Only two from each Company (ten from the battalion) are balloted for whenever a 'leave' train is despatched, so it will be 1917 before some of us arrive. We have been gradually moving up towards the trenches, and have already had our baptism of fire. This is rather nerve-racking at first, but one soon

becomes accustomed to the rattling and the whizzing and the thundering of guns, and it is really nothing to worry about. I had my first bath yesterday since arriving in this country. It was in hot water, too, and was simply delightful.

By this time, the battalion's machine-gunners had already been up to the front line. On 4 April, Richard Ormerod, in charge of two machine-gun crews, had gone with Lieutenant Ruttle into the trenches where he was fortunate to survive a near-miss from an enemy shell.

While in brigade reserve at Colincamps, the Pals were given the task of opening up and repairing trenches; it was gruesome work as the bodies and equipment of dead French soldiers were uncovered.

94 Brigade was relieved on 12 April, and 11/East Lancashire moved back into divisional reserve at Bertrancourt. Most of the following fifteen days saw men detailed to join working parties in the front or reserve trenches, or to carry stores and ammunition up to the line.

Percy Allsup, a textile mill worker from Clayton Green near Chorley, who had enlisted at the age of 17 alongside his elder brother, James, kept a diary in which he gave a succinct but evocative picture of the battalion's work at this time:

> 17 April: Rest through day. Parade 9.30PM, digging again in third line, wet through again, relieved at 3.00AM.
>
> 18 April: Got back 5.0AM, rest through day.
>
> 19 April: Parade 9.30PM. Digging in trenches again, wet through once more, got back 5.0AM, no sleep that day.
>
> 20 April: Fatigue 11.0AM. Parade 2.30PM. Parade 9.30PM, digging in trenches, got back 1.30AM.

An unnamed officer of the battalion gave a more detailed description of the hardships of working at night, whether it involved digging trenches or carrying ammunition:

> A working party by night was a miserable affair. Digging or revetting when you could scarcely see what you were doing resulted in very little being accomplished; often the walk to and from the work was a very long one; and even with people trying to do a job of work it seemed very doubtful whether a working party was worth while at all. Carrying parties were rather different; they did get something done, but some of the work was desperately hard. Only those who have tried to carry up to the line a trench-mortar shell along uneven and muddy trenches, probably with an occasional slip into a sump hole, can realize what it was like.

The work had to be done by night, as Richard Ormerod explained in a letter to his sister:

> Since I last wrote you I have had a spell in the trenches and we are now back resting, or should be resting but there is so much work to be done repairing trenches and digging new ones that the lads are at it nearly every night for they dare not throw clay on top of the trench in the day time as they run the danger of being shelled. Things have been rather quiet here since our arrival. The only activity being with the artillery and air-men. We gave the Germans a terrible 'straffing' the other night. Our artillery bombarded the enemies [*sic*] trenches for over an hour. It was like a perfect Hell.

On 23 April, four new subalterns joined the battalion: 22-year-old Lewis Hewitt Lewis, born at Fosdyke in Lincolnshire, Harry Clegg, a 24-year-old bank clerk from Burnley, Harry Noel Davies, a 21-year-old insurance clerk from Twickenham, and Bart Endean, a 22-year-old mason from Cramlington in Northumberland. Clegg was to enjoy only a short stay with the battalion, as he was to leave on 19 May to return to Britain for hospitalization following an injury caused by a fall from a horse.

The full list of the battalion's officers at this time was as follows:

Headquarters: Lieutenant Colonel A W Rickman, Major E L Reiss (second-in-command), Captain A Peltzer (adjutant), M Harlier (interpreter), Lieutenant J Smith (quartermaster), Lieutenant J H Ruttle (MG officer), Lieutenant F G Macalpine (signalling officer), Lieutenant H Bury (transport officer), Lieutenant J W N Roberts RAMC (medical officer).

W Company: Captain A G Watson, Captain H Livesey, Lieutenant H Ashworth (trench mortars), Lieutenant C Stonehouse, Second Lieutenant J C Palmer, Second Lieutenant H Brabin.

X Company: Captain P J Broadley, Captain A B Tough, Lieutenant T W Rawcliffe, Lieutenant F Bailey, Second Lieutenant G J Beaumont (bombers), Second Lieutenant L H Lewis.

Y Company: Major J C Milton, Captain J V Kershaw, Lieutenant G G Williams, Second Lieutenant E Ashwell, Second Lieutenant W A Kohn, Second Lieutenant J C Shorrock, Second Lieutenant H N Davies.

Z Company: Major R St G Ross, Captain H D Riley, Lieutenant L Ryden (snipers), Lieutenant F A Heys, Second Lieutenant W A Lewino, Second Lieutenant B Endean, Second Lieutenant H Clegg.

Another subaltern joined only a few days later: 16-year-old Reginald St John Beardsworth Battersby, a vicar's son from Blackley, Manchester, had contrived to enlist into the ranks of the Manchester Regiment four weeks shy of his 15th birthday and had gained a commission with the East Lancashire Regiment in May 1915.

The battalion went as a whole into the front-line trenches for the first time on 28 April when it took over a stretch of line midway between Beaumont-Hamel and Serre. Z Company was on the left, holding the line opposite the enemy strongpoint known as the Heidenkopf or Quadrilateral Redoubt, Y Company was in the centre and W Company was on the right. Over the first four days that the battalion held the line, the reserve company was provided by 12/York and Lancaster while over the second four days it was supplied by 14/York and Lancaster. The fact that 11/East Lancashire had to depend on another battalion to supply the reserve company suggests that X Company had still not returned, after being away for more than one month.

The battalion's first fatalities in action came when, at 11.30pm on 29 April, the enemy began a bombardment in reaction to a raid on the right of the battalion by 29th Division. Fred Sayer of Z Company was standing alongside Captain Riley in the second line when word came back that men had been buried in a trench blown in by shellfire. Sayer, first on the scene, dug away at the earth with his entrenching tool:

> Scratching and scraping the earth away exposed sufficient of the first man for me to know that he was dead. The second man however was alive and by sitting cross-legged on the surface I was able to move enough earth to drag him from the sticky mess. Feeling over his limbs, he did not appear to have any broken bones, but he felt very heavy and was difficult to move. He was of stocky bred and after taking off his steel helmet and equipment I was able to get him on my back ... The journey was a nightmare, but I delivered him to someone in a trench shelter, at the same time asking for help to bring in the dead man.

The dead man was Jack Clark, a 20-year-old member of the Burnley Lads' Club.

On the same night, 24-year-old Arthur Riley of Accrington was fatally wounded by shrapnel, dying on 30 April at a casualty clearing station (CCS); an unposted letter to his mother, written before the battalion went into the line, was forwarded by Sergeant Daniel Cotter of the RAMC:

> By the time you get this I fancy we shall have done here, and won't Accrington people be glad to hear the 'Pals' are in the trenches at last, but I don't mind telling you that we have been doing much dangerous work while we have been here. We have been out in awful weather and all we get is 'Aren't the "Pals" in the trenches yet?'

On the Mesopotamian front, General Townshend surrendered Kut-al-Amara to the Turks on 29 April. Opposite the Pals, the enemy took the opportunity to gloat, placing a board in no-man's-land which reportedly carried the words 'God straff England. Gen Townsend [*sic*] surrendered at Kut with 8,000 men'.

The battalion was relieved by 13/East Yorkshire on 6 May, and went into divisional reserve at Warnimont Wood. Casualties had been relatively light during this first tour of the front line; two had been killed, one had died of wounds, and fourteen had been wounded, two of whom remained at duty. The third fatality was Joseph George Hartley, a 34-year-old clerk from Barrowford. In the course of its occupation of the front line, the battalion had been heavily engaged in improving the trench system and the men were glad to be free of the waterlogged and muddy trenches, as later related by Crabtree and Sayer:

> In May the Battalion moved into some tarpaulin huts in [Warnimont Wood]. Spring was in the air and the leaves on the trees were showing. What a delight after the mud, cold and filth of the trenches. Men were able to clean their bodies and clothes and equipment, and lice were slain by the thousand and comfort obtained. Working parties still went forth each night. The woods brought peace and men were able to sit and enjoy the sunshine.

Adding to the good feeling was the arrival of 'heaps of tobacco and cigarettes for the Burnley lads' sent by the mayor and mayoress of Burnley, and shared out around the rest of the battalion. A lucky few were also enjoying a week's home leave.

In the middle of May, 94 Brigade was allotted the left sector of the front held by 31st Division, the front line of which ran from the southern end of Matthew Copse to the north-east corner of John Copse. The front was held by one battalion in the line, with a second in brigade reserve at Courcelles-au-Bois, the third in divisional reserve at Bus-lès-Artois, while the fourth was used for special duties. The Accrington Pals moved out of Warnimont Wood into brigade reserve on 15 May before relieving 12/York and Lancaster in the front line in the early hours of 20 May. The battalion worked on improvement of the front-line trench, and sent out wiring parties every night. Writing to a friend, Sergeant Martin Folan, a 30-year-old taper from Accrington, gave a vivid description of his experiences:

> One thing that is very nerve trying is 'standing to'. Firing goes on all day and when it stops everybody 'stands to'. This lasts for about an hour and a half; it's terrible. There is no moving about and you are always expecting an attack. A chap is told to 'shut up' if he talks above a whisper. You imagine all sorts of things. It is then you see what is known as 'trench stare' – chaps' eyes bulging out of their

heads, giving you the impression that they are going mad. It's a great relief when the order 'stand down' is given. By that time it's safe for a sentry to get up in each bay. Then machine guns start cracking, sweeping the front. This is followed by the wiring parties going out to fix up and repair the wire in front of the trenches, no easy job, I can assure you. I had five nights hard running at it ... The trouble starts when it is dark, for the Germans throw up star shells. Then we have to lie down and not move until the shells burn out ... Of course, when the shelling starts you can't come in. On the first occasion we were out for one and a half hours, and the second time for two hours, and when we got back we didn't know our own trenches, as they had been knocked in somewhat!

The battalion suffered no casualties over the first five days of the tour but on 27 May two men were killed and eight wounded. The dead men were 19-year-old Thomas Jackson from Clayton-le-Moors and 30-year-old Robert Pickering from Darwen, both of X Company. Although the two men were reported as having been killed in action, it has been claimed that both were accidentally shot by one of their pals. The story is remarkably similar to that of Charles Scorah of the Howitzers who was killed by the accidental discharge of a rifle on 8 June.

There were no further fatalities in the battalion before it was relieved by 14/York and Lancaster on 30 May, and went into brigade reserve. Lieutenant John Palmer had, however, been 'blown up by a shell' on the day that the battalion was relieved, and was returned to Britain for hospitalization; Palmer returned to active service after recovering from his wounds, and survived the war. Further personnel changes had also taken place while the battalion was in the trenches. There were seventy-eight men transferred from the Army Cyclist Corps, Major Raymond Ross had left to join the staff at 31st Division Headquarters, Major James Milton had been invalided home and Lieutenant Harry Bury had been struck off the strength of the battalion having been granted three months' leave by the War Office following the death of his father on 26 May. There was an unusual conclusion to Harry Bury's military service: on 31 July his leave was extended by the War Office, though without pay, so as to allow him to manage the family owned chemical manufacturing business of Henry Bury (Junr) & Co. at Church. The War Office then seems to have lost track of Bury, as he had no further correspondence with the military authorities until long after the war had ended, when he received a letter dated 27 July 1920 from the War Office asking whether he was performing military duties, on leave or if he had been demobilized. Bury was duly demobilized the following month.

Just as the Howitzers had by this time started to receive 'comforts' from home, the Pals too were the grateful recipients of goods funded by subscribers:

the list included 200 cap badges, canvas covers for both rifles and machine guns, 16 pieces of band music, 500 tins of cocoa for use in the trenches, 8 footballs, 900 pairs of socks, special stores to the value of £4 8s 7d and a gross of safety razors. Rickman, who had been in temporary command of 94 Brigade owing to Carter-Campbell's absence on sick leave, found time to write to John Harwood to express the battalion's appreciation:

> I have not had a minute in which to write, as I have been command-
> ing the brigade for the last fourteen days and shall probably continue
> to do so until the General comes back from sick leave, probably in
> three weeks time. The regiment were lucky in their spell of duty
> in the trenches, only losing two killed and twenty-three wounded.
> The lads have done awfully well, and are as cheery and as proud of
> themselves as when they first left England. And they have had to
> rough it. The cocoa was very much appreciated and the men liked it
> very much, especially at early morning 'stand to'. The socks will also
> be most useful when they arrive – and socks go so quickly out here.

Lieutenant Gerry Gorst, the East Lancashire officer who had been wounded at Aubers with the 2nd Battalion on 9 May 1915, but had by now been pronounced fit to return to the front, left Folkestone for Boulogne in the evening of 25 May and reached his new battalion, the 11th, in the mid-afternoon of 28 May. He immediately gained a good impression of the Accrington Pals while noting that the battalion he aspired to join, the 1st, was in close proximity:

> This is a very good battalion, I think, and I'm not a bit sorry I came
> now. I am taking over command of a company, only for the time
> being, as the captain thereof is away sick . . . Funnily enough the 1st
> have turned up, and are billeted in the next village [Bertrancourt].
> I am in the transport lines at present, as the regiment is coming out
> of the trenches to-morrow, probably for ten days. I've been up to
> the trenches to-day with the colonel (who is acting brigadier at the
> moment), and they're good, though there are a lot of shells about . . .
> I am already equipped with several kinds of gas-mask, and also a steel
> helmet, rather like a soup-plate!

After a brief spell at Courcelles-au-Bois during which the battalion provided working and carrying parties, the Pals marched on 5 June with full pack to Gézaincourt. Unaccustomed to hard marching, the recent arrivals from the Cyclist Corps fell out of the march in large numbers. Over the following week, the battalions of 94 Brigade took part in special training for the forthcoming Somme offensive, rehearsing their attack over ground on which the German trench system around Serre had been marked out with flags and tapes. Rickman had a better understanding than most of the enormity of the task that faced his battalion; early in June, he had remarked to Harwood that 'a hundred or two wire-cutters would come in very useful'.

In the evening of the battalion's arrival at Gézaincourt the Allied cause suffered a severe blow when Field Marshal Earl Kitchener lost his life when the battle cruiser HMS *Hampshire* on which he was travelling to Russia struck an enemy mine and capsized.

Gorst, meanwhile, had been manoeuvring unsuccessfully to gain a transfer to 1/East Lancashire, as he explained in a letter to his sister written from Gézaincourt on 7 June:

> I had dinner with the 1st [Battalion] last week, and had considerable difficulty in getting home afterwards! Their CO has been a perfect angel, and has done his best to get me transferred – he went to the Division and the Corps, and to the Colonel of the 11th; but the only result was that they became all the more certain that they'd got a good thing, and they wouldn't part! The CO here (Col Rickman) said he'd give me a company, promote me, etc. etc. – but there are such a lot of captains here already unluckily! However, I've stopped grousing about it. We're way back from the line. Twelve miles or more, for a few days; everything very peaceful, if there weren't so many generals bucking about! General Hunter-Weston watched us march past on the way here, and kept asking the CO questions; and every time the CO opened his mouth to answer, the old man snarled 'Don't argue!!!'

The spell at Gézaincourt was popular too with the men, as it offered the chance to go into Beauval or Doullens where it was possible to have 'a jolly good feed of steak, chips, and haricot beans – a delightful change from stew, stew, stew ...'.

The battalion returned on 14 June to divisional reserve at Warnimont Wood from where it provided working parties in the trenches while completing preparations for the forthcoming attack, the date of which had been set at 29 June. Richard Ormerod noted one fatigue in which it had taken 12 hours to carry one 60-pound trench-mortar bomb into the trenches. On 15 June, Rickman relinquished control of the brigade, not to Carter-Campbell who remained on sick leave but to the newly promoted Brigadier General Hubert Rees.

A further five new subalterns, all from 10/East Lancashire, joined the battalion at Warnimont Wood: 21-year-old James Foldys Hitchon from Hoghton Bank near Preston, 21-year Cecil Douglas Gay from Dagenham, 20-year-old Arthur Robert Cecil (Artie) Lett from Watlington, 21-year-old Herbert William Thompson, a bank clerk from Fulham, and Arthur Sidney Williams. Coincidentally, Cecil Gay and Gerry Gorst had studied together before the war at Trinity College, Cambridge.

Captain Arnold Tough had little time to spare, as he explained in a brief letter written on 18 June to his siblings in Accrington:

> Don't expect many letters just now – no time for anything. We are going to be very busy – but of course I can't say any more. Hope to be able to write more shortly. Broadley has discovered he has hammer toes so of course I am pretty busy as he has gone into hospital and I don't expect to see him again for months. Ruttle is also in Hospital – pretty bad I believe but not dangerous.

Remarkably, none of the four company commanders of three months previously were still with the battalion. Captain Andrew Watson – who had transferred to the RAMC – Captain Philip Broadley, Major James Milton and Major Raymond Ross had been replaced by Captain Harry Livesey (W Company), Captain Arnold Tough (X Company), Captain John Kershaw (Y Company) and Captain Henry Riley (Z Company) respectively. The services were lost of yet another officer when Lieutenant Shorrock left on 20 June following the onset four days earlier of trench fever.

The battalion went back into the trenches on 19 June taking over the line between Matthew Copse and John Copse from 12/York and Lancaster. Casualties escalated in this last tour before the offensive; twelve were killed and twenty-four wounded in the four days before the battalion was relieved on the night of 23/24 June. Gerry Gorst wrote to his sister from the trenches:

> We are in the line at the moment but our time is very nearly over now; it's been rather beastly this time. We had four men buried by a shell this afternoon and I helped to dig them out, with the result that I've been feeling rather sick ever since; they were all dead poor chaps; and one of my best sergeants wounded too.

News of tremendous Russian successes on the Eastern Front had also filtered through to the front line. The Russian Eighth Army (General Aleksei Alekseevich Brusilov) had struck against the Austrians on 4 June: in 3 days 44,000 prisoners had been taken, in 3 weeks 200,000 and, by the end of the campaign in September, 450,000. Yet the victorious advance came at a great cost: 1,000,000 Russian casualties over 4 months shattered morale. A fortnight into the offensive, however, the opportunity to gloat over the Germans in the trenches opposite was irresistible, as Gorst wrote to his sister: 'Aren't the Rooshians great. We stuck up a notice in front of Bosche, saying that 500,000 Austrians had been captured, and that they were offering unconditional surrender; it wasn't strictly true, but it annoyed Bosche awfully!'

The battalion was relieved by 10/East Yorkshire on 23/24 June and marched back to Warnimont Wood. Astonishingly, fifty-eight men from 12/East Lancashire joined the battalion with less than a week to go before the date fixed for the attack. Second Lieutenant Ernest Edgar Ritchie also rejoined the battalion at this time after a spell in the Army Cyclist Corps.

The final days at Warnimont Wood were spent in further preparation for the attack which, owing to unfavourable weather, was on 28 June postponed for two days to 1 July. Second Lieutenant Lewino became the last officer to be taken off the strength of the battalion before the attack when he was injured by a German HE shell on 27 June, possibly while leading a wire–examining patrol into no–man's–land. The posting to the battalion on 27 June of Second Lieutenant William Barrett, a 24-year-old clerk from Burnley who had already served as a battery quartermaster sergeant in the RFA, would certainly have come too late to see him take part in the attack.

Captain Tough wrote a last letter to his sister, Christina, on 29 June:

> Just snatched time for a hasty one. Many thanks for yours and Fathers. We have been more than busy and I hardly know whether I am on my head or my heels. Probably won't be able to write for some time so don't worry – will write as soon as possible – you'll know why. Had a pretty hot time last trip up. They found our dug out and didn't forget to let us know. Hit our dinner as it was cooking one night and knocked it to [blazes]. They are fond of such little jokes – [damned] amusing. Give my love to Tom and Peg – I haven't time to write everybody – and tell Tom not to be an ass – OH – here come more orders. Nothing much. With best love children and have a good time – there's a good time coming. Write as soon as you like – I'll probably get them all together.

In the early evening of 30 June 1916, the Accrington Pals left Warnimont Wood to begin a march of more than 6 miles to the front-line trenches opposite Serre.

Chapter 12

They Fought Like Heroes

In formulating a plan for the British Fourth Army's offensive on the Somme, Rawlinson had to take into account German defences which he knew to consist not only of a front-line system of trenches but also of a second line which lay between 2,000 and 5,000yd beyond. He was at this time unaware that the enemy was constructing a third line some 3,000yd farther back. Whereas the German front-line system could be well observed along almost all of the Fourth Army front, this was not true of the second line, parts of which could only be observed from the air. Both front- and second-line systems were well protected by barbed wire, and it was well known that the ground was ideal for the construction of deep dugouts. The German defences were further strengthened by a substantial number of villages which lay both in and behind the front-line system and had been strongly fortified.

Rawlinson's initial plan for the offensive, submitted to General Headquarters (GHQ) on 3 April 1916, was to attack with ten divisions on a front of 20,000yd extending from a point between Mametz and Montauban on the right to Serre on the left. His objective for the first phase of the offensive was to overrun the enemy front-line system along the entire 20,000yd and to take the enemy second line as far south as the Albert–Bapaume road. Rather than attempt to reach the objectives in a single rush, however, Rawlinson argued for an advance in two stages, the first of which would be limited to include the enemy's front-line system and certain tactically important positions beyond. This approach – which has become known as 'bite and hold' – counted on the loss of key positions forcing the enemy to counter-attack under conditions that would cause them to take heavy casualties. Rawlinson favoured a preliminary artillery bombardment of between 48 and 72 hours duration rather than a much shorter hurricane bombardment immediately prior to the assault; his argument was that a longer bombardment would allow the assaulting troops to move into position under cover of darkness. The use of poison gas was rejected, not least because of its dependence on a suitable wind. The plan seems to have foreseen few problems in overcoming the German front-line system and the further tactical positions: Rawlinson believed his field guns and trench mortars to be well capable of destroying the wire that lay in front of the line, and reckoned

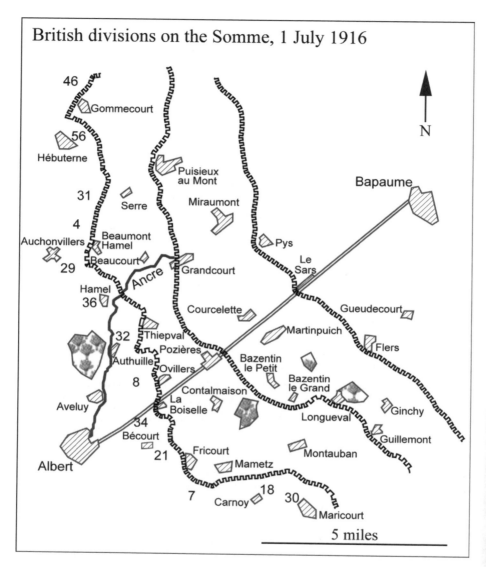

British divisions on the Somme, 1 July 1916

on the heavy artillery at his disposal to be sufficient to destroy a large portion of the defences.

Nine days elapsed before GHQ made a formal response to the Fourth Army plan. The feedback emphasized Haig's wish for Rawlinson to extend his initial advance to take in the farthest objectives of tactical value which had a reasonable chance of being held against counter-attack; highlighted were the Serre–Miraumont spur on the left of the attack, and the Montauban spur on the right. GHQ also asked Rawlinson to re-consider the option of preparing the attack with a hurricane bombardment both for its surprise value and for its effect on the enemy's morale. The response further advised a simultaneous operation against the Gommecourt salient in order to divert the enemy's artillery and reserves on the left flank of the main attack; the possibility of diversionary operations further to the north was also raised.

In his amended plan dated 19 April, Rawlinson reluctantly agreed to make provision to attempt the capture of his first-phase objectives in one attack. He was no more enthusiastic at the prospect of extending the front to be attacked to 22,500yd to take in Montauban, an amendment that would necessitate bringing in an extra division and diluting the concentration of heavy guns available to one or more corps elsewhere along the front. Not surprisingly, while agreeing that an operation against the Gommecourt salient would be of considerable assistance to the main attack, Rawlinson considered the Fourth Army to have insufficient resources to carry it out. Finally, Rawlinson held firm on the need for a prolonged bombardment, arguing that in any event it would take at least three days for the artillery to cut the wire and that the deprivation of sleep, food and ammunition for an extended period of time would have a greater impact on the enemy's morale that a shorter, more intense bombardment.

The dialogue between Rawlinson and Haig culminated in a memorandum from GHQ dated 16 May confirming that the first-phase objectives would extend to the capture of the Serre–Miraumont spur, Pozières, Contalmaison and Montauban. Rawlinson did, however, get agreement to a prolonged artillery bombardment, supposedly to 'be continued until the officers commanding the attacking units are satisfied that the obstacles to their advance have been adequately destroyed'. It was further decided that the diversionary attack on the Gommecourt salient would be carried out by Third Army (Lieutenant General Edmund Henry Hynman Allenby).

The task of forming the northern defensive flank of the main attack fell to 31st Division, with 94 Brigade on the left, 93 Brigade on the right and 92 Brigade in reserve. 94 Brigade was to attack on a two-battalion front with 11/East Lancashire on the right of 12/York and Lancaster given the key objective of capturing Serre village itself. Confronting 31st Division was the 169th (8th Baden) Infantry Regiment (hereafter referred to as IR169) whose headquarters were in Lahr, a town in the south-western German state of Baden-Württemberg.

11/East Lancashire was supposed to reach its assembly positions at 11.30pm on the eve of the attack. Two platoons from each of W and X companies were to assemble in the front line between Matthew Copse and Mark Copse to form the first wave of the attack, each company occupying a frontage of about 175yd. The remaining two platoons from each of the two companies were to gather in Copse Trench to form the second wave.

The attack was planned according to a strict timetable.

At **zero minus 10 minutes** (7.20am) the first wave was to advance into no-man's-land and lie down as close to the German wire as the artillery bombardment allowed.

At **zero minus 5 minutes** (7.25am) the second wave was to follow, and lie down 50yd behind the first wave.

At **zero** (7.30am) the divisional artillery was to lift its fire off the German front line and to creep forward 100yd every 2 minutes until it reached the fourth German line on which it was to continue firing until zero plus 20 minutes; by this time (7.50am) the first two waves – supported by trench-mortar teams – were expected to have advanced across three lines of enemy trenches, and to be in a position to occupy the fourth line which constituted the battalion's first of three objectives for the day. All the troops of 94 Brigade had been instructed to attack across the open, and not to enter trenches until their objective was reached.

Following behind the first and second waves from Copse Trench, two platoons from 13/York and Lancaster had the task of clearing the second and third enemy lines, as well as the communication trenches between the first and fourth enemy lines.

At **zero plus 5 minutes** (7.35am) the third and fourth waves were to leave Rob Roy and Campion trenches, and advance to the third and second German lines respectively, where they were to lie down until **zero plus 28 minutes** (7.58am) when they were to carry forward the attack along communication trenches until they had got as close as the artillery fire would allow to Munich Trench, the last trench that defended Serre village.

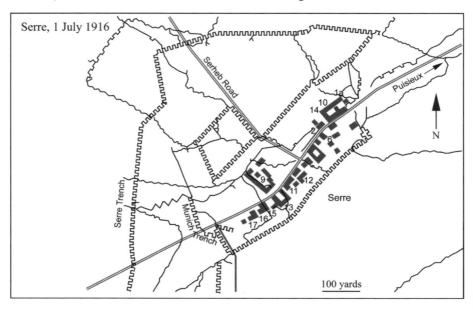

At **zero plus 40 minutes** (8.10am) the fire from the 18-pounder guns of the divisional artillery, having been directed on to Munich Trench for the previous 10 minutes, would begin to rake through Serre village. As the artillery lifted its fire from Munich Trench, the third and fourth waves, led by strong bombing parties, were to advance closely behind the barrage to reach the second objective, the capture of the village; Y Company was to work along the southern trench of Serre, while Z Company was to take the western edge of Serre, going forward along the two main communication trenches which led into House No. 9. (The owner of House No. 9 had told the British about large cellars and underground passages which were suspected to be occupied by the enemy.) House No. 9 was to be attacked by one platoon of Z Company with another platoon being sent against House No. 10 where resistance was also expected. Following behind Y Company, W Company was to stand by to attack the centre of the village; two platoons of X Company were to be sent forward to support the attack on House No. 9 and to secure all the exits from the house, with the remaining two platoons left behind in Munich Trench.

At **zero plus 1 hour 20 minutes** (8.50am), the divisional artillery was to lift from the eastern edge of the village to fire on Serre Orchard. Bombing parties were to lead Y and Z companies along the communication trenches running parallel to the Serre–Puisieux road and towards the Orchard.

At **zero plus 1 hour 40 minutes** (9.10am), the barrage would lift from the Orchard, the subsequent capture of which would see 11/East Lancashire reach its third and final objective for the day. Y and Z companies were to consolidate on the final line. After clearing the village, W Company was to dig in on the eastern edge of Serre. Two platoons of X Company were to remain in Munich Trench, while the remaining two platoons were to guard the exits from House No. 9.

The plan – in common with those of each and every other battalion taking part in the attack – assumed that the artillery would be able both to clear wide lanes through the wire and to render the enemy incapable of putting up any significant resistance; yet it was known that the dugouts beneath the enemy lines had been deliberately constructed to withstand an artillery bombardment. Tellingly, whereas the French XX Corps had on average one heavy artillery gun per 36yd of front, the British Fourth Army had only one heavy per 57yd.

The war diary of IR169 recorded that at 5am on 24 June artillery fire began to rain down over the whole of the regiment's sector, as well as to the north and south. The shellfire intensified over the course of the day as communication trenches, trench intersections and rear trenches were targeted. It was the start of a bombardment that was planned to extend over five days, with the infantry assault to go in on the morning of 29 June.

By 26 June, the bombardment – directed with the help of aerial observation – was at times reaching an intensity that in German accounts is graphically termed as *Trommelfeuer* (drumfire). IR169 reported dugouts blown in, underground cables torn up, wire entanglements in part heavily damaged and trenches in places filled in; the regiment's observation post on the edge of Serre village was destroyed by a direct hit, killing Second Lieutenant Schwendemann. The German infantry were experiencing a living hell, as Otto Lais, an 18-year-old machine-gunner from Wilferdingen near Karlsruhe, recollected: 'Those of us whose dugouts had not been crushed, crouched below on the alert, took breaths, whether of smoke, dust or shell-bursts, gasping and with difficulty, believed by the third day that the unrelenting booming, rolling, cracking and bursting, on top of the shaking and trembling of the earth, would drive us mad.'

For Major General Wanless O'Gowan at 31st Division Headquarters, however, there was disquieting news brought back from seven patrols which had been sent out to check the condition of the German front-line wire on the night of 27/28 June. On the front of 93 Brigade, the wire was reported to be impassable with the exception of one gap of 4yd width. The situation was little better on the front of 94 Brigade: only at one point had there been found a lane through the entanglements of about 20yd width, while elsewhere there were only 'one or two places' where the wire was seen as passable for small parties of infantry.

Adverse weather conditions on 27 and 28 June severely restricted the ability of the RFC to spot for the artillery, and at about 4pm on the 28th word was received at 94 Brigade Headquarters that the attack was to be postponed 48 hours to the morning of 1 July; to the consternation of Brigadier General Rees, the news was shouted down the village street for all to hear.

Mounting concern on 29 June – at least as far up as divisional level – that large stretches of the enemy wire on the front of 31st Division might remain impenetrable led to orders being sent out to 93 and 94 brigades to use their night-time patrols to 'make every effort to cut the enemy's wire' using Bangalore torpedoes and wire-cutters. Even this would be of no help were the troops to succeed in breaking through the enemy front line: 15th Squadron RFC reported that same day that stretches of wire behind the enemy front line had not been cut.

Patrols sent out over the night of 29/30 June brought back a mixed picture of the state of the enemy's defences. Lieutenant Frank Bailey led a patrol of the Accrington Pals along about 40yd of wire, finding only one stretch of concertina wire that merited use of a Bangalore torpedo. To Bailey's right, a patrol from 18/West Yorkshire reckoned the wire to be sufficiently cut to allow troops to pass through but ominously reported the enemy trenches to be 'very full of men'. Despite the evidence that the enemy defences had been far from adequately destroyed, no consideration seems to have been given to aborting the attack and, in reality, it would have been politically impossible at this late stage for the British to have done so.

While the Accrington Pals enjoyed a final night of rest before moving up into their assault positions, the guns of the Howitzers' C Battery were firing in support of a diversionary attack being made by 12 and 13/Royal Sussex against an enemy position known as the Boar's Head. In the attack, which went in at 3am on 30 June, the two battalions penetrated through to the enemy support line before being forced to withdraw. The battery's commanding officer, Captain Riley, gave a brief account of the action while writing to a friend on 27 July:

> We were firing continuously almost the whole night. The infantry were fairly successful in their effort, but not as much as we should have liked, and had many casualties. I went in the trenches next day myself, but the sights were most unpleasant. The artillery evidently played their part well, as the four batteries which remained behind received a glowing letter of praise; in fact, I considered it more glowing than the situation deserved. One of my men gained the Military Medal. He repeatedly repaired the telephone wires under heavy shell and machine-gun fire.

The Military Medallist was 20-year-old Driver James Farnworth, an electrical engineer from Barnoldswick.

In the early evening of 30 June, the Accrington Pals left Warnimont Wood to begin a march of more than 6 miles to the front-line trenches opposite Serre. Shortly after 7pm the battalion reached 31st Division Headquarters at Bus-lès-Artois Chateau, marching through the Chateau gates and along a pleasant tree-lined track before moving off towards Courcelles-au-Bois. At 8.30pm the column began to arrive at Courcelles where the men were given tea and biscuits, and allowed to rest. If each man wondered if he would live to see another sunset, there was optimism too, as Jack Hindle, a 22-year-old cotton weaver from Great Harwood, described:

> you may judge how cheerful we were when I tell you that as we were going to the trenches that night there were a lot of the RFA on the wayside and one of our chaps would say to one of them, 'What do you want bringing back – a German helmet or an officer's wrist watch?' and this was not the only joke, as all were promising to have a drink with each other at a village we had to take.

As the march resumed at 9.45pm, rolls of barbed wire, empty sandbags, shovels, pickaxes, rifle grenades, detonators and other equipment were distributed throughout the battalion. In addition to normal field service order, each soldier carried a groundsheet rolled up on the back of the belt with a mess tin on top, 2 gas helmets, 4 sandbags, 170 rounds of small-arms ammunition (SAA), 2 Mills bombs and rations for 2 days; 50 per cent of the men carried a shovel, and 25 per cent carried a pickaxe. In place of a pack, the men wore a haversack to the outside of which a tin disc was tied with string.

Darkness had now fallen and lamps were used to guide the column to a point just north of Colincamps where the men filed into the communication trench named Central Avenue. By this time Colincamps itself was coming under fire from HE and shrapnel shells.

The going now became considerably harder as the floor of the communication trench was a foot or more deep in glutinous mud. In many places the trench had been blown in by shellfire, and entangled telephone lines made progress even more difficult. By 12.30am the battalion had moved barely 1,000yd along Central Avenue; with the very real possibility that his men would start the attack in a state of complete exhaustion, Lieutenant Colonel Rickman ordered them out of the trench and led them overland until firing from the field artillery batteries forced them back into the trench system.

It was 2.40am – 4 hours later than planned – before Rickman at the head of the column reached the front line only to learn that new orders had been issued regarding two deep saps which had been driven across no-man's-land to within 30 or 40yd of the German front line; the saps should have been available to be used by the men of the first wave, but were now to be kept clear of troops. Rickman was consequently forced to place his first wave under Captain Tough in the fire-bays of the front line – which were already partially blown in by enemy artillery fire – and in the traffic trench behind. The second wave commanded by Captain Livesey gathered some 60yd back in Copse Trench while the third and fourth waves (led respectively by Second Lieutenant George Williams and Captain Henry Riley) were held 500yd back in Campion Trench and Monk Trench. Rickman established his headquarters at the mouth of one of the two saps (Sap C).

In the early hours of 1 July, German forces on the Somme were alerted to the imminency of the attack when their 'Moritz' listening station near Contalmaison intercepted an order from the British 34th Division. Only the exact hour was in doubt: at 3.30am IR169 Headquarters were advised to expect the attack in an hour's time. If further confirmation were needed that the attack was about to take place, it came when patrols from IR169 reported 'lively activity' in the British trenches.

As dawn broke at 4am, German artillery fire began to fall onto the British front line; for more than 3 hours, the men of the first wave hugged the floor of their blown-down trenches as the shellfire steadily stripped away their cover.

At 5am, the 60-pounder guns, 4.7in and heavy howitzers of the British VIII Corps heavy artillery opened fire, targeting enemy artillery batteries and selected spots in the German third and fourth lines. At 6.25am, some of the heavy howitzers were redirected onto the German front line which was now also coming under fire from the 18-pounder guns and 4.5in howitzers of the divisional artillery.

Walter Peart, a 22-year-old cotton weaver from Burnley, wrote after the attack that Z Company was singing at the time when word came around shortly after 7am that there were 'twenty minutes to go, boys' and that packs were to be got on. Waiting in Campion and Monk trenches, Z Company was far from safe from the enemy artillery fire as Will Marshall, a 23-year-old from Burnley explained:

> Ben [Sergeant Ben Ingham] and another Burnley man named Webster were occupying a dugout along with an officer [Second Lieutenant Bart Endean], when a shell came and burst right on them. I was further down the trench at the time, and word came that someone was wounded. I sent for the stretcher bearers, well knowing it was Ben. When the stretcher party passed me I could not tell who was the wounded man, as his head was covered. I could tell he was badly hurt.

Will Marshall, 24-year-old Ben Ingham and 33-year-old John Thomas Webster had all been prominent members of the Burnley Lads' Club, and were employed as weavers before the war. The explosion cost Ingham his life, while Webster suffered total blindness. Endean survived the explosion and after three months' convalescence in Britain was able to return to the battalion.

Regardless of the British artillery bombardment, German machine guns were firing at about 7am; Harry Bloor, then an 18-year-old clerk from Accrington, would later recall how machine-gun bullets tore at the sandbags on the parapet of his trench as he waited to go over the top with W Company.

With 10 minutes to go to zero, 40,000lb of ammonal were detonated under Hawthorn Ridge, 3,000yd south of the copses. At the same time – inexplicably 5 minutes ahead of schedule – the fire from the heavy howitzers began to lift away from the German front line along the entire 3½-mile frontage of VIII Corps from Serre through Beaumont-Hamel. The fire from the lighter divisional artillery onto the enemy front line however was intensified over the final 10 minutes before 7.30am: supporting 94 Brigade, CLXV Brigade RFA fired HE onto the front line before switching over to shrapnel and lifting at 7.30am. Furthermore, the light artillery barrage was joined at 7.20am by a hurricane mortar bombardment, 94 Brigade Light Trench Mortar Battery reporting the firing of 1,150 rounds onto the German front line in the 10 minutes that followed.

Watching events unfold from his advanced headquarters in front of Observation Wood, no more than 500yd behind the front line, Brigadier General Rees began to believe in the possibility of success: 'ten minutes before zero our guns opened an intense fire. I stood on top to watch. It was magnificent. The trenches in front of Serre changed shape and dissolved minute by minute under the terrific hail of steel.'

As the hurricane bombardment began, the men of the first waves from 12/York and Lancaster and 11/East Lancashire clambered into no-man's-land. Some 250yd away, German sentries were alert to the movement, as Otto Lais would vividly describe:

> But now men crawl out of half-crushed dugouts, now men squeeze through shot-through tunnels, through buried dugout entrances, through broken, shattered timber frames, now they rise up between the dead and dying and call and cry out: 'Get out! Get out! It's the attack!'
>
> 'They're coming'. The sentries, who had to remain outside through-out the drumfire, rise out of the shell-holes. Dust and dirt lie a centimetre-thick on their faces and uniforms. Their cry of warning rings piercingly in the narrow gaps that form the dugout entrance. 'Get out . . . get out . . . they're coming!' Now men rush to the surface and throw themselves into shell holes and craters; now they fling themselves in readiness at the crater's rim; now they rush forward under cover from the former second and third lines and place them-selves in the first line of defence. Hand grenades are being hauled by the box from shell-hole to shell-hole.

In the meantime, the men of the first wave of 11/East Lancashire had dropped to the ground 100yd into no-man's-land to wait for their own bombard-ment to lift from the German front line. At around 7.25am, the second wave followed, with two platoons from 13/York and Lancaster close behind.

In the remaining minutes before zero, casualties began to mount rapidly. On the extreme left of the advance, where A Company of 14/York and Lancaster was struggling to get into no-man's-land through the shell-shattered wreckage of Nairne Trench, the casualty rate before 7.30am is thought to have reached 30 per cent; a curtain of smoke released to the left of Nairne had done little to screen the left flank of 94 Brigade against fire coming from the north.

The third and fourth waves of 12/York and Lancaster and 11/East Lancashire moved forward from Campion and Monk Trenches at 7.29am. As James Henry Roberts, a 38-year-old colliery engineer from Burnley, described in a letter to his wife, both waves came under intense fire as they advanced slowly down the exposed face of the valley towards no-man's-land:

> Our sergeant called out, 'Ten minutes to go'. We stood in the trenches as you would stand with your head six inches below a wall. The Germans were sweeping the wall or trench top with their machine guns at the rate of over 400 bullets per minute, and shells were

bursting all around. Five minutes to go, and every man ready; joking and smoking . . . Three minutes to go; still they smoke and joke. And now, 'Over you go, lads.' Not a waver. We were in the last of four waves. And to see those waves! It was just as you would see four long lines of soldiers in peace times. On we went in a steady walk. The bullets from the German machine guns just looked like one big glistening fan as they flew through the air. I marvel at us getting so near the enemy as we did. With machine guns everywhere and thousands of shells bursting, how that choir of hell sang.

At 7.30am the British bombardment began to roll back towards the German fourth line. In no-man's-land, the men in the leading waves scrambled to their feet, took a moment to align themselves, and advanced towards the enemy. Edward Liveing, a 21-year-old subaltern who took part in the diversionary attack at Gommecourt, painted a vivid picture of the scene that met the British troops as they entered no-man's-land:

> A continuous hissing noise all around one, like a railway engine letting off steam, signified that the German machine-gunners had become aware of our advance . . . The scene that met my eyes as I stood on the parapet of our trench for that one second is almost indescribable. Just in front the ground was pitted by innumerable shell-holes. More holes opened suddenly every now and then . . . We had been told to walk. Our boys, however, rushed forward with splendid impetuosity to help their comrades and smash the German resistance in the front line . . . I kept up a fast walking pace and tried to keep the line together.

As Rees watched the battle unfold, his hopes turned rapidly to despair as hidden German artillery batteries opened fire, hurling an explosive torrent of shells onto the British trenches:

> as our infantry advanced, down came a perfect wall of explosive along the front trenches of my brigade and the 93rd. It was the most frightful artillery display that I had seen up to that time and in some ways I think it was the heaviest barrage I have seen put down by the defence on any occasion.

German machine-gunners were by now sending streams of bullets scything across no-man's-land. Otto Lais:

> One belt after another is raced through! 250 Shots 1,000 shots 3,000 shots. 'Bring up the spare gun-barrels' shouts the gun commander. The gun barrel's changed – carry on shooting! 5,000 shots – the gun-barrel has to be changed again. The barrel's scorching hot, the

coolant's boiling – the gunners' hands are nearly scorched, scalded. 'Carry on shooting' urges the gun commander 'or be shot yourself!' The coolant in the gun jacket boils, vaporized by the furious shooting. In the heat of battle, the steam hose comes away from the opening of the water can into which the steam's meant to re-condense. A tall jet of steam sprays upwards, a fine target for the enemy. It's lucky for us that the sun's shining in their eyes and that it's behind us.

On the left of the 94 Brigade attack, 47-year-old Captain William Arthur Colley had been hit by a shell burst and killed soon after leading C Company of 12/York and Lancaster into no-man's-land; the left half of C Company was wiped out before reaching the German wire. To the right of C Company, the men of A Company scurried along the wire desperately trying to find a way through; their commanding officer, 24-year-old Captain William Spenceley Clark, was cut down by machine-gun fire in front of the entanglements. Only on the battalion's right – where there were gaps in the wire – were men able to force their way into the German front-line trench.

Leading the Accrington Pals forward, Captain Tough had been wounded before 7.30am. Continuing to push on, he was wounded a second time before being fatally hit by a machine-gun bullet.

Frank Thomas, a 19-year-old apprentice iron moulder from Accrington, was in one of the first two waves of the attack:

> At 7.30 we had to go forward. We tried but were mown down by machine guns. I got to their wire and they were on the parapets with machine guns, rifles, bombs, and their shells were playing havoc with our men. We had to take cover as much as we could and wear them down. It was here I got a bit of shrapnel or a bullet through my heel. I kept on firing and got two of the devils. Then we tried to go forward and I got hit in the back and I thought I was done for. It laid me out but it didn't go far in and I could feel it and pulled it out.

Despite appalling losses, men from the first two waves of the Accrington Pals broke into the German front-line trench on the left and right. Lieutenant Cecil Gay may well have been the only officer in the first wave still on his feet as he led his platoon from X Company through the barbed wire entanglements into the German lines; in any event, the responsibility would have been short-lived as he was hit just below the right ear lobe by a bullet which flew on through the neck, exiting at the back. As his orderly dressed his wounds, he too was hit.

By 7.40am the remnants of the first two waves, now led by Captain Livesey – who had himself been wounded in crossing no-man's-land – were engaged in bitter fighting at close range in the German front-line trench. The third and fourth waves had suffered up to 50 per cent casualties from machine-gun and artillery fire before reaching the British front line but pressed on despite losing both their commanding officers: Captain Henry Riley was killed by machine-gun fire, while Lieutenant George Williams had been wounded in the right calf by a bullet. Albert Naylor, a 19-year-old tram conductor from Accrington, was in the third wave of the attack:

> We moved on and we caught up to [the first and second waves] in good time – what there was left of them. Well, we kept moving on until we got to the first German line. We started throwing bombs, but I was not so long before I was hit in the leg with a piece of German bomb, so I got out of the trench and got in a shell-hole just over the top of the trench.

For a while the intensity of machine-gun fire over no-man's-land slackened as fighting in the German trenches reached its height. Despite his wound, Lieutenant Gay was able to work his way back to the British lines where he reported to Rickman that his platoon was through the German first line.

On the extreme left of 94 Brigade, some of 14/York and Lancaster – sheltered by a Russian sap which had been dug across no-man's-land – reached the German lines only to find themselves isolated. 12/York and Lancaster remained largely trapped in front of the wire; only on the right – where Lieutenant Charles Elam, a 21-year-old Sheffield steelworker, was last seen leading a bombing party along a communication trench – had the battalion been able to make a significant breach into the enemy's front line.

On both flanks of the Accrington Pals, fighting continued in and beyond the German front-line trench. All attempts to bring telephone wires across no-man's-land had failed. Desperate for reinforcements, Captain Livesey could do no more than send a runner back with a message to Rickman; the message never arrived. Lieutenant Gerry Gorst, who as second-in-command of W Company had been held out of the attack, heard later of Livesey's gallantry and eventual death:

> We got mixed up in the advance: ours was the holding attack, and we drew every German gun for miles on to us! Luckily for me, Army orders said that officers 2nd in command of companies should be held in reserve; therefore I am still intact. We did our job and did it well (the regiment fought simply magnificently), but every officer who went in the attack is in hospital or in his grave, and the casualties among the men are much the same as May 9th [1915]. Livesey, who commanded my Coy, will I believe be recommended for the VC; a very gallant fellow, he was hit in the arm getting over the parapet, hit in the chest half way across, hit in the head on the German wire, and

he got into the German trench, cleared a part of it and held it till he was hit in the face by a rifle-grenade, and died.

I would not leave this battalion now for anything on earth: they fought like heroes, and I'm proud to belong to them.

Shortly after 7.40am, two platoons of A Company of 13/York and Lancaster were sent forward from Monk Trench to occupy the British front line. Behind them, the battalion's B Company led by 41-year-old, Manchester-born Major Thomas Heald Guest was ordered forward from Rolland Trench to follow the fourth wave of the Accrington Pals into no-man's-land. Incredulous German machine-gunners kept up their fire against each new wave of infantry that appeared in their sights:

The enemy's getting closer; we keep up our continuous fire! The steam dies away, again the barrel needs changing! The coolant's nearly all vaporized. 'Where's there water?' shouts the gunlayer. There's soda water (iron rations from the dugout) down below. 'There's none there, Corporal!' The iron rations were all used up in the week-long bombardment. Still the English attack; even though they already lie shot down in their hundreds in front of our lines, fresh waves continue to pour over from their jumping-off positions. We have to shoot! A gunner grabs the water can, jumps down into the shell-hole and relieves himself. A second then also pisses into the water can – it's quickly filled!

Some of the Accrington Pals – unwittingly in a hopeless position – were now pressing on towards Serre. At 7.50am, an artillery observer reported seeing infantry reach the German second-line trench.

It was not until 8am that IR169 Headquarters behind Serre received word that the regiment's lines had been penetrated in Sector S2, the sector under attack from the Accrington Pals. Minutes later, the regiment's 2nd Company was ordered to make an immediate counter-attack in platoon waves from the third line. By this time, it is likely that only isolated pockets of British troops remained in the German front line along the whole of the 94 Brigade front; those who had pressed on towards Serre were now completely cut off, and none would return.

Otto Lais tried to describe the scene of unimaginable horror that lay beyond the German wire:

Those following behind take cover behind their dead, groaning and moaning comrades. Many hang, mortally wounded, whimpering in the remains of the barbed wire and upon the hidden iron stakes of the barbed wire barricade. The survivors occupy the slight slope around and behind the remains of the barbed wire and shoot at us like things possessed, without much to aim at. They make cover for themselves from the bodies of their dead comrades and many of us fall in the fire. We shoot into the wire shreds, into the belt of barbed wire that winds to the earth. The hail of bullets breaks up at the wire and strikes downwards as an unpredictable crossfire into the protective slope. Soon the enemy fire dies out here as well.

Brigadier General Rees had no means of knowing the extent of the disaster that had befallen the leading battalions. If anything, the reports he was receiving from divisional artillery observers indicated that British troops were still advancing on Serre in force. In the absence of information to the contrary, he continued to push troops forward.

Shortly after 8am, the remnants of B Company of 13/York and Lancaster crossed the British front line amid a torrent of shellfire. Few, if any, reached the enemy lines: at their head, Major Guest was shot directly in front of the German front-line trench, never to be seen again.

Divisional observers continued to report sightings of British troops well inside the German lines. At 8.07am, infantry were sighted over the fourth line on the left of the brigade front. At 8.16am – and again at 8.25am – infantry were seen in Serre itself. The accuracy of these reports has never been verified.

As late as 8.45am, Rees was persuaded by reports of 93 Brigade and 4th Division pushing forward on his right to order C and D companies of 13/York and Lancaster to advance from Campion and Monk Trenches. The two companies suffered heavily before reaching the British front line, and were ultimately pulled back and ordered to re-form in Monk.

Rickman was hardly in a better position than Rees to follow the progress of the attack, as he was totally reliant on information being brought to him by runners or by the returning wounded. At 9am, he was told by wounded Corporal James Rigby that only seven of his platoon from the first wave had broken through to the enemy front line and that they had held it for about 20 minutes until they had run out of Mills bombs. Rigby told Rickman that he had seen the remains of the second wave lying in no-man's-land. Of the third and fourth waves, Rickman had no news whatsoever.

At 9.15am, IR169 was able to report to Brigade Headquarters that it was again in possession of Sectors S1 and S2. The battle for Serre was over. For the wounded who were lying out in no-man's-land, it was now a battle only for survival.

Will Clarke, a 28-year-old from Rishton, who had worked before the war in the Co-operative Society's grocery department, writing to his sister, Ivey:

Blinded almost with blood from my wound, I commenced to roll back to our own lines, but my equipment prevented me. In spite of the machine guns that were still playing on us (and, by the way, they killed many of our wounded), I knelt up, and God only knows how I threw off my equipment, but I did it, and crawling, pulling, stumbling over barbed wire, etc., I reached our own lines.

Frank Thomas writing to his father:

I was in a shell hole and decided to go back, for it was death to stop where I was as shells were falling all around. I hobbled across no man's land and I got half way when a lump of shrapnel hit me on the cheek taking pieces clean out. I was lucky to only get that for the air was filled with lead and iron. I could feel the bullets from their machine guns whistling round me and I was thankful when I threw myself in our front line close to the stretcher bearers who bandaged me up and sent me to the dressing station.

Jack Hindle writing to Thomas and Mary Iley, the parents of 25-year-old Jim Iley, a Yorkshire-born brickmaker from Accrington:

I am proud to say your son was one of my platoon and he died like a hero. I was wounded on the same day as Jim and as I was crawling back to our lines after being hit, I saw your son trying to work a machine gun on his own. He was badly hit then and bleeding on the head, so I tried to persuade him to go along with me, but he would not do so. He said there was no one to look after the gun and he could not leave it. I gave him a drink and he said he was all right. Whether it was that wound which caused his death or whether he was hit again afterwards, I cannot say. But you can always say he was a son to be proud of and a son who stuck to his gun to the last.

Jack Haining, a 26-year-old builder from West End, Oswaldtwistle, writing to his parents, Thomas and Mary:

We were in the worst of the fight and have lost a terrible lot of men. I had a miraculous escape, having to pass fourteen hours in a shell hole with three comrades, one of them being badly wounded. While we were there shells were dropping all around us and rifles and machine guns were blazing away as if they were alive. How many came back from the charge I don't know. Neither do I know how I got back. Poor Captain Tough was killed. I heard he was twice wounded but still kept going till he was killed. I think it was very courageous of him.

Albert Naylor writing to a friend in the Accrington Tramways Department:

I stopped [in a shell-hole] all day, but towards night a shell burst behind me and put a couple of pieces in my left arm, and a piece right through my shrapnel helmet into my head. Well, I bandaged myself up as best I could, and as soon as it went dark I made towards our line, in my way, but instead of landing there I got to another line of German trenches. I only found it out by them throwing a bomb which dropped beside my head, and it didn't half make blood fly – it poured out of my nose, ears and mouth – but there was very little shrapnel which I got about the face and into my right arm. After this I managed to get into our own lines, and I can tell you it was a great relief, as I was three days and a half without food, as I had to drop all my equipment as soon as I was hit.

As enemy shellfire continued to pound the British trenches throughout the day, Rickman began to make preparations to defend his front line against a possible counter-attack. In fact, a German infantry attack across no-man's-land would have encountered little opposition: shortly after 3pm, Rickman reported that very few of the firing bays along his front were defensible. An intensification of the enemy bombardment shortly before 4pm forced Rickman to move his men into Excema communication trench. By this time, he had with him only fifty-five men and two Lewis guns. The situation was little changed when he reported at 9.20pm that the few men with him were 'a good deal rattled'; 20 minutes later Rickman was knocked unconscious by the blast of an exploding shell.

From about 700 men from 11/East Lancashire who took part in the attack on 1 July, the regimental history states that 584 were killed, wounded or missing. Of the battalion's officers, nine were killed (Captains Livesey, Riley and Tough; Lieutenants Hitchon and Stonehouse; Second Lieutenants Beacall, Davies, Kohn and Thompson) and at least twelve were wounded (Lieutenant Colonel Rickman; Captains Peltzer and Roberts; Lieutenants Ashwell, Gay, Ryden and George Williams; Second Lieutenants Battersby, Endean, Lett, Ritchie and Arthur Williams).

The impact of the disaster on the town and people of Accrington will be discussed later; suffice it here to quote from the *Accrington Observer and Times* of 1 August:

Portraits of local men who have fallen have been received almost hourly until the number has reached overwhelming proportions. In some cases the photographs furnished are unsuitable for newspaper reproduction, and if the photographs do not appear relatives and friends may guess the reason. During July – that is since the great advance began – no fewer than 175 portraits of local men have appeared in the 'Observer' . . .

Gallantry awards to 11/East Lancashire for the period 24 June to 1 July included the DSO to Lieutenant Colonel Rickman, MCs to Lieutenants Lewis and Rawcliffe, DCMs to 26-year-old Sergeant Harold Kay, a regular soldier from Rawtenstall, 31-year-old Company Sergeant Major Arthur Leeming, a cotton weaver from Burnley, 20-year-old Lance Corporal Esmund Nowell, a cotton spinner from Withnell, and 31-year-old Church-born William Warburton who had returned from America to enlist when war broke out, and the MM to 22-year-old Holford Speak, a cotton weaver from Burnley. Countless more acts of bravery went unrecognized, their witnesses having been killed in the attack; neither the VC nor any other gallantry award was made to Captain Livesey.

The losses sustained by the whole of 31st Division on 1 July alone have been quoted as 3,600 killed, wounded, missing or taken prisoner. In stark contrast, IR169 gave their losses for the period of 24 June to 1 July as 591 killed, wounded or missing.

Significant gains of ground on the British front were only possible on the far right where the terrain was more favourable to the attacks by XV Corps and XIII Corps, and where the heavy guns of the French XX Corps were able to give support. British casualties on this blackest of days of the war totalled 57,470 of whom 19,240 were counted as having been killed in action or died of wounds.

The mayor of Accrington, Captain John Harwood, with officers of CLVIII Brigade RFA at Weeton Camp, 12 June 1915. Lieutenant Colonel Thomas Purvis Ritzema is standing on the mayor's left. (*Lancashire County Library, Accrington Local Studies Library*)

NCOs from CLVIII Brigade RFA at Weeton Camp, June 1915. (*Jane Ramagge*)

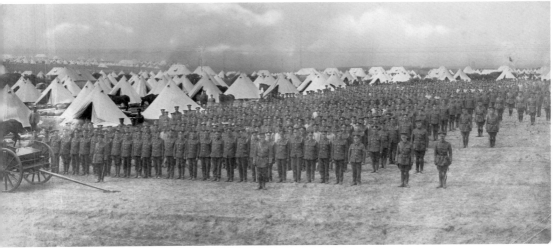

CLVIII Brigade RFA on parade at Weeton Camp, 12 June 1915. (*Jane Ramagge*)

Accrington Howitzers at Weeton Camp, June 1915.
(*Author's collection*)

Accrington Howitzers on inoculation parade at Weeton Camp, June 1915. L/757 Bombardier Tom Bent is tenth from left.
(*David and Derek Bent*)

Accrington Howitzer group at Weeton Camp, June 1915. L/757 Bombardier Tom Bent is third from left in the front row (kneeling).
(*David and Derek Bent*)

Burnley Howitzers from C Battery, CLVIII Brigade RFA, June 1915. (*Mike Townend and Towneley Hall Art Gallery & Museum, Burnley*)

Howitzers at physical drill, June 1915. (*Jane Ramagge*)

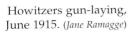

Howitzers gun-laying, June 1915. (*Jane Ramagge*)

Howitzers' shoesmiths at work, June 1915. (*Jane Ramagge*)

L/601 Gunner Herbert Chesters Bridge,
B Battery, CLVIII Brigade, RFA. (*Mike Townend and
Towneley Hall Art Gallery & Museum, Burnley*)

Lieutenant Colonel Ritzema's batman,
June 1915. (*Jane Ramagge*)

The 'Village Pirate Band' formed by men of X (District) Company, Accrington Pals, June 1915.
(*John Garwood*)

W (Accrington) Company group at Penkridge Bank Camp, 1915. 15224 Lance Corporal Percy Bury is standing at the back, with arm raised holding an entrenching tool.
(*Malcolm Bury*)

W (Accrington) Company group at Penkridge Bank Camp, 1915. (*Frances Morris*)

Y (Chorley) Company group at Penkridge Bank Camp, 1915. 15448 Richard Pendlebury and 15653 Edmund Hustings are third and fourth from left, respectively, in the second row from the front. *(John Garwood)*

15224 Lance Corporal Percy Bury (far left) on cleaning duty with three pals at Penkridge Bank Camp in 1915. *(Malcolm Bury)*

Accrington Pals group, probably at Penkridge Bank Camp, 1915. The barber (far left) is 17925 William Henry Bentley. 15045 Frank Thomas is fourth from right on the back row. *(Ian Thomas)*

Crowds greeting the Accrington Pals on the battalion's return to its home town on 1 August 1915. (*Ian Thomas*)

Family photograph at the wedding of Thomas Yates Harwood and Ida Belle Bradley, 29 September 1915. Standing, left to right: Robert Bradley, Bombardier John Richard Harwood, Lieutenant Thomas Yates Harwood and Ida Belle Harwood, Gladys Haworth, Captain John Harwood; seated, left to right: Sarah Jane Bradley, Miss Butterfield, Sarah Harwood. (*Anne and Paul Willett*)

15584 Fred Hacking, 11/East Lancashire. (*Frances Morris*)

W (Accrington) Company group at musketry practice on the firing range at Bishop Monkton near Ripon, August 1915. 15223 Lance Corporal Walter Briggs is standing second from right. (*Enid and Stuart Briggs*)

Z (Burnley) Company, led by Major Ross (location unknown but most likely to be Ripon), 1915. (*Nelly and Jacquie Ainslie*)

Lewis gunners of the Accrington Pals in Egypt, 1916. 18048 Stanley Bewsher is sat on the far right of the front row. (*John Garwood*)

Chapter 13

A Devilish Hot Time

The catastrophe that had befallen the British Army on 1 July 1916 had put paid to any immediate hopes that the Somme offensive could achieve a conclusive breakthrough. The very fact that the offensive had begun did, nevertheless, achieve the objective that Haig had confirmed to Prime Minister Asquith and Foreign Secretary Grey on 9 June: to relieve the pressure on Verdun. Already drained of divisions which were being diverted to support the Austrian army reeling from the Russian Brusilov offensive, the German army on the Western Front could no longer afford to maintain the Verdun offensive: on 11 July, von Falkenhayn met Crown Prince Wilhelm, commander of the German Fifth Army at Verdun, to bring the offensive to an end. On that same day, British artillery on the Somme began an intense bombardment in preparation for an infantry assault against the German second-line trench system on the Bazentin Ridge.

In the course of an acrimonious meeting on 3 July, Haig had resisted demands from Joffre that the British offensive be renewed north of the Albert–Bapaume road. Instead, he insisted on switching the direction of the offensive from the north-east to a drive northwards from south of the Albert–Bapaume road in order to take advantage of the limited British gains made over the previous two days. The new strategy for the Somme led to a plan for the capture of the Bazentin Ridge in which Haig had – with some reluctance – agreed to Rawlinson's proposal to start the infantry attack from as close to the enemy front line as possible, the attacking troops being pushed as far as possible into no-man's-land under cover of darkness. Yet it was the power of the artillery bombardment that would prove to be decisive: it has been estimated that the weight of shell per yard of trench to be attacked was eighteen times that of 1 July; nor was the enemy allowed any respite from the bombardment to make repairs to their defences and wire. The result was the capture of the German second-line system on 14 July along a front of 6,000yd; the villages of Bazentin-le-Petit and Bazentin-le-Grand fell to the British as did much of Longueval village and all of Trônes Wood.

CLVIII Brigade began its march south from La Thieuloye towards the Somme on 3 July, resting in billets in the villages of Grouches-Luchuèl and

Hem-Hardinval before reaching Authie six days later. By this time 35th Division had been allotted to VIII Corps, just when 11/East Lancashire had moved from VIII Corps to XI Corps. The division then found itself required to make a further move when it was placed under the orders of XIII Corps; CLVIII Brigade moved south around the town of Albert to Warly-Baillon on 14 July, and to Bois des Tailles between Morlancourt and Bray on the following day.

In the period between 5 and 14 July, there were a number of changes to the brigade's complement of officers, at least two of which suggest a degree of patronage on Fawcett's part. On 5 July, Second Lieutenant Hugh James Winder, a 28-year-old clerk from Ottery Saint Mary in Devon, joined the brigade from 25th divisional artillery in exchange for Second Lieutenant Bower and was posted to D Battery; a week later, his elder brother, Second Lieutenant George Maurice Winder, a 30-year-old valuer for the Inland Revenue, joined the brigade and was posted to C Battery, only to move between batteries to join his brother on 14 July. Given that the distance between Ottery Saint Mary and Fawcett's home in Uplyme was only 18 miles, it seems likely that he had an earlier acquaintance with the Winder family. The same period also saw Harold Bancroft promoted to captain to take command of A Battery in a belated replacement of Captain Gray, and A Battery reinforced by the transfer of Second Lieutenant Webster from the divisional ammunition column.

As a result of the advance made on 14 July, the British line south of the Albert–Bapaume road ran more or less eastwards from just below Pozières as far as Delville Wood, at which point it made a right-angle turn to the south before joining the French line in front of the farm of Maltzkorn-Duclerq, or Maltz Horn Farm as it was marked on British maps. Facing this farthermost stretch of the British line was a ridge running east of north from Maltz Horn Farm to the heavily fortified ruins of Guillemont village. On 19 July, CLVIII Brigade moved into position midway between Maricourt village and the Briqueterie in order to give artillery support to 30th Division on the Guillemont front.

The day after moving into position, all of the brigade's batteries were engaged in registration, their officers having made the best work possible of locating forward observation posts which could provide good views of the enemy line and to which telephone wires could be run without them being unnecessarily exposed to artillery fire. On 21 and 22 July, the brigade's three field-gun batteries worked on cutting the wire that guarded the approaches to Guillemont. Shrapnel remained the most effective means of cutting through wire entanglements, but was by no means a guarantor of success. HE shells of the time detonated only after burying themselves in the ground, sending the blast upwards where it had little effect other than to throw the wire up into the air from where it fell back to earth in an even more entangled state. It would be 1917 before HE shells using the 106 percussion fuse would provide a more effective means of cutting wire: the new fuse detonated the shell immediately on impact with the ground, sending out a destructive blast wave in a horizontal plane.

Despite the successes of 14 July, the British Army had a long way to travel up the learning curve as would be seen from the repeated attacks on the village of Guillemont, the first of which went in on 23 July. Following a preliminary artillery bombardment, the infantry assault began at 3.30am with 19/Manchester (4th Manchester City Battalion) advancing from the eastern edge of Trônes Wood and, further north, 2/Green Howards attacking in a south-easterly direction.

The orders for the divisional artillery, which included the Howitzers' guns, were to support the attack by providing a barrage to rake through the village ahead of the infantry in four lifts. Brigadier General William Cathcart Staveley, commanding 30th divisional artillery, would have preferred to adopt a 'creeping barrage' – already in use by the adjacent French artillery – in which a deep, rolling barrage of fire moved forward at a slow rate of about 25yd per minute; properly executed, the barrage minimized the duration of time that the infantry, following behind at a distance of less than a hundred yards, would be exposed to machine-gun and rifle fire when making the final rush on the enemy's position. Unfortunately – and for the foreseeable future – the many worn-out guns of the divisional artillery were simply not capable of providing an effective creeping barrage and, in any case, the ammunition supply was inadequate; a 'lifting barrage' would have to suffice.

Captain Neil Fraser-Tytler, who was commanding a 30th divisional battery alongside the Howitzers, recollected how the intensity of the German counter-barrage tested the ability of the signallers to maintain communication between the forward observation posts and the guns:

Macdonald had gone up at dawn with no less than fourteen linesmen, but even then communication was only possible in spasms. The Hun put down a terrific barrage, and the line had to be constantly relaid for the last 500 yards. The linesmen worked well, though the trench was choked with casualties and was being continually blown in. One of them twice ran the gauntlet of rifle fire from 400 yards by jumping over the parados, and then laying a line across the open, where it was less likely to get cut than in the trench.

19/Manchester suffered heavily while forcing a way through the largely intact enemy wire; the remnants of the left and centre companies of the battalion pressed on through Guillemont only to find themselves cut off by fire from hidden machine-gun nests. Only later was it realized that the Germans had improved their defensive tactics by moving their machine guns out of trenches and into shell holes where they were less likely to be targeted by artillery. The

Manchesters held on – some until 2pm – before they were overwhelmed by counter-attacks. In the meantime, 2/Green Howards had lost their direction in the dim light and smoke and were forced to fall back.

CLVIII Brigade reported only five casualties on 23 July. One was Gunner Ronald Denbigh, a 19-year-old apprentice plumber from Accrington, who was wounded in the right arm, neck and face; another was Driver James Thomas Clitheroe from Accrington. Denbigh was wounded by shrapnel from a shell explosion while taking a cart and horses away from a gas attack on B Battery; despite his wounds he managed to stop the horses from running away.

Gunner Herbert Chesters Bridge, a 22-year-old from Burnley who had worked as an assistant to a leather merchant before the war, gave his impressions of the day in a letter to his parents, Elijah and Kate, dated 24 July:

> Things are very lively here, and we had a dose of tear gas shell yesterday. At first I felt my eyes were smarting, then they started watering, and it was not long before I had my goggle on. Four or five of our chaps have been wounded, though only slightly, and no wonder, for shrapnel is flying about all day and night. Last night, two of us had to find a break in our wires, and we had rather an exciting time because of all the shrapnel, tear gas, barbed wire, and shell holes. However, we arrived back without a scratch, though how I don't know. The sight around the trenches was awful and the risk big. A continual roar is always going on, and our artillery must be playing havoc in the German lines. I think, on the whole, the news is good, and that our progress will be slow but sure.

The letter arrived in the same post as one informing Bridge's sister, Edith, that her brother had died of wounds on 27 July.

Enemy artillery fire on 24 July led to two more fatalities among the Howitzers. B Battery lost their commanding officer when Captain Hughes-Gibb was removed in a serious condition to hospital having been wounded in the wrist and stomach; he would lose his fight to survive the wounds on the following day. The manner in which Sergeant Harry Riley, a 27-year-old grocer's assistant from Burnley, was fatally wounded was described by Captain Bancroft in a letter to Riley's widow, Rachel:

> The day he received his wound he had been up to the front line, and his assistance enabled me to polish off a few Germans. He kept me in touch with my battery, and assisted me greatly. The way he met with his death was certainly most unfortunate. We were being shelled, and a shell which bursted [*sic*] about 200 yards away was the one which gave your husband his fatal injuries. I was talking to him at the

time, along with two other officers. When the shell burst, we all saw it, and paid no attention to it, when suddenly your husband fell back, struck in the left eye by a piece of splinter of the shell. Mr Jackson, son of Dr Jackson of Nelson, was present, and he rendered your husband first-aid immediately. As soon as Mr Jackson had dressed his wound, he was taken away to a dressing station ...

Lieutenant Reginald Jackson was to receive the MC for having 'voluntarily assisted wounded men with utter disregard of personal danger, while the batteries in the neighbourhood were under heavy shellfire'. Judging from a letter that Jackson wrote to his father on being presented with the award, he was somewhat embarrassed by the occasion:

You may be interested to know that I have got the Military Cross, and had the ribbon pinned on by General Pinney yesterday after-noon in the presence of General Staveley, the colonel, and others. I felt very self-conscious during the proceedings, especially when they read out of a book what I had done to get it, for I doubt very much if I deserved it. Every one of our people deserved it, I am sure, quite as much.

Sergeant Harry Riley, who succumbed to his wounds on 29 July, was posthumously awarded the MM.

On 26 July, CLVIII Brigade received orders to assist in an operation by 2nd and 5th divisions to capture Longueval village and Delville Wood on the following day. With support from the artillery of the French XX Corps, 35th divisional artillery was tasked with providing a diversionary bombardment over Guillemont so as to lead the enemy to expect a renewed attack against the village. From 6.10am until zero at 7.10am, the guns were to inflict as much damage as possible to trenches and wire in a bombardment of HE shells. At zero the bombardment was to be switched over to a 50:50 mixture of HE and shrapnel, and was to lift through Guillemont in the direction of Ginchy village.

The crushing weight of the preliminary bombardment on 27 July – estimated at 125,000 shells weighing 4.5 million pounds – cleared the path through Delville Wood, enabling 1/King's Royal Rifle Corps and 23/Royal Fusiliers from 2nd Division to reach their final objective, a line about 50yd inside the northern edge of the wood, by 9am. The inevitable German counter-attack succeeded only in forcing the right of the line to withdraw slightly. On the left of 2nd Division, 5th Division pushed well inside the western edge of the wood, but was unable to complete the capture of Longueval. Despite the undoubted success of the attack, it would be another month before Delville Wood was completely taken.

Some of the Howitzers' letters home gave more details of the horrors of warfare than were likely to be appreciated, as in this example from the *Accrington Observer and Times* of 8 August:

> I don't know what hell is like, but if it is hotter than this it is a mighty hot shop. When we were taking ammunition up to the guns on Thursday there was a two-horse ambulance wagon going up for the wounded. We had just got past it when a shell came and cut the two horses right in two and killed the driver on his seat. Up at the front of our guns there are hundreds of dead piled up. They don't half hum, I can tell you.

A fresh assault on Guillemont by 30th Division was planned to take place on 30 July as part of a larger-scale attack in which 2nd Division would attack on the left between Waterlot Farm and Guillemont station, while on the right the French 39th Division would attack Maurepas. The fire plan for the 35th divisional field guns differed little from that of a week previously. A short preliminary bombardment of HE shells over the enemy front line would lift at zero plus 8 minutes (4.53am) to advance in four steps through Guillemont until at zero plus 65 minutes (5.50am) the guns would switch to firing a 50:50 mixture of HE and shrapnel over a line beyond the village. The close similarity of the entire plan for the capture of Guillemont to that of 23 July practically ensured that the outcome would be no different.

2/Royal Scots Fusiliers sustained relatively light casualties in breaking through to Guillemont from the south-west; as the barrage lifted, the leading company pressed on to the north-eastern edge of the village where it dug in with help from some elements of 18/Manchester (3rd Manchester City Battalion). An enemy counter-attack was thrown back before two more companies of the Scots came up to consolidate the position. It was all to no avail; to the north, the attack had been broken up by machine-gun fire while, to the south, 19/King's – which despite heavy losses had succeeded in reaching an orchard on the south-eastern edge of Guillemont – fell back in the early afternoon believing itself to be isolated. The three beleaguered Scots companies – like the Manchesters before them – found themselves cut off by enemy fire and were eventually overwhelmed by German counter-attacks. At the end of the day, the only gains made by 30th Division were Maltz Horn Farm – captured by 2/Bedfordshire and the French 153rd Regiment – and the stretch of line which ran north from the farm as far as Arrowhead Copse.

For the Howitzers, 30 July was arguably their most arduous day on the Somme, the 4 batteries of CLVIII Brigade firing a total of 4,287 rounds. Neil Fraser-Tytler painted a vivid picture of a gun team in the heat of battle:

The scenes in the gun-pits were rather like the battle pictures of Nelson's day, a bunch of gunners stripped to the waist, covered with oil, a mountain of empty shell cases, clouds of steam rising from pools of water raised to boiling point even though poured only once through the bore; mops, rammers, more oil, dust, and debris of sandbags made up the picture, the whole being veiled by the green mist made by the bower of verdant spotted netting which encircles the gun-pit – netting which never loses an opportunity of catching fire.

There had still been only a few casualties among the Howitzers. Corporal Charles Henry Bradley, a 35-year-old draughtsman from Accrington, died on 29 July of wounds sustained while serving with B Battery of CLXIII Brigade. On 30 July, Lieutenant George Winder and Gunner George Eastham, a 23-year-old dental mechanic from Oswaldtwistle were wounded and evacuated.

Observations made from five enemy aeroplanes which were flying at low altitude over CLVIII Brigade between 5.30am and 7.30am on 31 July probably explained the heavy shellfire that broke over the brigade's gun batteries later in the day. Killed in the bombardment was D Battery's commanding officer, 44-year-old Captain Frederick Stevens, who had left the safety of a dugout to assist the drivers of an ammunition wagon which had been overturned by the explosion of a shell. According to Neil Fraser-Tytler, Stevens 'got knocked over by a big shell, and although apparently quite untouched, he died of shock an hour later. He had always been a sufferer from a wound in the head which he received in the South African War.' Fawcett described Stevens' action as 'one of purely unselfish self-sacrifice' made by 'a very gallant, efficient, and valuable officer'. Remarkably, one wounded man accounted for the brigade's only other casualty of the bombardment.

The third battery commander from CLVIII Brigade to lose his life on the Somme was Captain Riley of C Battery. The circumstances of Riley's fatal injury on 2 August were described in a letter from BQMS Allan Edmondson:

We had a very heavy strafe on Wednesday last – two gunners killed and five wounded. How the captain got his is not known, but it is surmised that in going to the aid of the wounded gunners he was hit by the following shell. No one knew until another gunner found him lying on the ground badly wounded. He was hit on the head, his left eye being clean cut out, his right eye badly damaged, and his forehead badly smashed. He never regained consciousness . . .

The two dead gunners were 26-year-old Harry Bailey, a cotton weaver from Colne, and Charles Fobester, a 20-year-old from Hackney. Of the wounded gunners, Fred Waddington, a 20-year-old warehouseman from Burnley, and his pal Ernest Draper, a 19-year-old cotton weaver from Whittlefield, Burnley, both died from their wounds in hospital at Corbie on 4 August. Riley died a day later.

The next four days were relatively quiet but on 7 August the preparatory bombardment for another attack on Guillemont began. On this occasion a 17-hour bombardment of the village by heavy artillery was supplemented by six 'Chinese attacks' delivered by gun batteries from 55th and 35th divisions. These consisted of sudden and intense lifting barrages of 15 minutes duration

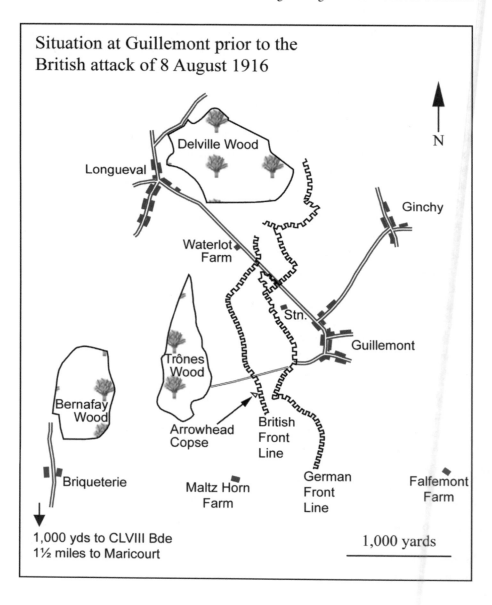

Situation at Guillemont prior to the British attack of 8 August 1916

N

Delville Wood

Longueval

Ginchy

Waterlot Farm

Stn.

Guillemont

Trônes Wood

Bernafay Wood

Arrowhead Copse

British Front Line

Briqueterie

Maltz Horn Farm

German Front Line

Falfemont Farm

1,000 yds to CLVIII Bde
1½ miles to Maricourt

1,000 yards

which were intended to deceive the enemy as to the real time of the attack as well as to destroy the enemy's defences.

The German counter-battery fire which began at about 8.30pm and continued until about 4am was itself inflicting damage and casualties as Gunner William Simpson, a 22-year-old butcher from Burnley, described in a letter to his parents, Frank and Sarah:

> On Monday night, August 7th, the Germans commenced a heavy bombardment on our batteries about 8.30pm, and continued till about 4am in the morning. It was a devilish hot time for us. I was in an old trench for cover, and was sitting in a small shelter dug in the trench side along with three other chaps. It was a pretty decent cover from shrapnel that kept continually flying in the trench. It would be about 2pm when a 5.9 shell hit the top of the shelter and burst. I just heard a deafening noise, and my heart seemed to stop beating, and when I tried to move I found I couldn't, for I was completely buried under planks and a few feet of earth. It was an awful situation. I thought my last day's work was done. One of the fellows managed to wriggle out, and then helped us out of it. It was a relief to get a breath of fresh air. I was thankful to come out alive, but I was badly bruised, and my right leg and thigh felt as if they had been stung by a thousand bees. I am now lying in the Royal Infirmary at Chester with shrapnel wounds in the right leg and thigh, also plenty of bruises.

Another casualty of the bombardment was 24-year-old Second Lieutenant Frederick Richmond Forster of B Battery, a grazier from Australia who had joined the brigade only two days before.

The artillery plan for the attack itself required the heavy guns to lift away from the enemy front line at 15 minutes before zero while the divisional artilleries were to adopt the familiar lifting barrage through Guillemont. The infantry attack that started at 4.20am on 8 August followed a depressingly predictable path. 1/8th King's fought their way into Guillemont only to be cut off, as were 1/King's who had reached Guillemont station; both battalions were overwhelmed by German counter-attacks on the following day.

The only recorded casualty of the day among the officers of CLVIII Brigade was Second Lieutenant Benton who was evacuated to a CCS with a head wound.

Two replacement officers joined the brigade before it was relieved in action four days later: Second Lieutenant George Gordon Douglas Scott was attached to D Battery (later to be made permanent); 34-year-old Bradshaw-born Second Lieutenant John Francis Mason joined from the Canadian Expeditionary Force and was posted to B Battery.

On being relieved by 24th divisional artillery on 12 August, CLVIII Brigade went first to Grove Town, an area midway between Méaulte and Bray-sur-Somme, before moving short distances over consecutive days to Bois des Tailles and then to Treux, a village on the Ancre River, south-west of Albert. The men of C and D batteries were unlucky enough to enjoy only one day's rest at Treux, as they were returned to action south of Montauban on 17 August to provide cover north of Guillemont for a renewed assault on the village which was to take place on the following day.

After a 36-hour bombardment, the infantry attack of 18 August against Guillemont started at 2.45pm and at last contained a degree of more imaginative planning. The later hour of attack and the absence of a quickening of the bombardment immediately prior to zero were intended to catch the enemy off-guard. Furthermore, the divisional artilleries were by this time able to offer better protection for the attacking troops through a creeping barrage rather than the lifting barrages that had been used previously. Despite the tactical innovations, the ground gained in the attack was modest when judged against the heavy casualties that were once more incurred. Advancing south of the track that ran from Trônes Wood to Guillemont, 12/Middlesex was stopped by intersecting machine-gun fire. North of the track, 7/Northamptonshire succeeded in breaking into the German front line, and was able to consolidate overnight. Further to the north, 3/Rifle Brigade made good use of the creeping barrage to overrun the enemy front line, and to advance further to take the station and to reach the road to Waterlot Farm. The Howitzers lost only three men wounded in the day: Second Lieutenant Hopkins, one sergeant and one gunner. It would be 3 September before the village was completely in British hands.

C and D batteries of CLVIII Brigade were relieved in the early evening of 22 August, and rejoined A and B batteries at Treux on the following day. In their absence, three officers had joined the brigade: Lieutenant Arthur Norman Haig RAMC, a 36-year-old physician and surgeon from Yeovil, Second Lieutenant Alan Richardson and Second Lieutenant Stanley Lionel Scovell, a 19-year-old from Southampton; both subalterns had been posted to A Battery.

All four batteries remained at Treux until their departure for Arras on 3 September. In the meantime, the brigade lost two of its original officers through sickness, Captain and Adjutant Renham (typhoid fever) and Lieutenant Mercer (colitis). Second Lieutenant Denys Vivian Hill, a 20-year-old from Wood Green in Middlesex joined the brigade on 26 August and was posted to C Battery.

In the five months that the brigade had been in action, it gained at least seven gallantry awards in addition to those described earlier which were made to Lieutenant Jackson and Sergeant Riley.

Awards of the MC were made to both of John Harwood's great-nephews, Lieutenant Frank Harwood and Second Lieutenant Edmund Mills Harwood. Their joint citation tells of the brothers voluntarily making a reconnaissance of hidden enemy defences; having dug themselves in overnight, they remained in position throughout the next day ranging a howitzer battery.

Bombardier Charles Edward Reeder, a cotton spinner from Oswaldtwistle who had enlisted for Army service alongside his younger brother Robert, was awarded the MM for the same operation in which the Harwood brothers each won the MC.

The DCM was awarded to 24-year-old Gunner Reuben Monk, a weaver from Great Harwood who had twice already been recommended for honours. Monk had been with Frank Harwood when the latter won his MC but gained his own award during a very heavy enemy bombardment which had cut all the telephone wires leading back from the front line; using a 'Lucas' daylight signalling lamp from an exposed position on the parapet of the front-line trench, Monk transmitted information in Morse code to the batteries. The citation also refers to a separate occasion when Monk, despite having been knocked out and badly shaken by a shell, stuck to his work, twelve times repairing broken wires under shellfire.

Gunner Thomas Henry Flannigan, a 30-year-old warehouseman from Accrington, was awarded the MM for repairing telephone wires throughout a 6-hour enemy bombardment, while other awards of the MM to CLVIII Brigade went to 36-year-old Lincolnshire-born Corporal Walter Edwin Bulley and 42-year-old Gunner William Rucastle, a bricklayer from Accrington.

From the brigade's original D Battery – that which had been exchanged in May for a howitzer battery of CLXIII Brigade – awards of the MM were made to 28-year-old Bombardier Harry Morgan, a beamer from Burnley, and Artificer Jack Lord, a 25-year-old engineer from Nelson. Lord's plea to his wife, Agnes, not to make too much of the award went unheeded as she proudly allowed his letter to her to be published in the local press:

> Well lass, I said I had a surprise in store for you, and I had to go on Thursday and be presented with the Military Medal by the General for 'coolness in action, repairing the guns under shellfire, and show-ing great devotion to duty'. That's what the Staff Captain read out. Well, lass, don't go and make a song about it, for I don't like being put up in the limelight. I would sooner go through any strafe and say nowt than keep being told about doing something that anyone else out here would do unconcernedly. Anything you have to do here has to be done and done quickly and normal, and it is only when things are quiet and normal again that you can study whether you did right or wrong.

CLXIII Brigade had taken up new positions 900yd south of Montauban on 1 and 2 August covering 2nd Division. In order to enable B Battery, the former D/CLVIII, to rest as many of its men as possible, its three remaining guns were attached to A and C batteries when the brigade was in action to support the infantry attacks on Guillemont of 8 and 9 August. After a short spell out of the line, CLXIII Brigade took up new battery positions in the orchard east of Maricourt on 16 August, B/CLXIII coming into action still with three guns only. During the attack by 3rd Division south of Guillemont on 18 August, the brigade's fire zone covered the area in which the division's only successes of the day were achieved, east of Maltz Horn Farm. CLXIII Brigade then remained in the line to support a French attack on 24 August which was ultimately forced back on the left by enfilade fire from Falfemont Farm. The brigade was withdrawn from action over the night of 25/26 August and moved to Bois des Tailles. As part of the divisional artillery reorganization on 8 September, B/CLXIII would return to CLVIII Brigade.

Chapter 14

The Old Spirit Still There

The tragedy that had engulfed the Accrington Pals on 1 July necessitated re-organization at every level of the battalion. Percy Allsup noted in his diary that he had been 'picked out as an NCO as we had lost almost all in the Advance'. Of the four company commanders, only Captain Kershaw (Y Company) had been spared. Although the names of the officers who took over command of W, X and Z companies were not recorded in the battalion's war diary, they are assumed to have been Lieutenants Gorst, Lewis and Heys, respectively. Owing to the wound suffered by Lieutenant Colonel Rickman late in the day, Major Reiss assumed command of the battalion. At brigade level, Brigadier General Rees learned on 2 July that Carter-Campbell had returned from sick leave and would resume command of 94 Brigade; Rees had hoped to retain command and described the news as 'a bitter blow'.

The remnants of 11/East Lancashire occupied Rolland trench until the night of 4/5 July when the battalion was relieved by 6/Gloucester and started on a journey by road and rail to Steenbecque where it detrained in the evening of 8 July. The men bivouacked overnight in a field before marching on the following day to Calonne-sur-la-Lys where they were billeted in barns; Allsup remarked that on the following night he 'slept first class'. The battalion spent six days at Calonne refitting and re-organizing, work which Gerry Gorst described as 'very exhausting and rather heart-breaking'. On 15 July, 11/East Lancashire marched to billets in Croix-Barbée, the village in which the Howitzers had been stationed only three months previously. As news of the successful British attack on the Bazentin Ridge reached the battalion, Gorst was prompted to write: 'The show has been a great success so far, hasn't it? I hope they will go on in the same way, and we'll beat Bosche yet before the winter.'

While at Croix-Barbée, working parties were provided for the trenches, and training was given to specialists, including the Lewis gunners and bombers. The battalion seems to have played no part in any of the several diversionary raids mounted by 31st Division ahead of the attack made by 61st and 5th Australian divisions on 19 July; in the action – which has become known as the Battle of Fromelles – the enemy front line was taken but could not be held. A draft of fifteen officers and a number of other ranks joined the battalion at Croix-Barbée, among them Second Lieutenant Robert Stanley Gordon, a

19-year-old from Blackrod near Chorley. At about the same time, the battalion lost one of its few remaining experienced officers when cardiac problems brought on by influenza led to Lieutenant Bailey being removed to hospital in Britain.

On 24 July, Y and Z companies temporarily combined to form a composite company of 6 officers and 160 other ranks under the command of Captain Kershaw for a 72-hour tour of the trenches. On three consecutive nights, Percy Allsup found himself assigned to a listening post in no-man's-land, which at this point was less than 100yd in width. The nights were fortunately relatively quiet with only occasional rounds of sniper fire to contend with. During the daytime, aggressive bursts of enemy shellfire – referred to by Allsup as 'the Kaiser's travelling managerie' – supplemented the ever-present dangers of rifle-grenade and mortar fire. On leaving the trenches, the two companies marched to billets in the village of Locon where they re-joined W and X companies in divisional reserve.

The battalion took over trenches in the Neuve-Chapelle sector on 4 August. Still well short of the manpower required to hold the length of trench system allotted to a battalion, it was necessary for 11/East Lancashire to form a composite battalion under the command of Major Reiss together with 12/York and Lancaster and one company of 13/York and Lancaster; the arrival of a draft of 182 other ranks for 11/East Lancashire between 5 and 7 August allowed the Barnsley company to be relieved.

A curious incident took place in the headquarters dugout of Z Company on the first day of the battalion's tour of the Neuve-Chapelle trenches when Second Lieutenant Gordon Peter Raeburn, a 19-year-old who had left his birthplace of Shanghai to volunteer for Army service, shot himself in the left hand with a Webley revolver. If Raeburn had been judged guilty of deliberately wounding himself, his punishment would have been severe. As it was, the two other officers who were present in the dugout at the time – Lieutenant Heys and the battalion's new medical officer, 26-year-old Irish-born Captain George Chambers Anglin – testified that they were convinced of an accidental discharge of the revolver. Major Reiss stated that Raeburn had 'shown himself an exceptionally keen officer and quite without fear or nervousness' and concurred that the subaltern was to blame only for carelessness. Neither Carter-Campbell nor Wanless O'Gowan saw any reason to come to a different conclusion, and Raeburn escaped further repercussions from the incident.

The poorly constructed trenches that the composite battalion occupied in the Neuve-Chapelle sector were subjected to frequent bombardment from trench mortars, the terrifying effects of which were described by newly promoted Captain Gerry Gorst:

> Bosche has an infernal machine here (three of them to be exact) called a 'Minenwerfer', politely known as Minnie, which is a singularly

unpleasant thing; it's a ten-inch mortar and throws a very large fat shell with a terrific explosion; you can feel the ground shake within three hundred yards of it; personally I've been within twenty yards, and I counted my legs and arms carefully afterwards to make sure they were all there still!

Among the conscripts who were joining the battalion were men who should never have been sent out to the front. A case in point was Richard Scholes, a 29-year-old labourer from Church, who had been called up on 11 April 1916 and found himself posted to 11/East Lancashire little more than three months later. There was a history of mental illness in Scholes' family and he himself had suffered a head wound at the age of 15, after which he had been unable to work for ten months; he would later be described as 'simple, childish and ignorant for his age'. On 14 August – ten days into the battalion's tour – Scholes made an unsuccessful attempt to desert; a Field General Court Martial held ten days later found him guilty and sentenced him to suffer death by being shot. Scholes was fortunate: not only was his sentence commuted on 16 September to two years' hard labour but, in the light of subsequent medical assessments, the unexpired portion of his sentence was written off. Scholes was discharged from the Army on 21 July 1917.

This first tour of the Neuve-Chapelle trenches lasted an unusually long fourteen days. It had cost two subalterns their lives: William Barrett and George Edwin Wighton, a 23-year-old railway engineer from Leytonstone. Of two other officers who escaped with wounds, one was 26-year-old Second Lieutenant Samuel Taylor, who had worked as a secretary in an Accrington cotton-spinning mill before joining the Howitzers in February 1915. Taylor had been promoted to Acting BQMS when in November 1915 he applied for a commission; despite the opposition of Lieutenant Colonel Ritzema to his transfer out of the brigade, he was discharged in January 1916 to a temporary commission with the East Lancashire Regiment. Taylor made a quick recovery from his wounds and returned to the battalion before the month was out. The battalion's other casualties during the tour amounted to eight other ranks killed and sixty-one wounded.

After 11/East Lancashire had left the trenches on 18 August and gone into divisional reserve at Locon, Gerry Gorst mentioned in a letter to his sister that 'a very nice fellow named Duff has come from the 3rd Battalion to my company'.

John Shire (Jack) Duff, a 26-year-old mining engineer, was one of two South Africans – the other being 23-year-old Spencer Richard Fleischer – whose applications for temporary commissions in the British Army had been supported by the South African High Commissioner in London in a letter addressed to the War Office on 21 December 1915. Both young men had travelled to Britain at their own expense, after being discharged from the Imperial Light Horse at the conclusion of the German South-West Africa Campaign. Their applications were quickly accepted; before the year came to an end, both men had been appointed as subalterns to 3/East Lancashire, and had received orders to join the School of Instruction at Bedford on 12 January 1916. The two South Africans were separated when posted overseas to different battalions, Fleischer going to 8/East Lancashire.

On completing a relatively uneventful time in brigade reserve between 26 August and 11 September, 11/East Lancashire had earned five days' rest in Army reserve at Vieille-Chapelle. The battalion war diary records the arrival of 25 officers and 349 other ranks in between leaving the Somme and moving to Vieille-Chapelle; even by this time, 11/East Lancashire can have recovered to only half of its full complement. Among the most recent draft of officers was Lieutenant Harold Wilton, a 28-year-old draper from East Keswick near Leeds who before the war had been employed as a store manager in Russia.

After only five days at Vieille-Chapelle, the battalion went into the front line in the Festubert sector. The trenches were in extremely poor condition and were entirely overlooked from the German lines. It was a situation made bearable, as Gerry Gorst explained to his sister, only because the enemy was disinclined to make trouble:

> it's rained every day since we came in, so the trenches (where there are any) are full of water, and dear brother Bosche is only sixty yards away and overlooks the whole line from an enormous crater on the right, and you get a picture of earthly bliss (very earthy too) which I've rarely met before. Fortunately the old Hun is of the Saxon variety, and fairly tame, besides which his trenches must be nearly as bad as ours. So we haven't much to contend with except the weather and the snipers, who are some of the poorest shots I've met; so far they've killed one of my men, and I can swear to a bag of nine of theirs, and a lot more probable too.'

As it turned out, his own Lewis gunners posed the greater threat to his life:

> I nearly tore it last night; I wandered out into No Man's Land after sending my runner to tell everyone I was doing so; unfortunately the ass never told the Lewis gunners, so they naturally thought I was a Hun, and did some pretty shooting on me at thirty yards. Of course, I was out of sight in about one fifth of a second, but they put one through the sleeve of my tunic, which was quite as close as I care about. To-night I'm giving No Man's Land a rest, as I've been out every night since we came in.

One of Gorst's officers, Lieutenant Richard Bunster Wayland, a 21-year-old clerk from Great Meols near Hoylake, was less fortunate: 'I lost another officer this last time in, shot in the tummy, poor lad. Plucky fellow too, as it must have hurt like blazes, and he never made a sound; he died next morning.' In addition to Wayland, four other ranks were killed and one wounded before the battalion was relieved on 24 September.

On top of the reverses suffered by the Central Powers at Verdun and in the Brusilov offensive, the entry into the war of Romania on the side of the Allies on 27 August had led two days later to the replacement of von Falkenhayn as Chief of the German General Staff by Field Marshal Paul von Hindenburg, the victor of Tannenberg. Working alongside von Hindenburg with the title of First Quartermaster-General, 51-year-old General Erich Friedrich Wilhelm Ludendorff effectively took on the role of head of operations.

A new British offensive on the Somme launched on 15 September at Flers–Courcelette prompted Gorst to write to his sister: 'By Jove, isn't the news from the south good?' The offensive, best remembered for the first use of tanks on the battlefield, achieved a breakthrough on the first day along an 8-mile front to a depth of up to 3,000yd.

A familiar face was welcomed back to the battalion on 28 September: Second Lieutenant Battersby re-joined having recovered from his wounds of 1 July.

After a further spell in the trenches from 1 to 4 October, during which time three other ranks were wounded, 11/East Lancashire moved by road and rail to Doullens; the final leg of the move was a 5-mile march to billets in the village of Sarton. Over the following ten days, the battalion practised making attacks, a novel feature of which was the use by signallers of flares and ground-shutters to allow aeroplanes to follow the infantry's progress. The mock attacks were in preparation for a renewed assault north of the Ancre River on the Somme battlefield, a prospect that the battalion's officers had been aware of before leaving the Neuve-Chapelle/Festubert area, as Gerry Gorst had written to his sister: 'I have indeed left that nasty dangerous spot, but I'm not sure yet whether in the long run it wouldn't have been better to stop there . . . daresay I may find myself somewhere on familiar ground'. So it proved. On 15 October, 31st Division returned to the Serre sector to take over the 1¼-mile stretch of front line that ran north from John Copse. 11/East Lancashire moved up into divisional reserve at Warnimont Wood four days later; for those who had been with the battalion on 1 July, it was an emotional return:

> Warnimont Wood came in sight, the steep slope from the road impressing its old familiarity on the 'veterans'. The same old huts, a little more worn and shabby, stood out plainly amid the half leafless trees. What strange old thoughts came back to the men. Here it was on the evening of 29 June that Captain Riley had gone round the huts and had a last talk to the men he would lead to attack on that fateful Saturday morning. His spoken words were probably forgotten – but

somehow the things he left unsaid, conjured up in Z men's minds the conviction that he would not survive the attack. A lump came into many throats and unspeakable thoughts flashed through men's minds at the sight of the old camp which only a few months before had heard the joyous ring of Lancashire voices ...

Before 11/East Lancashire went into the front line on the night of 30/31 October, Gerry Gorst, suffering from cardiac problems, had left the battalion. That there was only one fatality during this spell in the trenches which lasted until 3 November, 22-year-old Samuel Pilling from Bacup, says nothing of the appalling conditions that the men had to endure:

> This tour of the trenches was beastly in the extreme. Rain and mud harrassed the poor fellows, while five-nines dropped persistently on communication trenches. Bringing up water rations and [small-arms] ammunition was truly a nightmare, especially when these had to be carried to advanced posts. Gum boots were worn, but one fellow from Brunshaw floundered up to the waist in a mud-filled shell hole, not far from John Copse.

Trench Foot was a new hazard to be faced:

> A new ailment appeared – Trench Feet. Feet were sodden with mud and rain and had become cramped and swollen – some even bloated and painfully tender. Walking was almost impossible and several men were sent into hospital as stretcher cases. Then came an issue of Whale oil – nasty smelling stuff, but when well rubbed in the feet and the ankles it prevented the excruciating pain of Trench Feet.

The battalion was relieved on 3 November and played no part in the second attempt ten days later to capture Serre village, other than to provide two platoons to carry stores up to 92 Brigade. The situation in front of Serre was even less auspicious for the British than it had been before the attack of 1 July. The ground below the village was now a sea of deep, cloying mud overlayed with more sophisticated and more densely concentrated barbed wire entanglements. At 5am on 13 November, shrouded in fog, the leading battalions of 76 Brigade (3rd Division) moved into no-man's-land, crossing the same ground over which the men of 94 Brigade had fallen over four and a half months earlier. History was to repeat itself. On the left of the brigade front, few of 2/Suffolk were able to penetrate the German wire. Behind them, 8/King's Own were caught in no-man's-land by a devastating artillery barrage. On the right, men of 10/Royal Welch Fusiliers and 1/Gordon Highlanders fought their way as far as the German fourth line but were eventually overwhelmed. On the left of 76 Brigade, 12 and 13/East Yorkshire of 92 Brigade broke through the German front line but were eventually forced to retire when it became evident that 3rd Division were unable to make progress. As the Battle of the Somme drew to a close with the capture of Saint-Pierre Divion, Beaucourt and Beaumont-Hamel, Serre remained in German hands.

Over the winter of 1916–17, offensive operations were continued by means of trench raids. Raiding parties were used to gather information about the strength and identity of the units holding the opposing front line, to kill or capture the enemy, to bomb dugouts and to destroy machine-gun and trench-mortar emplacements. 11/East Lancashire took over the line again in the afternoon of 14 November and made preparations for a raid across no-man's-land that was to take place four nights later.

Friday, 17 November 1916 had been a generally clear, if cold, day. At 6.30pm, darkness having descended over the battlefield, 31st divisional artillery opened fire over a 2,000yd stretch of the enemy front line. The burst of fire lasted just 45 seconds. At 8pm, another 45-second burst of artillery fire broke over the enemy front line. Shortly before 9pm, a raiding party of one officer and fifty-five other ranks from 11/East Lancashire scrambled into no-man's-land 1,200yd north-west of Serre and took up position close to the British wire. Both flanks were protected by covering parties, each of which comprised at least twenty other ranks and a Lewis gun. At 9pm – with the enemy hopefully by now accustomed to short bursts of artillery fire followed without incident – the divisional artillery again opened fire on the enemy front line, and 45 seconds later, the artillery fire was checked, then diverted to form a pocket around the intended point of entry. At the same time, the raiding party rushed forward. Their orders were to identify the units holding the enemy line. Unfortunately, there seems to be no record of what followed, other than that the raiding party failed to enter the enemy trenches. Most likely the enemy were not after all taken by surprise and the raiding party ran into heavy fire. Four men from the battalion were posted as having been killed in action on either 17 or 18 November: John Markendale Clapham from Nelson, 25-year-old Herbert Hartley from Burnley, 19-year-old John Bramham Wadsworth from Nelson and 27-year-old Frederick (Fred) Westwell from Accrington; with the exception of Westwell, who had worked as a railway clerk before the war, all had been employed as cotton weavers. It must be likely that all four lost their lives during the over-night raid.

The battalion was relieved on the day following the raid, but had to under-take another tour of the front line before the month of November was done. Since going into the line on 30/31 October, 11/East Lancashire had lost at least eleven killed, thirty-two wounded and two missing; among the wounded were Second Lieutenants Leonard William Clarke, a 20-year-old who died of his wounds on 14 November, J C J O'Connor and Herbert Clifford Richardson, a 24-year-old architect from Ashton-on-Mersey.

With Rickman still unfit to resume command of the battalion, the responsibility passed on 3 December to Major George Boothby Wauhope after Reiss had been transferred to the General List. One Pal commented that the new commanding officer was 'one of the best' with 'many of the good qualities of Rickman, being a strict disciplinarian and devoted to his men'.

For the next six weeks, 94 Brigade held the right sector of the divisional front using a rotation system in which, at any one time, one battalion plus two companies of another held the trench system, one battalion less two companies were in reserve at Sailly-au-Bois, and the remaining two battalions were at Sailly Dell and Rossignol Farm. It was a system that was criticized not just for being intricate but also for doing nothing for battalion cohesion.

11/East Lancashire celebrated Christmas at Rossignol Farm on 24 December, as the battalion was due to go back into the trenches on Christmas Day itself. If the best efforts of the battalion's cooks to prepare a Christmas dinner fell short of the men's expectations, a plentiful supply of parcels from home enabled them to enjoy Christmas pudding four days running.

This particular spell at the front ended on 11 January when the battalion was withdrawn by bus to Beauval, a village 3½ miles south of Doullens in which three companies of the Pals had been billeted overnight on moving up to the line in late March of the previous year. Over the following six weeks, the battalion trained at Beauval, Fienvillers and Fieffes; a regime of route marching, rifle practice, close-order drill, specialist training, physical training and bayonet fighting was later supplemented by mock attacks on trench systems and villages in platoon, company, battalion and brigade formations. The training seems to have been limited to the mornings, with games of football being popular in the afternoons. It was a time that was remembered for the intense cold: snow that had fallen a month previously still lay thickly on the ground, and the ponds and rivers were said to have been covered with ice to a depth of between 12 and 18in; rifle practice had to be abandoned, and a ration of hot cocoa – a gift from the battalion's friends in its home towns – served mid-morning was more than welcome. It was only at the end of the training that 11/East Lancashire had more or less returned to its full strength; it had taken the arrival of at least 38 officers and 938 other ranks to recover from the catastrophic attack on Serre more than 7 months previously. Although the new recruits had mostly come from further afield than Accrington, Burnley and Chorley, the spirit of the original battalion lived on. Fred Sayer wrote of his feelings on leaving the battalion in 1917:

> Leaving the 11th East Lancs, even though it was not now the 'Pals', was an anticlimax. All the old 'Bombers' were casualties in July, but I had been in the forefront of the birth of the new 'First Aid Squad' and saw to it that the old spirit had survived. Somehow this happened

throughout the specialist groups, throughout the battalion, and the 1914 men, returning after recovery, found the old spirit still there.

Tragically, the specialist training for the bombers was to lead to a fatality among the Pals' officers. When 11/East Lancashire came out of the line on 11 January, Lieutenant Beaumont was posted as Chief Bombing Instructor to 31st Divisional School of Instruction where a course began on the 15th. At around 3pm on the fourth day of the course Beaumont was instructing George Wentworth Dimery, a 29-year-old subaltern from Moortown, Leeds who was serving with 15/West Yorkshire. Dimery was throwing live bombs from a specially prepared cage breastwork, with Beaumont standing about 3yd behind him. The remainder of those on the course waited behind a sandbag shelter some distance to the rear. The bombs they were using had been checked and charged by Lance Sergeant Robert Edmund Driver, a former warehouseman from Oswaldtwistle who had become an experienced bomber in his time with the Accrington Pals. There had been five bombs from the box safely thrown already, two of them by Dimery himself. On Beaumont's whistle, Dimery withdrew the pin from his third bomb and brought his arm back to throw. At least two eyewitnesses saw the bomb explode in his hand within about a second of the pin being pulled. Dimery – amazingly still on his feet – turned around aghast to see Beaumont lying on the ground unconscious with terrible wounds to the head. Beaumont was rushed to a CCS, but died there of his wounds on 24 January. Dimery was hospitalized with severe wounds to his right eye, right hand and right hip, but died of a gangrenous appendix at the London Hospital, Middlesex on 4 April. A Court of Inquiry held on the day of the accident concluded that neither officer was to blame and that the cause of the accident was the premature explosion of the bomb for reasons unknown.

Before 11/East Lancashire left Fieffes on 20 February, rumours were rife that the Germans were preparing to make a withdrawal from the Somme battlefield. The rumours proved to be correct: on the fine though misty morning of 24 February, three patrols from 21/Manchester reached the western outskirts of Serre without sighting the enemy. The commanding officer of the Manchesters, Colonel William Willie Norman, forwarded the patrol report to 91 Brigade headquarters with the footnote: 'The above report seems almost incredible but I am of an opinion that it is reliable. If so, it points to the evacuation of Serre by the enemy.' At 6.35am on the following day, A Company of 21/Manchester advanced on the ruins of the village, with C Company on its right. A Company came under enemy artillery fire while passing through the centre of Serre, and later encountered slight resistance from a small body of the enemy holding out in the northern part of the village; by 10.10am, however, A Company had reached its final objective and joined up with C Company across the Serre–Puisieux road. It had taken 239 days from 1 July 1916, but

Serre had finally fallen. The withdrawal was the prelude to the German retreat of 16–19 March to the *Siegfried Stellung*, or Hindenburg Line, a defensive position of daunting strength and depth which had been under construction since October 1916 and extended for 90 miles south from Arras.

On the night of 20/21 February, 31st Division took over the line between Serre and Gommecourt. 11/East Lancashire – going into divisional reserve as part of 94 Brigade – sent one company to Couin while battalion headquarters and the remaining three companies went to Coigneux. Every available man was now needed for working parties, either from Couin and Coigneux or in the back areas to where 400 men were detached on 26 February. A draft of three subalterns had joined the battalion during February: 24-year-old Thomas Edgar Cronshaw and 26-year-old William Farrer Lonsdale, both from Blackburn, and 23-year-old William Arthur Lauderdale from Ilford.

The battalion moved up on 1/2 March to Sailly Dell and was joined there by the detached working parties. On 6 March, 11/East Lancashire took over a stretch of line east of Puisieux having struggled forward overnight across shell-torn, treacherous ground which had been cleared of any landmarks. The position held by the battalion consisted of two lines of isolated posts backed by two former German trenches known as Orchard and Gudgeon and the *Wundt-Werk* strongpoint.

During the night of 7/8 March, Second Lieutenant Frederic James Wild, a 25-year-old from Shuttleworth, led a patrol of twenty men out into no-man's-land in order to examine a suspected enemy machine-gun emplacement and ascertain whether the enemy was holding Bucquoy trench in strength. An account of the events that followed was given by Wild in January 1919:

> When close to the [enemy] wire I went ahead with Corporal Bamber and Lance Corporal Kewley to reconnoitre it. We almost crawled into a working party in the wire and had to lie quiet for several minutes. Two of the working party looked towards us several times; then they all went back through the wire, and on our endeavouring to creep away back to the remainder singly we were challenged and fired upon. At the same time two men came through the wire and intercepted me. I got away by shooting the first with my revolver. The second fled. I emptied my revolver at him but missed. I ran back to the remainder of the patrol and found them commencing to scatter. By this time very heavy machine-gun and rifle fire had been opened upon us. I tried to rally the patrol, but had hardly commenced when I was hit in the thigh. I called for help and took cover with Lance Corporal Kewley and several men who came back to me. Daylight broke before any attempt to get away could be made. Numerous

parties of Germans spent the intervening time searching the ground, but apparently missed us.

The following evening we attempted to get back. Very heavy machine-gun and rifle fire was opened at once, killing one man and wounding Lance Corporal Kewley very severely. We again took cover, and when the fire died down I sent the remainder, who were unwounded, off individually, resolving to take my chance with the lance corporal. Early the following morning a German patrol found us and took us in.

In addition to Wild and Lance Corporal Herbert Kewley, a 24-year-old from the Isle of Man, two men were reported in the battalion war diary as missing from the patrol; the bodies of 28-year-old James Knowles and 32-year-old Frank Myers, both from Accrington, were never identified.

The other fatality suffered by the battalion during this spell in the front line occurred when the enemy artillery made a direct hit on Y Company headquarters, mortally wounding Second Lieutenant Cronshaw within ten days of his having joined the battalion; severely wounded in the same shell burst were Captain Frederick Kite ('Fog') Dodson, a 26-year-old teacher from Penwortham, and Second Lieutenant Battersby. Dodson lost his right leg and left foot as a result of the explosion, while Battersby – still only 17 years of age – lost his left leg.

The battalion was relieved on 9 March and went to billets in Courcelles-au-Bois from where over 13–16 March it was employed on working parties constructing a railway line near Serre. It was particularly grim work, as the bodies of several men who had been reported missing on 1 July of the previous year were uncovered.

On 18 March, 11/East Lancashire began a march northwards into the First Army area, reaching billets in Merville seven days later. From then until 8 April – the eve of the opening of the Battle of Arras – the battalion trained in wood fighting as well as carrying out the usual small-arms practice and specialists' training. Of the eight officers who joined at Merville, one – Second Lieutenant Lett – was returning to the battalion having recovered from his wounds of 1 July 1916; the others were Captain John Shaw Wyllie, Lieutenant Philip Lancelot Bathurst, and Second Lieutenants Joseph Albert Edmondson, E Harrison, Errol William Carlisle Leach, Harold Winder and Albert Edward Womersley. In addition, Captain Stanley Williams of 11/East Yorkshire was attached to the battalion from 1 April.

While the battalion was marching north, John Harwood resigned from the 'thankless and unenviable task' of Military Representative for Accrington. The *Accrington Observer and Times* opined that Harwood's services to the country deserved to be publically recognized by the War Minister: no such recognition was ever made.

Chapter 15

Ceased to Hope for Anything Better

Returning to the second weekend of September 1916, we find CLVIII Brigade moving into new battery positions on the Scarpe River, outside of Arras. The move of 35th Division from the Somme to Arras ended in a major reorganization of the divisional artillery: CLXIII Brigade was disbanded, and its guns and personnel were divided among the other three brigades so that each now comprised three six-gun 18-pounder batteries and one four-gun 4.5in howitzer battery. It was a complicated transition with A and B/CLVIII – the two Accrington batteries – being made up to six-gun batteries with two sections of B/CLXIII (originally the Burnley battery, D/CLVIII), and C/CLVIII (the second Burnley battery) leaving the brigade to be split between CLVII and CLIX brigades and to be replaced by D/CLXIII. Second Lieutenant George Slinger was among the officers who found themselves posted to CLIX Brigade. From this point forward, the narrative will focus on the two Accrington batteries.

In a further change, each divisional artillery brigade was assigned a specific infantry brigade to cover, CLVIII Brigade being assigned to 106 Brigade (17/Royal Scots, 17/West Yorkshire, 19/Durham Light Infantry and 18/Highland Light Infantry).

Throughout the remaining months of 1916, 35th Division pursued the aggressive policy of dominating no-man's-land by regularly mounting trench raids. The enemy occupying the trenches opposite 35th Division in the month of September were also recovering from fighting on the Somme and seemed to be short of either guns or ammunition for their artillery; enemy trench-mortar fire on the other hand reached new heights of intensity and accuracy.

On the night of 14 September, A Battery co-operated in a raid by 15/Cheshire (105 Brigade) on the Three Craters salient just north of the road to Bailleul-sir-Berthoult. The battery's role was to fire HE shells at the communication trench leading from the enemy's support line to its front line over the 60 minutes following zero (8pm). Three bombing parties followed by a clearing up party were then able to enter the enemy front line and began bombing outwards but, in the time available, were unable to widen the breach sufficiently to allow a team of New Zealand miners to achieve their objective of locating and destroying mine shafts. The raiding party, which was recalled at 9pm, suffered two killed, twenty-eight wounded and three missing.

If there was a suspicion with the arrival of the Winder brothers that Fawcett was able to wield a certain amount of influence when it came to the appointment of officers to his command, confirmation seemingly came on 14 October when Lieutenant Cecil Lyne, the junior officer with whom Fawcett had forged a good relationship during the closing months of 1915, joined the brigade.

Evidence that a new German division had moved into the line opposite 35th Division came on 17 October when abnormal enemy artillery activity was attributed to a new division registering its guns on the British trenches. The regiment now facing 35th Division was soon seen to be more aggressive than its predecessor; hostile patrols into no-man's-land were stepped up and – in addition to ever-increasing trench-mortar fire – a new hazard appeared in the form of aerial torpedoes.

On 25 October, CLVIII Brigade supported a raid made by 15/Sherwood Foresters (105 Brigade) against enemy trenches at a point just south of the Bailleul-sir-Berthoult road. Over the 45 minutes that followed zero (8pm), four guns from A Battery and two guns from B Battery fired on the enemy front-line and communication trenches at 20-second section fire (a total of 270 rounds), three guns from C Battery targeted trench intersections at one round per minute, while D Battery was engaged on counter-battery fire at one round per minute. Although the artillery had cleared a path through the two series of 40ft-thick enemy wire in front of the point of entry, only one of the three bombing parties was able to find the gap, the other two having lost their direction in the smoke and darkness. Following behind the bombing parties, two of three clearing parties managed to get into the enemy lines where they destroyed two dugouts and took a prisoner (who reportedly tried unsuccessfully to strangle one of his captors while being hauled across to the British lines).

Little more than a week later, the Howitzers co-operated with 17/West Yorkshire (106 Brigade) in a successful raid made about 100yd north of the Bailleul-sir-Berthoult road at about 1.45am on 3 November. The artillery held their fire until the raiding party discharged rockets to indicate that a path had been blown through the enemy wire. The raiding party rushed the trenches, killed six of the enemy, bombed two dugouts and returned practically unscathed having recovered shoulder-strap identification of the 89th Grenadier Regiment.

Subsequent to Captain Crocker's departure to take up an appointment in Britain, 29-year-old Captain Hugh Smithson, a Regular Army officer from Sculcoates, joined the brigade on 21 November to take command of B Battery.

A period of relative calm enlivened only by occasional minor operations aimed at the destruction of enemy strongpoints and trench mortars was broken when the brigade was called upon to support a raid north-east of Roclincourt by 19/Durham Light Infantry (106 Brigade) at 3am on 26 November. One gun from A Battery was to provide enfilade fire along a communication trench, three guns from C Battery and three howitzers from D Battery were to target the support line and trench-mortar positions, while the remaining five guns of A Battery were to provide diversionary fire to the south of Roclincourt. Most of the raiding party failed to reach the German trenches, allegedly because of friendly artillery fire falling short in no-man's-land and around the point of entry. The two officers and eight men from the raiding party who did succeed in breaking into the enemy front line – apparently without difficulty – could do little more than bomb a dugout before being forced to withdraw through a lack of support. The largely fruitless raid cost the lives of two of the raiding party; nine more were wounded during the operation.

On 28 November, a sniper's bullet claimed the life of Second Lieutenant George Nicholas Slinger, the second son of Major Slinger and the first man to have been enlisted into the ranks of the Howitzers. Slinger and a fellow officer from CLIX Brigade, Lieutenant John Howard Hanrick, had taken advantage of the dense morning fog to examine the state of the enemy wire. The two officers were about to return when two shots were fired, one of which hit Slinger in the head, killing him instantly. During the following night Hanrick and a subaltern from 15/Cheshire, Harold Edward FitzGerald, went out to recover Slinger's body but, after losing their direction in the darkness, had to leave him in a shell hole. The two officers, moving away in completely the wrong direction, stumbled onto a German sap. A sentry on guard shouted in alarm, giving Hanrick and FitzGerald the chance to drop flat on the ground before the sky was lit by a flare. FitzGerald was slightly wounded in the arm by rifle fire before the pair took advantage of the returning darkness to escape back to their own lines. Another subaltern from the Cheshires, named Walker, went out early the following morning and again during the night but was unable to find Slinger's body. Following the British advance at Arras in 1917, Slinger's grave, well cared for by the enemy, was found marked by an inscribed cross in the grounds of the Chateau d'Immercourt at Saint-Laurent-Blangy.

At a meeting held at Advanced General Headquarters on 10 November 1916, the decision had been taken to reduce the number of field artillery brigades allocated to a division from four to two, and to use the surplus batteries to form Army Field Artillery (AFA) brigades which could be employed to reinforce sectors of the front without breaking up the divisional structure. It may well be that CLVIII Brigade had already been marked for disbandment when on 4 December Lieutenant Colonel Fawcett left Smithson in temporary command of the brigade in order to take charge himself of 48th Heavy Artillery Group, Royal Garrison Artillery.

Although 35th Division was relieved by 9th Division over the first few days of December, the divisional artillery remained in the line, CLVIII Brigade co-operating in a successful daylight raid on the enemy's trenches about 1,500yd north-north-east of Roclincourt by 3rd Canadian Division between 3 and 5pm on 20 December.

As Major George Richard Balston arrived to take over command on 25 December, the brigade's artillery activity for the day was drolly summarized in its war diary by: 'Xmas Greetings sent across to the German to interfere with his communications and inflict casualties on ration parties.' It would prove to be a valedictory shoot: on the following day, 35th divisional artillery began to be withdrawn from the line having been in continuous action for more than fifteen weeks. Between 8 and 11 January, CLVIII Brigade was broken up as the re-organization into AFA brigades took effect: the two Accrington batteries survived intact, A Battery becoming C Battery of XLVIII Brigade (hereafter C/XLVIII) and B Battery becoming C Battery of LXIV Brigade (hereafter C/LXIV); C Battery was absorbed into CLVII Brigade and, while one section of D Battery went to LII Brigade, the other joined D Battery of LXIV Brigade. Amid the reorganization, Second Lieutenant Edmund Mills Harwood left on being posted to the RFC on 23 January.

C/XLVIII moved up into action at Arras over the night of 9/10 January; its officers were Major H Bancroft, Captain D R Worsley, Second Lieutenant R Jackson, Second Lieutenant W T Beardsley, Second Lieutenant D V Hill and Second Lieutenant N Tomlinson. It was almost one month later before C/LXIV first went into action at Maroeuil; although the names of its officers were not recorded at the time, they can be presumed to have included Major H Smithson, Lieutenant C C Morgan, Lieutenant F Harwood, Lieutenant C E L Lyne, Second Lieutenant J F Mason, Second Lieutenant P J D Flecknoe and Second Lieutenant S Knocker.

December 1916 had brought two changes to the political and military leader-ship of the Allies that were to shape the future direction of the war. In Britain, David Lloyd George had replaced Asquith as Prime Minister, while across the Channel General Robert Georges Nivelle had superseded Joffre as commander-in-chief of the French armies. Lloyd George, in his determination to avoid British casualties on the scale of the Somme campaign from a renewed offensive by Haig in 1917, was easily seduced by Nivelle's promise of a breakthrough from a French spring offensive on the Chemin des Dames; nothing more than a diversionary attack one week earlier would be required of the British.

The diversionary attack – the Battle of Arras – was to be launched by ten divisions of Allenby's British Third Army on a 10-mile front astride the Scarpe River. In order to protect the left flank of the Third Army attack, four Canadian divisions were given the task of assaulting Vimy Ridge. The Third Army attack was expected to break through three consecutive lines of German trenches – codenamed Black, Blue and Brown – and to reach the so-called Green Line, an advance of up to 7,000yd, all on the first day.

The preliminary bombardment for the attack – to take place at 5.30am on Z Day, which was planned to be Easter Sunday, 8 April – began on V Day, 4 April. In the event, a lack of preparedness on the part of Nivelle coupled with unseasonable falls of sleet and snow forced a delay of 24 hours. Both Accrington batteries took part in the bombardment, for which LXIV Brigade (Lieutenant Colonel Patterson Barton DSO) recorded firing 3,500, 2,500, 2,000, 2,000 and 8,000 rounds in the five days leading up to the assault.

North of the Scarpe River, LXIV Brigade had its gun positions by the Madagascar crossroads, on the reverse slope behind the village of Écurie. From a forward position, Lieutenant Lyne was able to see the destruction being wrought by the British heavy artillery: 'There's a village [Thélus] on the ridge in front of us that until yesterday was just picturesquely ruined, during the morning our heavies strafed it for 40 minutes, during that time it was hidden in a smother of bursting shells, and clouds of brick; when over, nothing but a wilderness of broken stone remained.'

Aeroplanes of the RFC flew continuously over the enemy lines spotting for the artillery. It was a hazardous undertaking, as Lyne witnessed on 8 April: 'One of our observing machines was suddenly attacked by two fast fighters, vainly it circled and dived, trying to get to the ground, suddenly it burst into flames and fell headlong, then righted itself and blazing fiercely tried to land but all at once it crumpled up and smashed to the ground, a mass of flames.'

Two days after the aerial combat watched by Lyne, Second Lieutenant Edmund Mills Harwood was fortunate to escape unharmed when the BE2c from 8 Squadron from which he was spotting for the artillery was forced down after being damaged by shellfire over Bullecourt. His pilot, 27-year-old Second Lieutenant Pierre Bouillier Pattisson, was wounded in the action.

The role of LXIV Brigade on the opening day of the Arras offensive was to provide artillery cover for 152 Brigade which, together with 154 Brigade, would lead the attack of 51st (Highland) Division alongside that of the 1st Canadian Division. On Easter Monday, 9 April, 4 minutes after the gun batteries opened fire at 5.30am, the infantry attack went in, and 40 minutes later, 152 Brigade reported that it had taken the Black Line. Its two leading battalions, 6/Seaforth Highlanders and 6/Gordon Highlanders, had however suffered heavy casualties in the process. Pressing on to the Blue Line, 8/Argyll and Sutherland Highlanders and 5/Seaforth Highlanders were held up by machine-gun fire and fell behind the creeping artillery barrage. Major Arthur Travers Saulez of D/LXIV, realizing that the infantry had lost the barrage, re-directed the fire of one of his sections onto a machine gun that was holding up the advance and saw it destroyed. Even so, it took until about 2pm before 152 Brigade cleared the enemy out of the Blue Line. By the end of the day, the infantry brigade had pushed on only as far as a trench lying less than halfway between the Blue and Brown lines.

South of the Scarpe at Beaurains, XLVIII Brigade's task in the attack was to cover 42 and 43 brigades of 14th (Light) Division. Confronting the division, the Hindenburg Line climbed Telegraph Hill from the south before running into a redoubt known from its shape as The Harp. Looking out across no-man's-land on Easter Sunday, 22-year-old Captain Thomas Clive Tanner of 5/King's Shropshire Light Infantry (42 Brigade) was chilled by the sight of 'a dense mass of German wire. It must have been over fifty yards thick and my heart sank. I thought to myself, "My God, they've got an impossible task."' In the event, Tanner's worst fears were not realized; going forward at 7.34am on the following day, hugging the creeping barrage, his company broke into The Harp and by 8.45am had taken all its objectives. Between them, 42 and 43 brigades stormed Telegraph Hill, shells from the barrage passing over the heads of the infantry by no more than a few feet as they cleared the top of the hill and surged on to take the Blue Line. The artillery now formed a pro-tective barrage 300yd east of the Blue Line to which the infantry closed up in readiness to continue the advance. At 12.30pm 43 Brigade attacked the Brown Line as the barrage lifted but were stopped by heavy machine-gun fire from the right. Later in the afternoon, C/XLVIII moved forward to take up new gun positions on the south-western slope of Telegraph Hill.

Easter Monday 1917 is chiefly remembered for the achievement of the Canadians in taking Vimy Ridge. Yet the British Third Army made comparable territorial gains, pushing the line forward by between 2,000 and 6,000yd. The contrast between 9 April 1917 and 1 July 1916 was stark: a much higher concentration of heavy guns, the introduction of the 106 fuse, a well-developed creeping barrage and the fact that the enemy – not expecting the attack for another week – had held their reserves too far back all contributed to the day's successes. A breakthrough, however, remained elusive: in the remaining days of the first phase of the Battle of Arras – the first Battle of the Scarpe – the British advance gradually ground to a halt as German reserves came into the line while the British artillery struggled to move up guns and ammunition. Lyne gave a vivid description of the problems faced in bringing up ammunition to the guns:

> The further we advance the more difficult becomes the getting of ammunition to the guns. Roads have disappeared, probably mined in many places, and in some cases, as many as three or four divisions have to follow and use the same track and with this awful weather to deviate even a foot from the road puts you into a morass from which in many cases you can never extract the horses ... This morning I started with ammunition at 10am to go three miles. I have just returned at 6pm. A giant tractor with a 6-inch gun had stuck in the middle of a gangway, an [ammunition supply] wagon had tried to pass it, slipped off the track and become embedded up to the wheel tops; further on another lorry had got mixed up with a water cart while in various places pack animals, mired to the neck, were being

dug out (in many cases, a bullet was the only thing); ceaseless rain, cold winds, one has ceased to hope for anything better.

51st Division completed its capture of the Brown Line on 11 April. On 13 April, LXIV Brigade moved up to new gun positions about 3,000yd east of Roclincourt from where on the afternoon of 14 April all four batteries began to register on the Oppy Line. In front of XLVIII Brigade, 14th Division had still not taken the Brown Line by 13 April when it was relieved by 50th Division; the field artillery, however, remained in action.

Nivelle's great offensive had already been compromised twelve days before its launch at 6am on 16 April by the loss of a copy of the orders for the attack in a German trench raid. The French bombardment consequently fell over ground from which German troops had largely been withdrawn. Although the offensive succeeded in pushing back the German lines – the furthest advance after a month of fighting was of 4 miles – it had failed to meet Nivelle's promise of a breakthrough within two days. Nivelle's persistence with the offensive necessitated the continuation of the British offensive at Arras. Demoralization set in among the French troops as their casualty figures – estimated at 134,000 in the first 10 days alone – were reported and even inflated by their own press. Incidents of troops refusing to obey orders grew in both number and severity until well after General Philippe Pétain had replaced Nivelle on 15 May. From this time on, it was left to the British Army to bear the brunt of the responsibility for offensive action on the Western Front.

When the British offensive at Arras was renewed on 23 April – the second Battle of the Scarpe – LXIV Brigade was one of six field artillery brigades in support of 63rd (Royal Naval) Division at Gavrelle, while, south of the Scarpe, XLVIII Brigade was part of the artillery support to 50th (Northumbrian) Division. On this occasion there was no chance of the enemy being taken by surprise. The German artillery was very active on the day before the attack – Y Day – as Lyne was to experience while making preparations for his battery to fire on a new zone:

> We had a fearful strafing all day, quite merciless. They chased me round the country for hours in the morning. Knocker and I had to lay a telephone wire to a new [observation post] from which I could do some shooting on a new Zone. But the last 500 yards was in full view of every Hun between here and the Rhine! Beautifully clear day, so of course they spotted us, and chased us merrily till we had to subside into a shell hole where we could luckily observe from.

LXIV Brigade expended about 600 rounds per battery on wire-cutting during Y Day, an activity which, at a range of 4,200yd, was described in the brigade war diary as useless. Casualties mounted as enemy counter-battery fire

both Oppy Trench and Wood Trench in an attempt to capture Bird Alley. Both parties reached Bird Alley only to find it filled with wire, making further progress impossible and – after a 20-minute bombing duel – the only option left was to withdraw. An enemy counter-attack at 5.30am on the 15th was driven back after a 'very hot' action. Second Lieutenants Leach and Winder and six other ranks lost their lives in the overnight actions, while a further man went missing. After the enemy strongpoint in Oppy Trench had been shelled by heavy artillery fire during the 16th, Lott again led a bombing party against it. The party immediately came under heavy attack from bombs, and within 15 minutes it became apparent that further advance along the trench was impossible. As enemy machine-gun fire chattered overhead, to attempt to go over the top in conditions of heavy mud and total darkness would have been suicidal, and Lott's party was again forced to withdraw. The battalion's casualties during its five-day tour in the front line totalled ten killed, thirty-six wounded and one missing.

The Battle of Arras officially ended on 17 May. Judged by the average daily rate of British casualties (4,070), the 39-day campaign would prove to be the deadliest of the war until the German spring offensives of 1918. Still the fighting went on. C/XLVIII – its complement of officers reinforced by the arrival on 18 May of 21-year-old, South African-born Second Lieutenant Guy Peel Millar – co-operated with assaults against Infantry Hill on 19 May and again on 14 June, and against Greenland Hill on 3 June. News reached the battery on 11 June that Captain Worsley had been awarded the MC; on an occasion when the battery was being heavily shelled, with four guns out of action and a dump set on fire, Worsley kept his remaining guns in action until his whole ammunition exploded.

After being absent from his battalion since 1 July 1916, Lieutenant Colonel Rickman made a welcome return to resume command of 11/East Lancashire on 31 May. Following a period of more than three weeks during which time the battalion was largely employed either in training or in providing night-time working parties, 11/East Lancashire returned to the Oppy sub-sector on 10 June. The largely uneventful nine-day tour in the forward lines ended when the battalion was withdrawn to camp near Écurie in order to prepare for an attack to be made by 94 Brigade and 15 Brigade (5th Division) on a front extending from Oppy Wood to Gavrelle. The attack had three objectives: to mislead the enemy into believing that the offensive east of Arras was being continued, to divert the enemy's attention from a simultaneous attack being made near Lens, and to capture ground from which the enemy had close observation over the British lines. Practice attacks were carried out on a marked system of trenches at Brunehaut Farm, first by officers and NCOs only, then by companies, afterwards by battalions, and lastly by the whole brigade. Major Kershaw, who had led 11/East Lancashire from 10 to 17 June while Rickman was absent at a

First Army Conference, was given command of the battalion for the attack, as Rickman was under brigade orders to stay behind with the reinforcements.

On the night of 26/27 June, 94 Brigade moved into the forward lines in readiness to attack at 7.10pm on the 28th. It seems likely that the enemy was

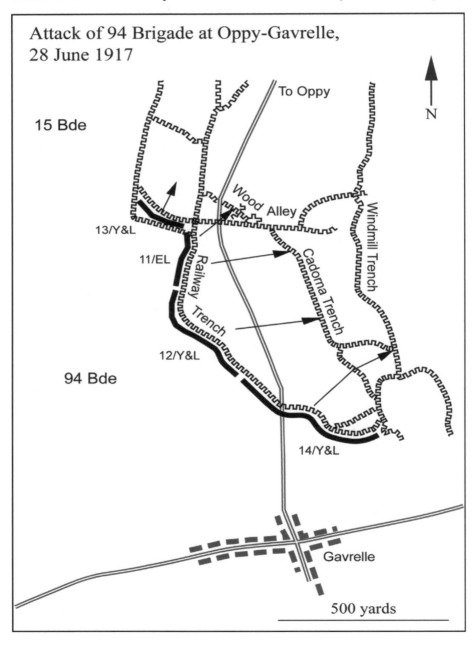

Attack of 94 Brigade at Oppy-Gavrelle, 28 June 1917

15 Bde

To Oppy

N

Wood Alley

13/Y&L

11/EL

Railway Trench

Windmill Trench

Cadorna Trench

12/Y&L

94 Bde

14/Y&L

Gavrelle

500 yards

alerted to the imminency of an attack by the large increase in telephone and telegraph messages and, at 5.30pm on the 27th, the brigade front came under a short but heavy searching barrage which caused fifty casualties. As a result of shrapnel wounds to Lieutenant Wilton, it fell to Second Lieutenant Lott to take command of X Company of 11/East Lancashire.

The enemy barrage was repeated at 5pm on the 28th but – as far as 11/East Lancashire was concerned – more casualties were caused closer to zero hour when British shells fired from a heavy artillery battery dropped short into the trench held by Z Company.

The plan for the attack confirmed that much had been learned from the Somme offensive of the previous year. The artillery bombardment would begin only at zero hour – so as to retain some element of surprise – and would take the form of a double-banked creeping barrage designed to prevent enemy machine guns from firing through the curtain of shellfire. The infantry would be closely supported by Lewis–gun fire, while the exposed right flank of the attack would be covered by a 300-round Thermite barrage.

At 7.10pm, British guns of all calibres began a systematic and devastating bombardment of the enemy positions. Machine-gun posts and strongpoints were smashed, while some parts of the enemy trenches were completely obliterated. At the same moment that the artillery opened fire, infantry from 11/East Lancashire, and 12 and 14/York and Lancaster scrambled up ladders into no–man's–land and moved forward, shells screaming close overhead, until they were as near as 60yd from the closer barrage line. They were joined on their left by 13/York and Lancaster 2 minutes later. The leading infantry paused momentarily to wait for the barrage to lift from the enemy front line, then pushed onward under cover of Lewis–gun and machine-gun fire.

On the right of the brigade attack, the success of the Thermite barrage in completely suppressing flanking machine-gun fire enabled 14/York and Lancaster to reach its objectives with very few casualties. To its left, 12/York and Lancaster remarkably reported no casualties at all in reaching all its objectives and taking twenty-eight prisoners.

Next in line, 11/East Lancashire attacked with Z Company (Captain Heys) on the right, X Company (Second Lieutenant Lott) in the centre and W Company (Lieutenant Jackson) on the left. The battalion's left flank met with most resistance. Second Lieutenant Frederick Lawrence Wheeldon, a 24–year–old from Chorlton, led his platoon into the enemy's trench where he found himself confronted by four of the enemy, all of whom he killed, despite being severely wounded by a bomb thrown by one of them. Following closely behind, Sergeant Thomas Southworth, a 25–year–old labourer at Howard and Bullough's, killed three of the enemy, and took over command of the platoon from the wounded Wheeldon. The battalion gained all its objectives at a cost of eight killed and forty-two wounded.

On the left of the brigade attack, 13/York and Lancaster reported taking the enemy's front line with only two killed, thirty-six wounded and two missing. To its left, 15 Brigade was no less successful, all battalions reaching their objectives.

Enemy artillery fire opened up at 7.12pm and gradually increased in intensity over the next 18 minutes. At 7.30pm, heavy rain and thunderstorms began to sweep across the battlefield. By this time, consolidation of the captured positions was already underway; Lewis guns were being pushed forward to provide cover, strongpoints were being made and forward-leading trenches were being blocked. Second Lieutenant Lott was later commended for setting 'a splendid example of coolness and disregard of danger, moving about on the top and encouraging his men'. Another East Lancashire officer picked out for his actions was Second Lieutenant William Farrer Lonsdale who 'continued to set a fine example of pluck and determination until having to finally give in due to the effects of his wound'.

At 8.54pm, 14/York and Lancaster fired an SOS signal on seeing the enemy preparing to counter-attack. An artillery barrage was quickly brought down, and within 15 minutes the danger had receded. The threat of a counter-attack against the left flank of the brigade at around 10pm was soon dispersed by heavy fire from rifles, Lewis guns and machine guns.

Consolidation was continued throughout the night. Although the enemy hurried forward reserves, no further counter-attacks were attempted, and the following days were comparatively quiet. On the night of 2/3 July, 94 Brigade was withdrawn to the vicinity of Roclincourt.

By any measure, 94 Brigade's attack at Oppy-Gavrelle has to be regarded as a complete success. All the objectives were met at the relatively light cost of 29 killed and 160 wounded.

For 11/East Lancashire the fighting at Arras was over; the battalion was relieved in the line over the night of 1/2 July, and on 3 July reached camp at Maroeuil.

C/XLVIII remained in the line at Arras; a routine of harassing fire and targeting enemy trench-mortar positions was broken by occasional barrages in support of the infantry. The number of men in the battery wounded over the four months of July through October could be counted on the fingers of one hand. It was a period of relative quiet which came to an end on 29 October when XLVIII Brigade entrained at Arras to join the Fifth Army at Ypres.

Chapter 16

The Hottest Show

The failure of the Nivelle offensive to achieve a breakthrough and the subsequent insurrection within the French armies allowed – arguably even compelled – Haig to return to the offensive after closing down the Battle of Arras. On this occasion, the battleground was to be of Haig's choosing: the Ypres salient.

In the spring of 1917, the British lines at Ypres formed a semi-circle around the eastern side of the town. In order to break out of the salient towards the Belgian coast, the British would have to capture Pilckem Ridge – a stretch of higher ground that runs in a north-westerly direction from the Gheluvelt plateau – then cross the Steenbeek valley before advancing gradually uphill to take the northern end of the ridge on which lie the villages of Passchendaele and Westroosebeke.

However unfavourable the topography, there was – in contrast to the rationale behind the Somme campaign of the previous year – a genuine strategic objective to be gained from a breakthrough at Ypres: the elimination of the German U-boat bases on the Flanders coast. Unrestricted submarine warfare by Germany had accounted for the loss of 526,000 tons of British shipping in April 1917 alone; on 20 June, the First Sea Lord, Admiral John Rushworth Jellicoe, had shocked the War Cabinet by suggesting that shipping losses from submarine warfare would render it impossible for Britain to continue the war in 1918.

On 7 May, Haig announced at a meeting with his army commanders that the Flanders offensive would commence with an attack on the Messines–Wytschaete Ridge to the south of Ypres on or about 7 June followed, some weeks later, by the main attack against the Passchendaele–Westroosebeke Ridge. Haig had already decided to entrust the main attack to the Fifth Army commanded by 46-year-old Lieutenant General Sir Hubert de la Poer Gough, rather than to the Fourth or Second armies, commanded respectively by the more-cautious 53-year-old Rawlinson and 60-year-old General Sir Hubert Charles Onslow Plumer.

The task of capturing the Messines–Wytschaete Ridge was left to Plumer, whose tunnelling companies had been working for more than a year to place twenty-one explosive charges under the ridge. The largest of the mines, charged with a staggering 95,600lb of ammonal, was completed as late as 28 May. The final plan was to explode nineteen of the charges simultaneously at zero hour across a 10-mile stretch of the ridge; the assaulting infantry would then follow a creeping barrage to limited objectives which were to be consolidated with the aid of reserves.

Over 15 and 16 May, LXIV Brigade had marched north from Arras via Noeux-les-Mines to Mont-Bernanchon. Three days of rest followed the 26-mile march before, in the evenings of 20, 21 and 22 May, the brigade marched a total of 28 miles through Hazebrouck, Saint-Sylvestre-Cappel, Eecke and Steenvoorde to reach its wagon lines in the neighbourhood of Reninghelst, about 3 miles south-east of Poperinghe. Over 26 and 27 May, five guns from each battery were taken up into firing positions between Lankhof and Chester farms on the north bank of the Ypres–Comines Canal; the remaining guns were kept in reserve.

By 1 June, all four batteries had joined in the systematic artillery bombardment of the enemy positions that had begun on 21 May, and which had stepped up in intensity on the previous day. The brigade's target zone was towards the northern end of the Messines–Wytschaete front, extending a distance of 400yd in a south-westerly direction from the Ypres–Comines Canal. During the last 2 hours of daylight on the 1st, two guns were knocked out of action when the batteries were heavily shelled by an enemy 5.9in howitzer battery firing from the north-east. Lyne described the experience as being worse than at Arras:

> This is about the hottest show we have been in yet, makes one look upon the last fight as a rest cure. We've already had more casualties than in the whole of the Arras battle. Night before last they sprayed our battery with 5.9, and put the wind up most people, got a direct hit on a dug out in which six men and two sergeants were sleeping, and blew a hole in the roof you could drive a wagon through, but not a man was hurt. The most extraordinary thing I have ever seen! Pitched another two yards from the Mess, wounded two men seriously, and a third.

Casualties to the brigade's men and horses were also mounting as the enemy artillery targeted the roads and tracks between the wagon lines and the guns; among the early casualties was 21-year-old Driver Hugh Crouch Houston from Church who before enlisting had been employed in a calico print works. A letter from an officer to Houston's mother, Annie, described how her son had been severely wounded when several heavy calibre shells landed on the road along which the wagon teams were riding on their way back from the guns in the early morning of 27 May. Houston died of his wounds later on the same day.

Lyne wrote on 3 June of the bravery of an unnamed gunner on another occasion in which the wagon teams had come under heavy shellfire:

Yesterday morning I came down to the wagon line and we had a convoy of eighteen empty wagons to get up last night. The start was disastrous. A shell hit in the middle of the road between two teams just as we were starting, smashed up eight horses, and two wagons, killed the bombardier [20-year-old John Hollingworth from New Birchwood near Alfreton], and seriously wounded the back driver ... took out the poor fellows eyes, and wounded the gunner. The teams couldn't go on till the mess had been cleared up, and meanwhile more shells were dropping ... I was rather pleased with the gunner who was wounded. He was helping to clear the horses and wagons out of the way, and when they were clear he came up to me, and said, 'They've smashed up the wagon I was on Sir, shall I go on with the next?' He was all covered with blood, and wounded in several places. I told him to go and get himself seen to. Rather fine of him, wasn't it?

The use by the enemy of gas shells brought additional terror, as Lyne described on 4 June:

Last night was absolutely the record for convoys. I took up a *dozen* wagons, and a matter of 1,100 rounds. Got up alright, and were just moving away, when a perfect hurricane of shells came over. We started to make a bolt for it, before realising they were gas shells, and we were right on the cloud; it's hard to appreciate the difficulties of controlling two frenzied horses, getting your steel helmet off and your gas mask on with only the normal allowance of fingers and hands. All in the space of what time you can hold your breath without bursting. However, on they were got somehow, and off we went; all of a sudden a shell hit a dump alongside the road, and there was a blinding flash, and a terrific explosion, and most of us were blown into the ditch amongst a perfect deluge of debris.

The artillery preparation for the assault on the ridge incorporated at least one full-dress rehearsal of the creeping barrage for LXIV Brigade on the afternoon of 4 June. The idea behind the simulated attack was to induce the enemy to reveal the location of its hidden gun batteries which would then be targeted over the last day or so of the bombardment. On the evening of 4 June, the brigade's remaining guns were brought into action.

At 3.10am on Z Day, 7 June, the Messines–Wytschaete Ridge was torn asunder by the detonation of more than 400 tons of explosives in the nineteen mines, the shock from which was said to have been felt distinctly in London. Lyne was one of thousands to be awestruck by the spectacle:

> This show has been quite unlike [either the Somme or Arras]. Our previous bombardment had been very intermittent, and during the night preceding the attack, the gun fire dropped, until absolute quiet reigned. Hour succeeded hour, and gradually the weary Hun must have fallen asleep; all of a sudden just after 3am the night was shattered by a tremendous roar; sheets of flame shot skyward, the whole earth shook, and rocked. Then for twenty seconds not a sound, then all of a sudden every gun on the front spoke out. The line was lit from right to left, with the flicker of thousands of guns, as we threw a barrage on the German line, the like of which had never been seen before.

Writing to a friend, Sergeant Ted Crawshaw, a 30-year-old house painter from Accrington, compared the sight to the spectacular firework reconstructions of battles that regularly thrilled crowds at Manchester's Belle Vue Gardens: 'By jove, Tom, you should have seen the mines go up. Talk about Belle Vue fireworks! My word!'

A staggering 3,561,530 rounds had been fired over the 12 days preceding the assault. Now the 18-pounder field guns covered the infantry attack with a creeping barrage that, as each objective was reached, switched to a protective barrage which swept the area searching for enemy troop concentrations. A machine-gun barrage laid 400yd ahead of the creeping barrage further aided the advance. Attacking astride the Ypres–Comines Canal, 47th (2nd London) Division captured all of its objectives within the zone of LXIV Brigade by 9.30am. It was a success that was repeated along almost the entire length of the Messines–Wytschaete Ridge. The last objectives for the battle were reached seven days later when the Spoil Bank on the north side of the canal and – in an attack supported by LXIV Brigade – Olive and Optic trenches on the south side of the canal were taken.

Haig had every reason to be delighted with the results of the operation to capture the Messines–Wytschaete Ridge. Not only had all the objectives been gained but 144 officers, 7,210 other ranks, 48 guns, 218 machine guns and 60 trench mortars had been captured from the enemy. British casualties over the period 1–12 June numbering 24,562 were matched or exceeded by German losses. Yet the opportunity to press on to capture the Gheluvelt plateau, the platform from which hostile artillery would be able to direct enfilade fire against an advance to the north, was already being lost. The need for urgency – fully appreciated by Haig before the battle – had somehow been lost as the commander-in-chief passed responsibility for capture of the plateau from Plumer to Gough. After several days' deliberation, Gough asked on 14 June that he be allowed to postpone the attack on the plateau until the date of the main offensive to the north; Haig accepted the request. The delay, which would be drawn out to one of more than six weeks' duration, was to the enemy's advantage.

LXIV Brigade, in action continuously since the beginning of March, began to be withdrawn from the line over the night of 24/25 June. For the sections that were still in the line, the 25th was 'a terror of a day'. The batteries began to come under fire from 5.9 and 8in shells early on; servants carrying a breakfast of coffee, porridge and fish across to C Battery's telephone pit were throwing themselves to the ground every few yards to avoid the shell bursts. Lyne observed the destruction wrought by the bombardment at close quarters:

> After bombarding for half an hour they set D Battery on fire. I stood on top to watch what was happening, when there was a tremendous explosion, hit me in the face like a sledge hammer, and toppled me all of a heap in the dugout . . . 1,500 rounds had gone up in one burst, not so many yards away . . . D Battery still burned, and occasionally exploded. To add to the gaiety of the occasion, A Battery in front was also set on fire; burnt beautifully, and occasionally exploded . . .

The brigade's war diary wryly notes that over the following night 'the two remaining sections of all batteries, or what was left of them, withdrew to wagon lines'. On 27 June the brigade marched into rest at Reninghelst. Advantage was taken of the week's rest that followed to organize a football competition in which C Battery narrowly lost 2–1 to the eventual winners from A Battery.

The ground that lies between Ypres and the Passchendaele–Westroosebeke Ridge is divided by a number of streams, principally the Steenbeek, Hanebeek and Stroombeek. By the summer of 1917, the low ridges above the streams, held by the enemy, were guarded by lines of concrete pillboxes while trenches and artillery batteries were concealed on their reverse slopes. Preceding the main offensive, the British bombardment, in which 3,106 guns combined to fire almost 3 million shells, had considerable success in neutralizing the enemy defences but inevitably also resulted in the destruction of the local drainage system and turned the shallow valleys through which the streams flowed into areas of swamp. The postponement of the attack from 25 to 31 July, requested by both Gough and General François Paul Anthoine of the French First Army, increased the likelihood that autumnal heavy rain would transform the battlefield into a landscape of water-filled shell holes linked by narrow tracts of glutinous mud.

LXIV Brigade had learned on 6 July that it was to return to action just north of Zillebeke Lake from where it would support 8th Division in the forthcoming attack. The guns were taken up to the new positions on 11 July and were registered on the following day. By 13 July, more than 7,000 rounds had been brought up to each of the brigade's 3 18-pounder batteries. Gunners, drivers and horses were constantly at risk from hostile HE, shrapnel and gas shells. The brigade took its place in the bombardment on 16 July, a fine and very hot day. The next fifteen days which led up to the attack were exhausting in the extreme for the gun crews, who had to work day and night while wearing gas masks. On 18 July, 31-year-old Corporal Charles Edward Reeder MM and 21-year-old Acting Bombardier Wilfred Bowling Cocker, a cotton weaver from Nelson, were both killed by an enemy shell. Gunner Arthur Baldwin, a 21-year-old blacksmith from Burnley, was killed six days later during an enemy bombardment of the battery positions.

At 3.50am on 31 July, two divisions of Anthoine's First Army, nine divisions and one brigade of Gough's Fifth Army and five divisions of Plumer's Second Army attacked on a 15-mile front. Once more employed was the tactic of interspersing successive infantry advances behind a creeping barrage with protective barrages which scoured the ground ahead in search of enemy troops concentrating for a counter-attack. Still missing, however, was a reliable and fast means of communication between infantry and artillery. Less than an hour into the attack, the telephone line between LXIV Brigade's batteries and its observation post had been broken; from then on, the brigade's FOO had to rely on either pigeons or runners to send back messages. In the zone of LXIV Brigade, 8th Division reported the capture and consolidation of its first objective, Bellewaarde Ridge, at 5.55am. At 6.30am, the brigade received a report that the division had taken its second objective, Westhoek Ridge; in fact, heavy enemy machine-gun fire rendered the ridge untenable except on the left, and prevented any further advance towards the third objective. Nevertheless, the line had been advanced by about a mile; further north, the line had been pushed forwards by up to 2 miles on Pilckem Ridge.

Although the gains of 31 July had fallen short of the day's objectives, they were still considerable, especially when judged against the opening day of the Battle of the Somme, little more than a year previously. It was more evidence of the gradual, if erratic, progression along the 'learning curve' that would eventually lead to the British Army's mastery of the battlefield. But now the weather intervened on the side of the enemy. For the next three days, the rain was continuous; the roads and tracks turned to mud, and it proved impossible to move the guns quickly up into positions from where they could support a renewal of the offensive. LXIV Brigade was shelled on each of those days, seven of its guns being knocked out on 2 August; on 3 August – a day on which the batteries were shelled from 11.30am until 8pm – Sergeant Ernest Bartholomew, a 31-year-old from Accrington, was fatally wounded in the head, and died in the early hours of the following morning.

Although the first phase of the main offensive officially ended on 2 August, LXIV Brigade co-operated with 74 Brigade (25th Division) in an attack on

10 August which secured Westhoek Ridge. Four days later, 8th Division – having enjoyed less than fourteen days' rest – relieved 25th Division in the line to take part in a Fifth Army attack on Zonnebeke Ridge. As on 31 July, 8th Division would be covered in the attack by the guns of LXIV Brigade. At zero hour, 4.45am on 16 August, 23 Brigade (on the left) and 25 Brigade advanced from Westhoek Ridge, crossed the Hanebeek by means of portable bridges, and surged up the eastern slope of the valley to take their objectives. Yet the inability of the infantry to communicate directly with the guns again allowed the enemy to recover the situation. SOS flares fired from Very pistols at the sight of the enemy concentrating for a counter-attack apparently went unseen by the FOOs in the smoke of battle; in any event, LXIV Brigade reported that it had no communication with its FOO throughout the morning. By the time artillery support arrived, it was too late; 25 Brigade, attacked from front and right, fell back after taking heavy losses causing 23 Brigade to follow as its right flank was enveloped in turn. The two brigades eventually re-grouped, only about 200yd in front of their starting line.

Only on the northern flank of the Fifth Army attack were the day's objectives reached by 20th and 29th divisions at Langemarck. Before the month had ended, Haig had transferred responsibility for the front facing the Gheluvelt plateau from Gough to Plumer.

Over 22 and 23 August, the batteries of LXIV Brigade effectively side-slipped to the north, taking up new positions 2 miles east of Ypres and ½ mile north of the Ypres–Roulers railway. In the period before the start of the next phase of the offensive, the brigade was returned practically to full strength by the arrival of 59 other ranks and 125 horses. Although it was a relatively quiet time for the guns, there were casualties nevertheless. Acting Bombardier James Wilkinson, a 24-year-old cotton weaver from Stacksteads, died of wounds on 1 September and 34-year-old Driver James Read from Burnley was killed in action four days later. Corporal Harry Riley, a 29-year-old weaver from Burnley, and Corporal George Thomas Guy, a 25-year-old Howard and Bullough's employee from Clayton-le-Moors, were both killed when a shell laden with poison gas exploded in the entrance to the dugout where they were sleeping. For Guy, it was third-time unlucky, as he had twice previously survived gas attacks.

A key element in the artillery preparation for the next attack was an attempt to wear down and exhaust the enemy by rehearsing the barrage programme on each of the last seven days leading up to Z Day, set for 20 September. LXIV Brigade's zone for the battle was the ground to be attacked by the South African Brigade, which now incongruously formed a part of 9th (Scottish) Division. In order to achieve their objectives, the South Africans would have to overcome the defences of Borry Farm, which had held out against an attack by 16th Division on 16 August when it was thought to have been defended by a

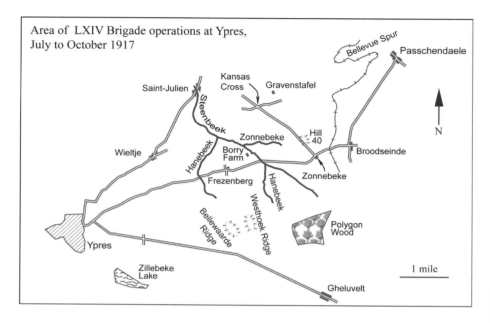

Area of LXIV Brigade operations at Ypres,
July to October 1917

hundred men and five machine guns, cross the Hanebeek, a belt of swamp
and water-filled shell holes, then climb the opposite side of the valley to take
the strongpoints of Waterend House and the Bremen Redoubt.

At 5.40am on 20 September, eleven divisions attacked on a front of 14,500yd,
9th Division forming part of the five-division attack by Gough's Fifth Army in
support of the main attack on the Gheluvelt plateau by Plumer's Second Army.
The artillery support for the assault now extended to providing three belts of
fire: 100 to 400yd ahead of the creeping barrage fired by 18-pounder guns was a
searching barrage fired by 18-pounder guns and 4.5in howitzers, while further
forward again was a sweeping, destructive barrage fired by 60-pounder guns
and 6in howitzers. The South Africans took Borry Farm, aided by the tactical
innovation of maintaining a barrage of HE and smoke over the strongpoint
while leaving a lane clear for an infantry column to move up into a position
from which the defences could be stormed as soon as the barrage was lifted.
Despite being swept by machine-gun fire from the left where the adjoining
division had failed to reach its first objectives, the South Africans pressed on to
complete the capture of Waterend House and the Bremen Redoubt.

The final objectives for the day were reached along almost the entire front. It
was a classic example of a successful 'bite and hold' operation.

The weather stayed fair for the second 'bite and hold' attack, the main
thrust of which would see 5th and 4th Australian divisions of the Second Army
respectively clear Polygon Wood and reach the southern end of Zonnebeke
village. The attack of the two Australian divisions was supported on the left

by 3rd and 59th divisions of the Fifth Army. Zero hour was at 5.50am on 26 September. In the zone of LXIV Brigade, 8 Brigade (3rd Division) was held up by the Zonnebeke stream, impassable in places, and was eventually stopped by machine-gun fire near the foot of Hill 40, short of its final objective; nevertheless, the new line was up to 1,000yd farther forward on what was another successful day for the Second and Fifth armies.

Over the three days from 30 September to 2 October, LXIV Brigade moved its guns forward into new positions 900yd south-west of the Frezenberg cross-roads. In the course of the move, 28-year-old Bombardier Harold Gregson from Hapton, who before the war had worked alongside his father, Henry, a dealer in jewellery and fancy goods, was hit in the head and leg by fragments from an enemy shell; Gregson died of his wounds the same day, 1 October.

The third of the successful 'bite and hold' operations took place on 4 October with the responsibility for the main assault given to four Anzac divisions of the Second Army. At 6am, 11 Australian Brigade (3rd Australian Division) – covered by a barrage provided in part by LXIV Brigade – overcame deter-mined opposition to drive the enemy off Hill 40 and into the barrage of HE that lay beyond. Fresh battalions took over the attack and fought their way up on to the Broodseinde Ridge. At 10am, LXIV Brigade reported that an estimated 700 prisoners had been taken on its front; 15 minutes later, a wounded NCO brought back news that the Australians were digging in on the line of their final objective. The morning's fighting had advanced the line by a further 1,500–2,000yd.

With the benefit of hindsight this was the point at which the whole campaign should have been brought to a close and indeed both Gough and Plumer argued as much at a conference with Haig on 7 October. Haig, however, was insistent that the successes of the previous three attacks could be repeated to drive the enemy from its dominating position along the ridge between Passchendaele and Westroosebeke. There can be little doubt that Haig was influenced by his experience at Gheluvelt on 31 October 1914 when one more attack by the enemy would have broken through the British lines.

In preparation for the next attack, and amid terrible weather, LXIV Brigade managed to find forward positions for its guns 800yd west-south-west of Gravenstafel, on either side of the road to Wieltje. The brigade's batteries may well have been the most forward of the Corps sector, whose field artillery was largely farther back where there was firmer ground; even here some guns were muzzle-deep in mud until they could be lifted onto hastily constructed platforms. Ammunition had to be brought up to the guns in pouring rain along forward roads and tracks which were in a wretched condition.

At 5.20am on 9 October, five divisions of the Second Army – the 5th, 7th, 2nd Australian, 66th and 49th – attacked alongside six divisions of the Fifth Army. On this occasion, it was 66th (2nd East Lancashire) Division that found itself covered by LXIV Brigade. On the left of the divisional front, 198 Brigade could advance only slowly across a landscape of glutinous mud in which every shell-hole and abandoned trench had been filled with water. Enfiladed by machine-gun fire from pillboxes on the higher ground of Bellevue Spur, between 500 and 800yd distant on the left, 198 Brigade stopped about 300yd short of its first objective. Word of the attack's progress was reaching the battery positions only through returning infantry, and it was from a wounded corporal that LXIV Brigade learned at 9.45am that some troops had got to within 50yd of their day's objectives. Attacking across higher and drier ground to the right, 197 Brigade reached its final objective at about 10am; one patrol even ventured farther forward to find that the enemy had fled from the ruins of Passchendaele village. Yet the infantry were unable to consolidate their gains; as the leading units came under artillery fire and, from the right, enfilade machine-gun fire, 197 Brigade was forced to withdraw and ended the day only 500yd forward of its starting line.

The inability of the artillery both to clear paths through two freshly erected belts of wire entanglements and to destroy the pillboxes on Bellevue Spur doomed the next attempt to capture Passchendaele on 12 October. 3rd Australian Division – having relieved 66th Division in the line – attacked in heavy rain at 5.20am. LXIV Brigade received a report at 10.25am that 10 Australian Brigade on the left of the divisional front had been stopped by the wire and by enfilade machine-gun fire, a situation that was apparently unchanged at 12.50pm. On the right, 9 Australian Brigade initially made better progress but by 2.30pm the whole of the divisional line was retiring and the day ended with the Australians back in their starting positions.

In between attacks on Passchendaele, LXIV Brigade suffered nine casualties at Lancer Farm on 18 October from a bomb dropped from an enemy aeroplane. Among the fatalities were Corporal Robert Higgin MM and Gunner Henry John Farrer, a 28-year-old cotton manufacturer's clerk from Nelson, who died on 19 October following the amputation of his leg.

On 26 October, following a sequence of days on which the weather had been generally fine, LXIV Brigade was one of seven field artillery brigades supporting 10 Canadian Infantry Brigade (4th Canadian Division) in the first of three 'bite and hold' operations to secure the capture of Passchendaele. Steady and continuous rain had returned before the Canadians attacked at 5.40am. Despite the appalling conditions, the infantry advanced 400yd to reach their objectives by 7.15am, a success confirmed to LXIV Brigade by the firing of Very flares. Yet again, however, the new line could not be held as a deluge of enemy artillery fire forced the Canadians back to within 100yd of where they had begun the day. Farther left, infantry had fought their way on to the Bellevue Spur, depriving the enemy of the enfilade fire that had broken up previous attacks against Passchendaele.

Over the following three days – throughout which fine weather prevailed – 17,900 rounds of ammunition were brought up to LXIV Brigade's guns in readiness for the next operation. This time, the weather held for the attack of 12 Canadian Infantry Brigade at daybreak (5.50am) on 30 October. The Canadians succeeded in reaching and consolidating all their objectives, including the vital Crest Farm Ridge, stormed behind the creeping barrage before the enemy had any chance to react. The Canadians' new line was just 400yd short of Passchendaele church.

Killed at the guns of C/LXIV on 30 October was Gunner Harold Shaw, a 22-year-old cotton weaver from Church. The brigade's gunners – having been continually in action for sixteen weeks – were relieved over the next two days. The brigade played no direct role in either the third 'bite and hold' operation in which the Canadians captured Passchendaele village on 6 November, or the attack four days later which advanced the line 500yd northwards along the ridge towards Westroosebeke bringing the third Battle of Ypres to its official end.

British casualties over the 64 days of the battle up to 3 October totalled 138,787; the final 37 days raised the number to 244,897. The number of German casualties in the battle may have reached 400,000.

While LXIV Brigade was in the process of being relieved, XLVIII Brigade, having detrained at Pezelhoek outside of Poperinghe on 30 October, coincidentally began to go into action close to the Steenbeek stream south of Langemarck over the night of 31 October/1 November. It was to be a traumatic introduction to the Ypres battlefield as the battery positions immediately came under a bombardment of HE, gas and incendiary shells. Conditions were so bad that the brigade's detachments at the guns had to be withdrawn within 24 hours of their arrival. Major Harold Bancroft and Lieutenant Reginald Jackson, two of the officers who had joined the Howitzers on the brigade's formation, were evacuated with gas poisoning. The guns had to remain in place as the sea of mud made it almost impossible to move them.

The entries in the brigade's war diary paint a vivid picture of the conditions at the front. On 4 November:

> Front line very unsettled, held by posts and strong points. No trenches of any kind. Communication very difficult. Roads constantly full of holes from shelling, and repair work very slow. Pack animals only means of getting supplies and ammunition forward. Shell holes fill with water immediately, and no deep dugouts possible. Concrete 'pillboxes' numerous and afford the only shelter available. The light railways are continually being blown up and cannot be relied upon for transporting supplies and material. One gun [from A/XLVIII] damaged by shellfire. Hauled out by salvage party on sleds. Steenbeek positions constantly shelled.

On 5 November:

> Headquarters moved to Lancashire Farm [at map reference] C14c05.20. Cupola shelters with electric light. Too far back; telephone lines (buried cables) forward are continually being broken. 7,000 yards to nearest battery. Duckboard walks only means of getting to them. Weather from 1st to 5th continued fine. Detachments withdrawn from Steenbeek on 1st returned and guns kept in action in case of SOS only. Salvage party hauling them out [of the mud] as opportunity permits.

It was not until 14 November that C/XLVIII got five of its six guns into action in new positions on platforms at Malta House, 1,100yd south-west of Poelcappelle, and west of the road to Saint-Julien. The task of getting the guns into position can barely be imagined. It required the use of a light railway which at various times was broken in five places by direct hits from enemy shells. One gun fell from the rails into a deep shell hole where it lay upside-down with only its spade and the top of its wheels visible above the mud and water. A working party of eighty men was unable to salvage the gun after toiling for 4 hours and finally could do no more than mark its location by attaching a buoy to its spade.

C/XLVIII remained in action until 10 December after which the battery was withdrawn to the brigade's wagon lines. The battery positions at Malta House had periodically been subjected to bombardments, in one of which Second Lieutenant Guy Millar had been severely wounded. The battery's only part in an offensive operation at Ypres took place on 2 December when it provided an enfilade barrage to support an infantry attack towards Westroosebeke; a lack of progress on either flank of the attack necessitated the withdrawal from ground gained in the centre. After spending Christmas Day at the wagon lines, sections of C/XLVIII went back into action between Zonnebeke and Kansas Cross for a further nine or ten days. On 7 January 1917, XLVIII Brigade left the Ypres salient, moving south over four days to reach Valhoun, 4½ miles north of Saint-Pol-sur-Ternoise, on 10 January.

Of the two Accrington batteries, C/LXIV had endured by far the greater share of action in 1917. After the battery returned to the line at Gallipoli Farm on 22 and 23 November, the casualty list grew steadily longer until LXIV Brigade was finally withdrawn between 12 and 14 December. Driver Stanley Bassinder, a 23-year-old assistant at Veevers' grocery store in Accrington, was wounded in the head by a shell while taking a wagon up to the line on 23 November. That same day, Accrington-born Sergeant Charles Stewart Royston, a 33-year-old who had been employed in a chemist's shop, was killed in action. On the following day, Lieutenant Flecknoe was wounded at the battery position and died at a CCS in the early morning of 25 November.

On 29 November, Driver Thomas Parkinson, a 29-year-old collier from Burnley, died from his wounds. A direct hit from a shell on a dugout on 11 December killed the occupants; among the fatalities were Bombardier Fred Chadwick, a 28-year-old cotton weaver from Haslingden, Corporal John Daniel Condry, a 21-year-old from Church, and Corporal Thomas Henry Flannigan MM.

When finally withdrawn from the line, LXIV Brigade moved first to Oudezeele, 9½ miles west of Poperinghe, before shifting 5 miles eastwards on 21 December to billets in Watou. Christmas Eve saw C Battery overcome B Battery 2–0 in the first round of the Brigade Football Shield, while Christmas Day was celebrated with a full day's holiday, good dinners and concerts. C Battery narrowly failed to win the Brigade Shield, being beaten 3–2 by D Battery in the New Year's Day final.

LXIV Brigade remained at Watou until 7 January 1918 when it began a 23-mile march southwards through Steenvoorde, Hazebrouck and Morbecque to reach the area of Guarbecque on the following day.

Chapter 17

This Gallant Officer

After making its successful attack at Oppy-Gavrelle on 28 June 1917, 31st Division side-stepped north to occupy the line opposite the German-held villages of Acheville and Méricourt, east of Vimy Ridge. For 11/East Lancashire, much of July was taken up with training and reorganization, first at Maroeuil and later at Mont-Saint-Éloi. While at Maroeuil, the battalion was temporarily reorganized into three fighting companies – apparently designated W, X and Z – and one headquarters company. A break from routine took place on 11 July, when the battalion lined the Arras–Souchez road for the visit of His Majesty King George V, an event described by an unnamed correspondent for the *Accrington Gazette*: 'We paraded along a well war-worn road last week to see King George. He drove past in his motor, nice and slowly. He had an escort of aeroplanes to keep back a too inquisitive enemy from seeing what was going on, as the cheering that resulted from the visit might have aroused Fritz's suspicions.'

Some 50 miles to the north at Nieuport, the enemy was preparing to make its first use of mustard gas in warfare. Chemical weapons had been deployed on the battlefield as early in the war as October 1914 when shrapnel shells containing an irritant substance were fired by German artillery at Neuve-Chapelle. In January 1915, shells containing xylyl bromide (tear gas) were fired against Russian troops at Bolimow on the Eastern Front. The use of chemical weapons escalated massively when, on 22 April 1915, 168 tons of chlorine gas were released from 4,000 cylinders on a 4-mile front against French and Canadian divisions in the Ypres salient. French-Algerian troops fled in panic as the gas was carried by the wind into the Allied trenches. The first British deployment of chlorine gas, on 25 September 1915 at Loos, demonstrated the fallibility of using cylinders when a change in wind direction drove the gas back towards the British trenches. From 1916 onwards, both sides made increasing use of artillery shells to deliver the gas directly onto the target.

Following its first use at Nieuport, mustard gas – also known as Yellow Cross because of the coloured cross marked on the artillery shell – was used to deluge the town of Ypres on the night of 12/13 July 1917, causing 2,014 casualties. The gas shells burst on impact to release the liquid contents which evaporated to give a virtually odourless gas. Inhalation of the gas was rarely fatal, but caused severe pains in the head, throat and eyes, vomiting and bronchial irritation. Many victims would suffer from chronic bronchitis in later years.

11/East Lancashire received reinforcements of 7 officers and 112 other ranks in the month of July, while casualties amounted to just 2 men killed and 3 wounded. Among five officers who joined on 18 July was Second Lieutenant Ernest David Kay who had been wounded with the battalion as a sergeant on 1 July 1916 and had been appointed to a commission on 25 April 1917.

A telegram dated 24 July brought news to the Slinger family in Accrington of the death in action of a second son of Major Slinger. Lieutenant William Slinger had been posted overseas from 12/East Lancashire to join 1/East Lancashire in September 1916. He was killed by enemy shellfire while leading a working party up to the lines on 23 July, the day after he had returned to the battalion from leave.

A substantial part of 11/East Lancashire's time from early August until the end of the year was taken up in strengthening the Vimy Ridge defences. It would later be said of the battalion's work: 'A splendid system of trenches was constructed and better and more complete wire entanglements than the battalion had ever seen before, and it is to be noted that this line was one of the few parts of the whole British line which held during the German attacks of 1918.' It was also a period that included seven tours of the front line, each normally of six days' duration. On the night of 4/5 September, the battalion was relieved in the front line by 13/York and Lancaster and went into brigade reserve with battalion headquarters and one company at Thélus caves, and two companies in the railway embankment near Vimy station. During the relief the enemy bombarded Vimy and the embankment with mustard gas shells wounding 5 officers and 114 other ranks. Such was the effect on the battalion's fighting strength that it returned to the front line for its next tour only on 24 September, having spent the previous twenty days largely on working parties.

The battalion suffered a further thirty-five casualties when on 16 October it came under a heavy bombardment of HE and gas shells while in brigade support east of Willerval. On 13 November, battalion headquarters again came under bombardment from HE and gas shells; two men were killed and forty-seven wounded or gassed, including the commanding officer, Lieutenant Colonel Rickman. Major Lewis temporarily took over command of the battalion until Major Kershaw returned from leave.

The casualty number for the battalion over the fourth months of August through November was recorded as 234, while only about 180 officers and men joined. Among the five officers who joined 11/East Lancashire during October was 30-year-old Second Lieutenant Basil Arthur Horsfall who had served with the Ceylon Engineer Volunteers before returning to Britain to enlist in July

1916; appointed to a commission in December 1916, he had been wounded with 1/East Lancashire at Rouex on 11 May.

While 11/East Lancashire was in the front line at Oppy-Gavrelle on 4 December, 24-year-old Captain Charles Heathcote Mallinson, a native of Little Lever near Bolton, was taken prisoner by a hostile raiding party. Mallinson had been born Emil August Hennig Schloesser but had changed his name by deed poll in September 1915. Tragically, Mallinson would die as a prisoner of war in Germany on 26 or 27 June 1918. The battalion was to suffer no further casualties in November, though five other officers were to leave for various reasons. In the continuing absence of Lieutenant Colonel Rickman, Major William Douglas Lowe MC took over command of 11/East Lancashire on 8 December. The best part of three weeks' training, first at Écoivres and then at Neuville-Saint-Vaast, followed the tour in which the unfortunate Mallinson had been taken prisoner. The first five weeks of 1918 saw the battalion make two tours of the front line, the remainder of its time being spent in brigade reserve or support. The end of the heavy frost on 16 January resulted in trenches being knee-deep in icy water, and the battalion being set to work on trench clearance and improvement. There were fourteen recorded casualties in the battalion during January; replacements in the two months of December and January had totalled fourteen officers and fifty-seven other ranks.

Just ten days after the third Battle of Ypres was brought to an unsatisfactory close on 10 November, the British Army mounted one final offensive operation in 1917. The nineteen-day Battle of Cambrai that followed would show that technology and tactics were ready to combine to enable after three years a return to mobile warfare. There was no preliminary bombardment. Enemy gun batteries were located by a combination of aerial observation, flash spotting and sound ranging. Working from calculated ranges and bearings, carefully calibrated guns were directed against their targets without the need for prior registration, a technique known as 'predicted fire'. At 6.20am on 20 November, nearly 1,000 guns opened fire along a 6-mile front. Gas shells were extensively used to neutralize battery positions without creating a landscape of water-filled craters. Behind the barrage, 5 infantry divisions and 216 tanks of the Third Army (General Julian Hedworth George Byng) went forward. The initial success was astonishing: an outpost line and two strong trench systems of the Hindenburg Line were overcome in little more than 4 hours in an advance of between 3 and 4 miles. Yet after the advance had run out of steam, a surprise counter-attack by eighteen divisions of the German Second Army (General Georg von der Marwitz) on 30 November wiped out the earlier British gains. Innovative tactics were by no means restricted to the British; Marwitz had successfully tried out a new form of infiltration tactic in which small, rapidly moving squads of infantry – later to be known as stormtroops – by-passed strongpoints to rush the battery positions and communication centres that lay beyond.

Although the German army on the Western Front had been pushed close to breaking point at Ypres, it had held while events elsewhere had largely gone in Germany's favour.

On the Italian front the Austro-Hungarian forces had been pushed to the point of collapse in the eleventh of the battles of the Isonzo fought in August and September 1917. Yet a newly formed Austro-German Fourteenth Army drove back the Italians more than 50 miles to the Piave River in the Caporetto counter-offensive launched on 24 October. At a cost of between 65,000 and 70,000 casualties the Fourteenth Army captured in the space of 4 weeks 294,000 prisoners and 3,136 guns. Italy appealed to her allies for assistance with the result that five British and six French divisions were transferred from the Western Front.

In Russia, the 'February Revolution' had resulted in Nicholas standing down as Czar and an unstable political situation in which the Provisional Government of Duma vied for power with the socialist revolutionaries of the Petrograd Soviet. The unilateral imposition by the Petrograd Soviet of Army Order No. 1 required all units of the Russian army at company level and above to elect soldiers' committees, a move that had a corrosive effect on the troops' willingness to fight. The Kerensky offensive of the summer – launched as an attempt by the new Russian Minister of War, Alexander Fyodorovich Kerensky, to convince Britain and France of his country's credibility as an ally in war – advanced up to 20 miles only to be driven back by an Austro-German counter-offensive which regained the ground conceded to Brusilov in the previous year. Following the 'October Revolution' and the rise to power in Russia of the Bolsheviks, a general armistice was agreed with the Central Powers on 15 December.

The British Army on the Western Front, weakened by the events of 1917, was further stretched when it was obliged to extend its front by 25 per cent in January 1918 by taking over 25 miles from the French. Although adequate numbers of reinforcements were available in Britain, Lloyd George refused to sanction their transfer in order to ensure that Haig was incapable of launching a fresh offensive in 1918. The situation was managed early in 1918 by bringing the battalions up to strength using men released by disbanding or merging no less than 153 battalions, an upheaval that necessitated reducing the number of battalions in each infantry brigade from 4 to 3. At the beginning of February 1918, 11/East Lancashire was able to reorganize itself into headquarters and 4 fighting companies, following the arrival of 20 officers and 400 other ranks from 8/East Lancashire. Among the officers transferred was Captain Spencer Fleischer, the South African who had travelled to Britain with Jack Duff to enlist late in 1915. On 11 February, the battalion joined 10 and

11/East Yorkshire to form 92 Brigade. Of the other three battalions that had been a part of 94 Brigade since May 1915, 12 and 14/York and Lancaster were disbanded while 13/York and Lancaster went to 93 Brigade. With 94 Brigade having been dissolved, its place in 31st Division was taken by 4 Guards Brigade.

Set against these favourable developments for Germany was the inescapable fact that the entry of the United States into the war in April 1917, motivated in part by Germany's declaration of unrestricted submarine warfare, would ultimately spell defeat through sheer weight of numbers. The build-up of American forces in Europe had, on the other hand, been slow: only five US divisions had reached France by the beginning of February 1918. Ludendorff saw a window of opportunity in which to make a last bid for victory. Between 1 November 1917 and 21 March 1918, 38 of 85 German divisions were withdrawn from the Eastern Front where the Russian army no longer posed a tangible threat, while on the Western Front the number of German divisions was raised from 147 to 191.

On 21 March 1918, the German Seventeenth, Second and Eighteenth armies were launched against the British lines on a 54-mile front from Arras to La Fère. In a bold attempt to punch through the lines and to drive the British armies north to the Channel, the German Michael offensive threw 500,000 troops against 160,000 men of the British Third and Fifth armies.

Although Byng's Third Army stood its ground well, the attack to the south forced the overstretched Fifth Army under Gough to concede up to 4½ miles of ground on the first day of the offensive; 21,000 British troops were taken prisoner. Despite intensely fought rearguard actions, the Fifth Army was compelled to fall back day after day. Within 48 hours, the Germans had thrown 750,000 men into the battle.

The Third Army, which continued to withstand the onslaught, was forced to drop back to safeguard its right flank as the Fifth Army retreated. On 23 March, five French divisions were brought in to reinforce the southern end of the line; still the retreat continued. On 25 March, the Fifth Army was pushed back across the 1916 Somme battlefield. The following day saw Albert fall to the enemy but, on 27 March, the Fifth Army finally held its line. The afternoon of 26 March had also seen General Foch appointed by the French and British governments to co-ordinate the activities of the Allied armies on the Western Front.

From 5–16 February, 11/East Lancashire had been employed on working parties and training while in brigade reserve at Springvale Camp, Écurie. The battalion then spent six-day tours of the support line and the front line in which three other ranks were killed. Over 3 and 4 March, 11/East Lancashire marched to Marquay (headquarters and two companies) and Bailleul-aux-Cornailles (two companies) for training. Command of the battalion passed temporarily to Major Kershaw when Lieutenant Colonel Lowe went on leave on 11 February then, on 5 March, to Lieutenant Colonel Walter Backhouse Hulke DSO when Lowe returned from leave to re-join 18/Durham Light Infantry. On 21 March, Lieutenant Colonel Rickman resumed command of 11/East Lancashire; there was to be no chance of his easing himself back into the responsibilities of command, for at 10pm he received orders that the battalion should be prepared to move on the following morning. At 9am on 22 March, buses were boarded and the battalion was taken to Bailleulval, 8 miles south-west of Arras. The battalion remained there – with the unnerving sounds of battle carrying from 12 miles away – until orders received at 11pm sent the men forward by a 10-mile route march to the so-called Green Line east of the village of Boisleux-Saint-Marc, 5½ miles south of Arras. On reaching its allocated position in the early hours of 23 March only to find it already occupied by the Guards Division, the tired battalion took up a fresh position west of the village at 6am. The men were able to rest during the day until orders were received for 92 Brigade to move southwards to Ervillers in order to protect the right flank of 4 Guards Brigade which, along with 93 Brigade on its left, was in the front line west of Saint-Léger.

By 1am on 24 March, 11/East Lancashire was in its new position with – from right to left – Y, W and Z companies in line just east of the Ervillers–Hamelincourt road; battalion headquarters and X Company were on the Gomiécourt–Hamelincourt road. Of the other two battalions in 92 Brigade, 11/East Yorkshire was on the right holding Ervillers, while 10/East Yorkshire was in reserve. At about 10pm on 24 March, the enemy delivered a very strong attack during which the 91st Reserve Infantry Regiment succeeded in breaking through to Ervillers beyond the right flank of 4 Guards Brigade at about midnight; two companies of 10/East Yorkshire were sent forward to clear the enemy from Ervillers while X and Y companies of 11/East Lancashire were re-deployed to form a defensive flank facing south. On the morning of 25 March, with the immediate danger over, X and Y companies were withdrawn to the so-called Yellow Line south of Hamelincourt and east of the railway line. Although further attacks on Ervillers made by the 77th Reserve Infantry Regiment on 25 March were driven off, a deteriorating situation to the south dictated the withdrawal of the whole of 92 Brigade: W and Z companies of 11/East Lancashire fell back to the Yellow Line, with X and Z companies on their right where they once more formed a defensive flank facing south. By 4.30am on 26 March, a further withdrawal was necessary. Under cover of a thick ground mist 92 Brigade dug in along the ridge line between Ablainzevelle and Moyenneville with 11/East Lancashire on the right of 11/East Yorkshire, and 10/East Yorkshire in reserve. 11/East Lancashire held a line extending from 500yd north-east of Ablainzevelle as far as the road leading from Courcelles-le-Comte to Ayette with W Company (Captain Duff) on the right, Y Company

(Captain Bentley) in the centre, X Company (Captain McKenzie) on the left and Z Company (Captain Fleischer) in reserve. Later in the day, two enemy attacks were both driven off. At 6pm, W Company took over an additional 1,500yd of frontage with the support of one company from 10/East Yorkshire.

At dawn on 27 March the situation was already critical; the left flank of 92 Brigade was under threat from German troops advancing through Moyenneville, no wire was available to protect the line, and the right flank was severely stretched by the need to keep in touch with 126 Brigade to the south. To make matters worse, the brigade's positions had been hit by short-falling British artillery fire during the previous afternoon and night.

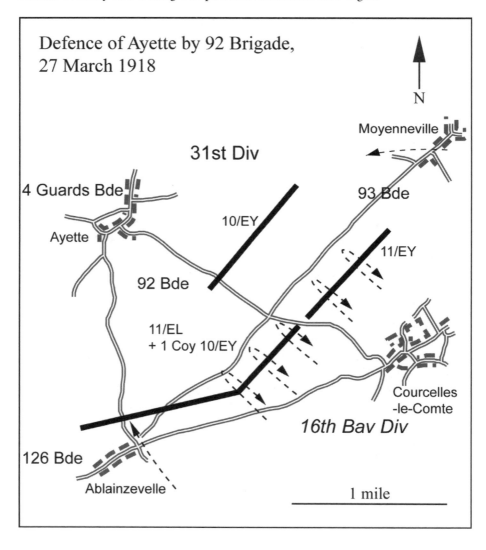

Defence of Ayette by 92 Brigade, 27 March 1918

Following an intense artillery bombardment, the German 16th Bavarian Division made its first infantry attack on the 92 Brigade front at 11.17am. After more than 30 minutes of desperate fighting at close range – during which 11/East Yorkshire was forced back – the entire brigade line was restored by a local counter-attack. The attacks were renewed at noon and at 12.20pm. At about this time, the forward sections of the platoon led by Second Lieutenant Horsfall at the centre-left of the East Lancashires' front were driven back from the crest of the ridge. Although Horsfall had been severely wounded in the head, he immediately organized the remainder of his men and successfully counter-attacked to recover the original position. On hearing that of the remaining three officers of his company two had been killed and one wounded, he refused to go to the dressing station. Later his platoon had to fall back to escape very heavy shellfire but, as soon as the shelling lifted, he made a second counter-attack and again recovered the position.

Fighting alongside Horsfall, Lance Corporal James Johnson Moore, a 34-year-old collier from Chorley, was credited with saving the left flank of the battalion by keeping his Lewis gun in action until ordered to withdraw. Moore would be awarded the MM.

In the early afternoon, considerable German forces were seen to be collecting in Ablainzevelle, posing a serious threat to the right flank of the brigade. A company of 10/East Yorkshire was sent forward in support but was stopped short by heavy machine-gun fire from the village.

Throughout the battle for the ridge the wounded were taken clear of the fighting, an operation that had to be done across open ground where the stretcher bearers were exposed to shellfire and flanking machine-gun fire. Awards of the MM were made to stretcher bearers Harry Collison, a 21-year-old from Burnley who had worked as a farrier with his father before the war, and Isaac Thompson, a 19-year-old from Blackpool. Communication between the front line and battalion headquarters depended on runners carrying messages across the same open ground, an act that contributed towards the award of the MM to 25-year-old Thomas Catlow from Oswaldtwistle.

By 2.40pm the Germans had gained a foothold on the ridge at the junction of the two forward battalions. The remainder of the supporting battalion, 10/East Yorkshire, was used up in a successful counter-attack. As late in the afternoon as 3.45pm, hopes remained high that the brigade's position could be held. Finally, however, the pressure told and both flanks gave way. By 4.25pm, 92 Brigade's situation finally became untenable; with telephone wires hopelessly cut and with mist rendering signalling impossible, Lieutenant Colonel Rickman – as the senior officer on the spot – informed divisional headquarters by pigeon of his decision to withdraw the brigade. Horsfall was the last East Lancashire officer to leave his position and, although exhausted, said he could have held on. This gallant officer was killed during the retirement. The subsequent award of the VC to Horsfall was one of only four gained by the East Lancashire Regiment during the war, and the only one awarded to the battalion.

To the right of Horsfall's position, 27-year-old Second Lieutenant Herbert Cecil Laycock from Burnley had held his platoon's line intact, despite it having been under enfilade fire for 3 hours. When the time came for the battalion to withdraw, Laycock covered the retirement of the remaining wounded and the medical staff by taking up a position with two Lewis guns in front of the aid post, an action for which he would be awarded the MC.

In their stubborn defence of the Ablainzevelle–Moyeneville Ridge in front of Ayette, 350 officers and men of 11/East Lancashire were killed, wounded or missing. The battalion took no further part in the first German offensive of 1918.

LXIV Brigade was not involved in the offensive. From training in the Guarbecque area, the brigade had moved up on 19 January along roads flooded by the recent thaw through Haverskerque, Saint-Venant, Calonne-sur-la-Lys and Merville to the area of Steenwerck; on 22 January, C/LXIV moved into new gun positions in Armentières. The batteries then side-slipped to the south on 16 and 17 February to take up positions south of the Lys River in the Fleurbaix sector. Following the departure of Lieutenant Colonel Barton to take over command of XLI Brigade on 6 March, command of LXIV Brigade was assumed by 35-year-old Lieutenant Colonel Vivian Allan Batchelor DSO. As early as 10 March, the anticipation of an enemy breakthrough prompted the inspection of reserve battery positions north of the Lys River. Sixteen days later, two guns of C/LXIV were brought into new positions in the factory about 1,600yd north-west of the bridge over the Lys at Bac Saint-Maur; the battery's remaining guns followed on the night of 27/28 March.

XLVIII Brigade, however, had been drawn into the thick of the fighting on the Somme. On 19 January, C/XLVIII had moved up from Valhoun to Arras where it was joined a week later by D/XLVIII to work on gun positions east of Roclincourt. The battery was still working outside of Roclincourt – having enjoyed only three days' respite at Valhoun – when XLVIII Brigade was recalled to Vedrel, 9 miles west of Lens, from where it moved south over the next four days to take up positions in front of the village of Bouzincourt, 2¼ miles north-west of Albert; there it was placed at the disposal of 12th Division which was under orders to hold the line of the Ancre River between Albert and Hamel. The brigade came into action on 27 March: while under heavy counter-battery fire, it helped to break up three desperate attacks made by the German 54th Reserve Division between the northern suburbs of Albert and Aveluy. At 8.30am on the following day, a determined attempt by the enemy to break out of the bridgehead at Aveluy in a north-westerly direction along the valley towards Martinsart was repulsed with heavy losses by the brigade's artillery fire. By about 10am, however, the enemy had been able to position three machine guns on a crest within 1,500yd of the gun positions, forcing the batteries to withdraw to new positions about 2 miles to the west in front of Senlis. Among the fatalities suffered by C Battery as it pulled back under heavy machine-gun fire was Bombardier Robert Reeder, a 29-year-old cotton spinner from Oswaldtwistle whose elder brother, Charles, had been killed in action with LXIV Brigade in July of 1917. In addition, two Accrington men were killed while attempting to repair one of the battery's guns: Bombardier Andrew William Kirkham, a 27-year-old cotton mill overlooker, and his friend Artificer James Frederick Morris MSM, a 28-year-old iron fitter who had worked at Howard and Bullough's before enlisting. On 2 April, 21-year-old Major Marcus Menus ('Marto') O'Keeffe MC was killed just one day after taking over command of C Battery.

Local enemy attacks on 29 March and 4 April were driven off, as was a more widespread attack on 5 April, the day on which Ludendorff called off the Michael Offensive. Until XLVIII Brigade pulled back behind Senlis on 15 April to act as a 'silent' brigade on the front of 38th (Welsh) Division, the daily routine was largely one of harassing fire by day and night and opportunistic shooting. A sequence of quiet days followed before an enemy attack in the afternoon of 21 April north of Aveluy Wood which required a sharp counter-attack in order to recover the front line; it was an eventful day which included a report from the Australian Corps that the German flying ace, Baron Manfred von Richthofen, had been brought down by Lewis-gun fire from the ground. An attempt by 38th and 35th divisions on 22 April to recapture the higher ground between Bouzincourt and Aveluy, supported by all available guns on the fronts of both divisions, met with only partial success. On 27 April, LXVIII Brigade was withdrawn to wagon lines at Vadencourt near Contay as Division Mobile Reserve.

For both 11/East Lancashire and LXIV Brigade, the month of April had been a considerably more torrid experience, as both units had been engaged in a fresh German attempt to achieve a breakthrough, this time in the zone of the Lys River.

Chapter 18

With Our Backs to the Wall

Shortly after 4am on 9 April, Acting Major Cecil Lyne, commanding C/LXIV, was woken by the sound of heavy gun fire. Lyne's first thought was to connect the noise of the guns with a raid by two companies of 20/Middlesex which was planned to take place at around that time. C/LXIV had in fact been moved up across the Lys River to a forward position near Barlette Farm in order to support the raid; one of the six guns from the battery had been positioned just behind the trenches in order to provide close support to the infantry, while the remaining five guns were sited some 500yd farther back. Lyne, having received no intelligence of any heightened activity in the enemy lines, had left his captain in charge of the guns for what was expected to be a routine operation. Lyne himself had remained with the brigade's wagon lines.

The reality was that Lyne had been woken by the opening salvoes of the heavy bombardment that began the second great German offensive of 1918, known as Georgette. From 4.15am, the German artillery targeted battery positions, road junctions and communication centres with HE and phosgene-gas shells. Lyne soon received an urgent wire to send forward gun teams and limbers in readiness to withdraw the guns from Barlette Farm; reaching brigade headquarters 600yd north-east of the bridge at Bac Saint-Maur, Lyne found a scene of total chaos. At around 5am, the headquarters had been hit by shellfire; the adjutant, Captain Atkins, had been severely wounded and blood was everywhere. Along with Lieutenant Stanley Knocker, Lyne crossed the river by foot to reconnoitre a way forward to his guns. Although the pair found the main routes out of Bac Saint-Maur to be impassable, they were able to find an infantry track running across country which looked capable of taking the limbers. Lyne returned to collect his gun teams and had only just got under way when Knocker rode up at a gallop with orders to return to headquarters. While information from the front line was scarce, reports suggested that infantry were falling back through the guns and that German troops were pushing through.

At 8am, the full, terrifying intensity of the German bombardment had been re-directed onto the forward positions along a 10-mile front held from south to north by 55th Division, 2nd Portuguese Division (both of XI Corps), 40th Division and 34th Division (both of XV Corps). Following a final

Trench at Serre held by
5th Company, 2nd Battalion,
169th (8th Baden) Infantry
Regiment, 1916. (*Hardy Huber*)

5th Company, 2nd Battalion,
169th (8th Baden) Infantry
Regiment, 1916. (*Hardy Huber*)

Captain Arnold Bannatyne Tough,
11/East Lancashire. (*Marjorie Lloyd-Jones*)

Second Lieutenant Reginald St John
Beardsworth Battersby, 11/East Lancashire.
(*Peter Bell*)

15173 Corporal Richard Ormerod,
11/East Lancashire. (*John Garwood*)

15504 Samuel Davies (Sam) Hardman,
11/East Lancashire.
(*Tracey Gardner and Dorothy Parkinson*)

15708 Robert (Bob) Bullen, 11/East Lancashire.
(*Terry Whittaker*)

15045 Corporal Francis Joseph (Frank) Thomas
MM, 11/East Lancashire. (*Ian Thomas*)

Lieutenant Frank Harwood MC, RFA.
(*Nin Harwood*)

Frank, Valérie and Joan Harwood, *c*. 1924.
(*Nin Harwood*)

Officers of 11/East Lancashire at Grammont, 11 November 1918. Captain John Shire (Jack) Duff MC and Bar is standing in the centre at the front (on the padre's left); Captain Spencer Richard Fleischer DSO, MC is standing second from the right at the front. (*Jane Maclean*)

From left, Second Lieutenant Edmund Mills Harwood RFA, Kate Hollis (née Harwood) and Second Lieutenant Frank Harwood RFA, 1915. (*Nin Harwood*)

Second Lieutenant Basil Arthur Horsfall VC, 11/East Lancashire. (*Lancashire Infantry Museum*)

Lieutenant Ernest David Kay MC, 11/East Lancashire. (*Pat and Roger Kay*)

Brigadier General Hubert Conway Rees (right) being questioned by the Kaiser on the California Plateau, 28 May 1918. (*Diana Stockford*)

38099 Corporal William Hill, 11/East Lancashire. (*Barbara Rogers*)

Captain Bart Endean, 11/East Lancashire. (*Peter Bell*)

Captain John Shire (Jack) Duff MC and Bar, 11/East Lancashire. (*Jane Maclean*)

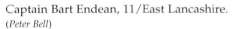

Lieutenant Colonel Percy Harrison Fawcett (second from left) on his final expedition, 1925. (*Royal Geographical Society, S0005734*)

The memorial to the Accrington Pals at Serre, 1990. (*Alyson Jackson*)

bridgehead. Foch had earlier declined to relieve any part of the British line, forcing Haig to take 29th and 49th divisions out of the Ypres front; before much longer, he would have to call on 31st Division, despite it still being under-strength from the Somme offensive.

LXIV Brigade continued to direct fire against the Sailly–Estaires road overnight; little information was coming in to brigade headquarters, prompting Lyne to send out an armed reconnoitring patrol under Corporal Reuben Monk, who had already won the DCM with CLVIII Brigade in 1916; Lyne regarded him as 'the best and bravest fellow' he'd ever known.

It dawned chilly and misty on 10 April. At about 7.30am, infantry of the German 35th Division scrambled under cover of the mist across the damaged Pont Levis bridge outside Estaires. Before long, the enemy were pushing out of the new bridgehead towards both Neuf Berquin in the west and, ominously for LXIV Brigade, Cul-de-Sac Farm in the north. Some 2 hours after the German success at Estaires, a breakthrough in the Bac Saint-Maur sector forced 74 Brigade to fall back in a north-westerly direction. At 1pm, LXIV Brigade began to withdraw to the north as it came under threat on both flanks; the situation remained very confused, and no sooner had C/LXIV passed through Le Doulieu than Lyne received fresh orders to go back into action south of the village. Writing home a few weeks later, Lyne described how the village was 'under occasional fire and the streets were packed, there was a big ammunition dump on fire in the centre, wagon lines were pouring through, civilians in country carts and afoot, some driving cattle, some carrying children, reinforce-ments coming up, ammunition wagons going away. People stood in the door-ways and watched helplessly the moving traffic, they didn't want to go and feared to stay.' Returning to action at about 3pm in a marshy field south of Le Doulieu, C/LXIV endured an uncomfortable 3–4 hours exposed to rifle and machine-gun fire on both flanks until ordered to pull back to a new position between Le Doulieu and La Brielle Farm at about 6.30pm. By this time, the gunners were not only suffering from exhaustion and hunger, but were beginning to feel the full effects of the poison gas to which they had been exposed throughout the day's fighting. Lyne himself 'was as sick as anything, could only speak in a hoarse whisper; and what with coughing and choking all night, a continual flow of orderlies and calls to the telephone, spent a sleepless night of singular misery'. LXIV Brigade's guns continued to fire during the night at the approach roads to Estaires, and the crossings over the Lys.

After the fierce engagement in front of Ayette on 27 March, 11/East Lancashire was rebuilding and training at Bailleul-aux-Cornailles when at 11am on 10 April it received orders from 31st Division to move by bus to the XV Corps area in order to help counter the rapidly developing German threat against the strategically important railway centre of Hazebrouck. The battalion embussed at 7pm, travelling via Lillers and Hazebrouck to Le Paradis where it debussed on the Vieux Berquin–Strazeele road before daybreak on 11 April. Packs were dumped, and the battalion marched through Vieux Berquin and La Couronne to Bleu where it took up a defensive position on the east and south sides of the hamlet.

The British line on the front of XV Corps on the morning of 11 April was held by 149 and 150 brigades between Estaires and Sailly, then by 40th Division as far as Steenwerck. Behind 150 Brigade were 86 and 87 brigades of 29th Division, with the newly arrived 92 and 93 brigades of 31st Division a further 3 miles back.

By 9am, 150 Brigade – which had already been driven back around 1,000yd from the Lys on the previous afternoon – was again being forced back in the mist and gradually fell back through the lines of 87 Brigade, ending up by 10.30pm on the west side of the road from Estaires to Neuf Berquin. Shortly after 150 Brigade began to fall back, the Germans broke through on the right flank of 149 Brigade in front of Neuf Berquin.

At 11.15am, 92 Brigade was pushed forward to dig in on a line behind Le Doulieu. 11/East Lancashire was kept in reserve, 1,000yd behind the forward positions held by 10 and 11/East Yorkshire. 93 Brigade, which had first been ordered to move into a position to support 92 Brigade, was at 2pm given orders to make a counter-attack on the left of 11/East Yorkshire. The attack, made by 13/York and Lancaster and 18/Durham Light Infantry in failing light at 7pm and without artillery preparation, caught the enemy completely by surprise and succeeded in re-taking La Becque and La Rose Farm.

By mid-afternoon, the German breakthrough in front of Neuf Berquin had left the right flank of 29th Division dangerously exposed forcing 86 and 87 brigades to pull back and to re-form on the right of 31st Division.

After enduring his 'sleepless night of singular misery', Lyne had at least been able to get his first meal since the battle started, a breakfast of eggs cooked in the farm kitchen. Later in the morning, he and Monk went forward to where, from the loft of a farm, they were able to observe the attack developing against the front of 86 and 87 brigades. After directing fire for 30 minutes, the pair began to come under shellfire themselves and returned hastily to the guns. The next hour was an anxious one as Lyne, watching infantry falling back on his left, feared that a sudden attack by the enemy would leave his battery completely exposed to machine-gun fire. By the time orders came through to evacuate, Lyne had only two guns left in action. At 4pm, LXIV Brigade retired through the lines of 10/East Yorkshire and 11/East Lancashire to the hamlet of Bleu. Lyne described the retirement:

> a wearisome affair, the roads were congested and choked by every sort of vehicle and traffic. Broken down civilian wagons, ditched motor lorries, and with it all wounded in hundreds, some on stretchers,

others helping each other on their toilsome way; coated with dust, caked with blood. Some of them had been on the road for the last two days with never a chance of getting their wounds dressed.

With German forces now within 6 miles of Hazebrouck, and with few reserves at his disposal, Haig issued his special Order of the Day which has gone into history as the 'backs to the wall' message. The concluding paragraph of the order left no doubt as to the severity of the situation facing the British Army:

> There is no other course open to us but to fight it out. Every position must be held to the last man: there must be no retirement. With our backs to the wall and believing in the justice of our cause each one of us must fight on to the end. The safety of our homes and the Freedom of mankind alike depend upon the conduct of each one of us at this critical moment.

Whether or not the message influenced the outcome of the battle, it certainly provided material for the wits among the British troops; one Accrington Pal was remembered as bursting out laughing before exclaiming 'Backs to the wall, we never saw a [bloody] wall, it was all rivers of muck and blasted manure dumps.'

Overnight, 11/East Yorkshire moved forward to relieve the remnants of 40th Division and to re-establish contact with 93 Brigade at Du Bois Farm. At daybreak on 12 April, 150 and 149 brigades held the line to the west of the road between the Berquins, both brigades being covered by the newly arrived 4 Guards Brigade of 31st Division. 12/KOYLI had been slotted into the gap between 149 and 87 brigades. Further to the left, 86 Brigade bridged the gap to where 92 and 93 brigades took over.

The ground fog of early morning soon gave way to a clear day. On the right of the XV Corps sector, 149 Brigade was soon being driven back northwards onto 12/KOYLI as a fresh German division (12th Reserve) was brought into the attack between the Lys and the road to Vieux Berquin. 4 Guards Brigade held the line throughout the day, and at dark took on an extended front to cover both 150 and 149 brigades.

At about 7.30am, enemy shelling began along the entire front held by 29th and 31st divisions. At Bleu, where LXIV Brigade's batteries were now firing in support of 92 and 93 brigades, Lyne was growing increasingly anxious for the safety of his men, horses and guns. As the mist cleared, an enemy aeroplane spotted the battery's location and directed artillery fire onto it: in a short time, three horses had been maimed, a driver hit and a sergeant struck in the neck by a shell fragment. With the infantry in front of the battery holding on, Lyne held his position until ordered to pull back some time after 10am to a new position on the railway line south of Merris; there the guns returned to action to fire on Neuf Berquin and the road running north from the village.

By around 9am, a gap had opened up between 86 and 92 brigades as casualties rapidly mounted from an enemy field gun firing at a range of less than 1,000yd. At the same time, the right battalion of 93 Brigade (13/York and Lancaster) began to retire as enemy troops pressed forward, working down roads and hedges, closely supported by machine guns, mobile trench mortars and light artillery. With both flanks in danger of being turned, the two forward battalions of 92 Brigade were ordered to start withdrawing to the north-west at 10am.

The withdrawal under heavy shelling and machine-gun fire was made all the more difficult by the dykes and hedges that divided the landscape; men drowned while attempting to cross the deep and broad ditches. There was no hiding in the flat, open landscape from the artillery fire as the German guns were kept in contact with troop movements both from observation balloons, some not more than 2,500yd away, and by the use of Very flares by their infantry as they worked their way forward. After allowing 10/East Yorkshire to pass through its lines, 11/East Lancashire moved to cover the withdrawal of the brigade by extending its own front to the left. Lieutenant Harold Wilton was later awarded the MC for leading his company to the battalion's left flank under point-blank artillery fire and a hail of bullets from rifles and machine guns. The fire from Wilton's company was so effective that the enemy was forced to dig in. Wilton had returned from Russia to enlist, having emigrated in 1911 to take up a position as a store manager; he had re-joined the battalion only three months earlier after recovering from wounds sustained at Oppy-Gavrelle on 27 June 1917. At 11.30am, the battalion received orders to withdraw to a line on the right flank of 10/East Yorkshire running west from Haute Maison.

By noon on 12 April, the situation had deteriorated still further as a result of confusion over where 92 Brigade should make a stand; 11/East Yorkshire – expected to extend the brigade line to the left along the Rau du Leet – continued to fall back as far as Merris where it eventually joined a composite battalion formed from brigade details and stragglers. The yawning gap left between 92 and 93 brigades made the line of the Rau du Leet completely untenable. As 93 Brigade pulled back to the railway line east of Outtersteene, 10/East Yorkshire swung around its left to face east. Orders received by the composite battalion of 92 Brigade at 1.15pm to fill in the line along the railway between the left flank of 10/East Yorkshire and 93 Brigade were soon counter-manded as it became clear that the enemy were already across the railway and in possession of Outtersteene. As machine-gun fire swept over their exposed position along the railway line, the remnants of 93 Brigade were now in danger of being enveloped from the right and were compelled to withdraw northwards. As LXIV Brigade also came under machine-gun fire from Outtersteene, all four batteries were forced at about 3pm to pull back to the high ground east of Strazeele.

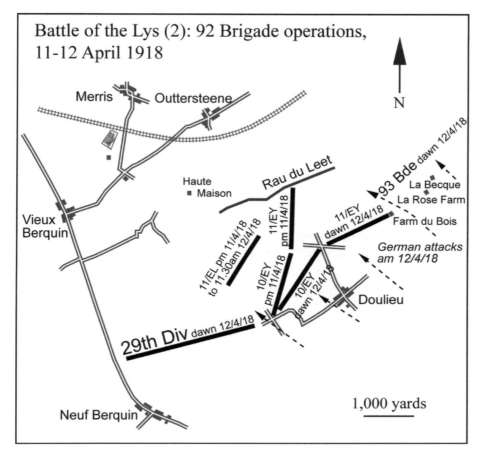

Battle of the Lys (2): 92 Brigade operations, 11-12 April 1918

With 10/East Yorkshire also in danger of being outflanked, 92 Brigade was forced to withdraw at around 3.30pm. 11/East Lancashire – having earlier swung around its right so as to make contact with 29th Division – was now ordered back to form a line extending north-west from Labis Farm as far as the railway. For a time, W Company led by Captain Duff and Z Company under Captain Fleischer were left isolated as the runner carrying the orders to withdraw failed to reach them; fortunately a second runner, Charles Nutt, a 19-year-old from Chorlton, Manchester, evaded the forward patrols of the enemy and succeeded in reaching the two companies before it was too late. Under exceptionally heavy fire, both officers successfully led their companies back to safety. Captain Duff, wounded in the arm, had later to be evacuated owing to loss of blood.

11/East Lancashire had by now established battalion headquarters in a cellar in Le Paradis. From there it was possible to communicate with both brigade and company headquarters by telephone, though the lines were constantly being broken and required signallers to make repairs while exposed to heavy artillery and machine-gun fire. Lance Corporal William Albert Stuart from Burnley would later be awarded the MM for this vital repair work.

The brigade front was extended north of the railway by 10/East Yorkshire and by the composite battalion, which by now was dug in west of Merris.

By 7pm the new line had been established, with forward posts held on the east edge of Celery Copse (Bois de Merris) by 11/East Lancashire and to the east of Merris by a company of a composite battalion formed from 93 Brigade. Over a relatively quiet night, rifle pits, hastily dug by the exhausted troops, were first deepened and improved, then converted into a continuous line of traversed trench.

As dawn broke on a cold, overcast 13 April, the weakly held British lines lay just 5 miles outside of Hazebrouck. Supporting the battle-weary 29th and 31st divisions were only four Australian battalions spread across a front of 1,200yd. It was vital that the line should hold until the arrival of the remainder of 1st Australian Division.

The first enemy attack of the day came to nothing as an ammunition dump caught fire close to where the troops were forming up, causing great confusion and attracting a destructive hail of artillery, rifle and machine-gun fire.

At 8.30am the enemy launched a strong attack along the entire front of 92 Brigade. On the edge of Celery Copse, the Lewis-gun team commanded by Sergeant Walter Beckett of 11/East Lancashire, a 25-year-old cotton weaver from Sabden, fired at the enemy until practically surrounded. Beckett stayed with his gun to cover the withdrawal of his men before retiring himself. Already possessing the DCM, Beckett was awarded a MM for his actions on 13 April. Although the forward posts in front of Merris and Celery Copse had been driven back by around 10am, the enemy were held up by artillery fire and made no further progress; at one point, LXIV Brigade sent a gun down the road towards Vieux Berquin from where it fired 100 rounds against enemy positions around Hullebert Farm at an average range of 1,800yd.

At 11.30am a fresh attack against the front of 11/East Lancashire came to nothing as the enemy were caught in enfilade fire from Lewis guns sited at Labis Farm. At one point, Second Lieutenant Kay took three Lewis-gun teams forward 150yd into the open to where he could direct enfilade fire into enemy troops gathering in a hollow. Kay was to be awarded the MC for his actions.

To the right of 92 Brigade, a critical situation was fast developing. 12/KOYLI, defending the approach to Vieux Berquin along the road, had been blown out of its positions at La Couronne by artillery fire. Further to the right, 4 Guards Brigade now had to defend against both frontal and flank attacks.

Desperate to exploit the situation at La Couronne, the enemy launched a fresh attack at 2.35pm against the two right companies of 11/East Lancashire and the left of 29th Division. As 11/East Lancashire held its positions while

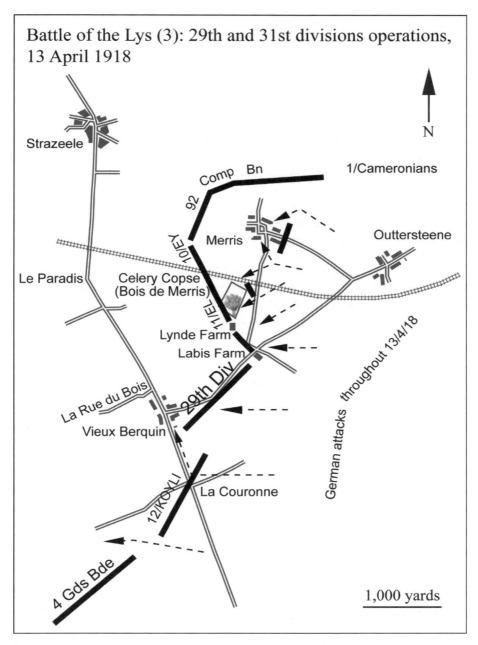

Battle of the Lys (3): 29th and 31st divisions operations, 13 April 1918

N

Strazeele

92 Comp Bn

1/Cameronians

Merris

Outtersteene

Le Paradis

Celery Copse
(Bois de Merris)

10/EY

11/EL

Lynde Farm

Labis Farm

29th Div

La Rue du Bois

Vieux Berquin

La Couronne

12/KOYLI

German attacks throughout 13/4/18

4 Gds Bde

1,000 yards

inflicting heavy losses on the enemy, Lieutenant Colonel Rickman was alarmed to see on his right about 800 men from 12/KOYLI and 29th Division streaming north out of Vieux Berquin. Rickman promptly sent Major Lewis and Captain Macalpine to recover the situation. In the face of heavy machine-gun fire coming up the road from Vieux Berquin, the 2 officers collected around 400 stragglers, formed them into a position commanding the exits to the village and saw them issued with ammunition. Lewis and Macalpine were respectively awarded the DSC and the MC.

Throughout the day 1st Australian Division had been digging in behind Vieux Berquin. By 6pm, the left front of 4 Guards Brigade had been broken, and was forced to fall back through the Australians. On the right, the Guards continued to fight late into the evening, Acting Captain Thomas Tannatt Pryce MC of 4/Grenadier Guards losing his life while winning the VC for the gallantry displayed by his depleted company in holding back at least one enemy battalion for over 10 hours.

With the enemy in possession of Vieux Berquin, 11/East Lancashire was again in danger of being outflanked. The battalion remained in position until after dusk, at which point Rickman was ordered to withdraw his battalion after warning the troops on his right.

The stubborn fight put up by 29th and 31st divisions over 11–13 April had bought enough time for 1st Australian Division to form a new line running from Strazeele through Le Paradis to La Rue de Bois. At 4am on 14 April, 92 Brigade withdrew through the Australian line.

Table: 92 Infantry Brigade casualties, April 1918. (TNA WO 95/2356)

Unit	Killed	Wounded	Missing	Total
Brigade HQ		3		3
10/East Yorkshire	13	141	214	368
11/East Yorkshire	9	79	338	426
11/East Lancashire	34	149	84	267
92 Trench Mortar Battery	3	8	4	15
	59	380	640	1,079

Among the dead from 11/East Lancashire was Second Lieutenant John Cyprian Lott MC. A 23-year-old born in De Aar, South Africa, Lott had volunteered to join the ranks of 18/Royal Fusiliers (1/Public Schools) in September 1914. After serving with the battalion in France for five months, he was posted Home to join an Officers Cadet Battalion in April 1916, and was granted a commission in the East Lancashire Regiment the following September. Lott won the MC for gallantry at Oppy-Gavrelle in May and June 1917; wounded at Ayette on 27 March 1918, he remained at duty only to be killed in action on 13 April.

The morning of 14 April was bitterly cold and windy. LXIV Brigade, which in the previous afternoon had been withdrawn 2 miles to the south-west, now supported 1 Australian Brigade from positions between Petit Sec Bois and the railway. German attacks from 8am aimed at gaining the Strazeele Ridge rarely came within 900yd of the Australian line owing to concentrated artillery and machine-gun fire. Renewed attacks at 2pm and 7pm were largely fruitless.

The following two days were generally quiet, though a successful local attack at Merris by the Australians at dusk on 16 April brought down a heavy retaliatory barrage from the enemy.

On 17 April, a terrific enemy bombardment over the ground held by 1 Australian Brigade preceded a series of infantry attacks, each of which was driven back by intense fire of every description. The line in this sector was to remain substantially unchanged for the next two months. LXIV Brigade, which for a time was the most advanced brigade on the Australian front, was relieved on 26 April and marched to wagon lines in the area of Staple, west of Hazebrouck.

After being withdrawn from the line of battle in the early hours of 14 April, 11/East Lancashire marched to billets near Honeghem, north of Hazebrouck. Casualties had been so great during the battle that the battalion was for a short time amalgamated with 13/York and Lancaster to form 94/Composite Battalion under the command of Major Lewis. On 17 April the Composite Battalion took over part of the Hazebrouck defences east of the town. On 19 April 11/East Lancashire recovered its identity and took over a section of the line on the north-eastern corner of Aval Wood.

As the German offensive on the Lys drew to a close, few imagined that the war would be over within seven months. While recovering from an arm wound, 27-year-old Corporal William Hill wrote to his father John on 28 April:

> My arm is almost better again, don't expect I shall be here [in hospital] above another week at the most, you get short mercy here if there is nothing the matter with you. We don't appear to be exactly winning the War at present but one never knows what the game is, perhaps the Yankees will polish them off.

Writing to the parents of his best friend, Wilf Kitchen, a 19-year-old talented art student from Macclesfield, had a more optimistic outlook:

> I shall be jolly glad when this is over. I'm fed up already and have only been out six weeks, however it won't be long now, the Bosche has done about as much as he can do. Well, up to now I've not done so bad, we get good grub and are billeted in a pretty decent barn. We are in supports at present, but I suppose it won't be long before we're in the front line again. I've been pretty lucky while we've been in action, except for being grazed by a piece of shrapnel I was untouched and we had a pretty hot time.

Chapter 19
Peaceful Penetration

With the failure of the German army to break through to Hazebrouck, the focus of the Georgette offensive shifted northwards to the Ypres salient where on 15 April the British were forced to abandon the Passchendaele–Westroosebeke Ridge and on 25 April the French lost Mount Kemmel. By this time, Ludendorff had already set in motion preparations for a new offensive (named Blücher) in the Chemin des Dames sector and after a last strike on 29 April he brought Georgette to a close.

British Army casualties in the months of April and May 1918 totalled 316,889. Yet German losses were no less severe, with 303,450 casualties reported in the 3 main assaulting armies in the period from 21 March to 10 April alone.

Ludendorff's intention in striking at the French Sixth Army in the Chemin des Dames sector was to induce Foch to move his reserves southwards in order to protect Paris, thereby leaving the British-held front to the north vulnerable to a fresh onslaught. The more immediate objectives were to capture the Chemin des Dames Ridge, cross the Aisne River and push beyond the line of the Vesle River between Soissons and Rheims. Ironically, the blow would fall not only on the French 61st, 21st and 22nd divisions, but on three British divisions, the 50th, 8th and 21st, which had been sent to this supposedly quiet area of the front in order to rest and recuperate after being mauled in the April (Lys) offensive. At the extreme left of the line held by the British divisions, 150 Brigade, still commanded by Hubert Rees, defended the California Plateau, seen by the Germans as 'the key of the Chemin des Dames position'. At 1am on 27 May, the greatest concentration of artillery yet assembled in the war opened fire on Allied positions across a front of 24 miles. Over the next 4½ hours, 1,100 German batteries fired an estimated 2 million shells, effectively paralysing all opposition within the Allied forward zone where General Denis Duchêne, commanding the French Sixth Army, had insisted on concentrating his forces. The infantry assault began at 3.40am, led under cover of mist, smoke and gas by seventeen divisions. Success was complete. At the California Plateau, 150 Brigade had effectively ceased to exist by 8am; Hubert Rees, after a series of adventures, was eventually taken prisoner while attempting to cross the Aisne. By the following morning, the German advance had in several places reached the Vesle, some 10 miles forward; a further two days saw the depth of the advance extended by up to 20 miles.

By the time the Blücher offensive ran out of steam on 3 June, the Germans had penetrated by as much as 30 miles. Yet the Allies had again stabilized the line and, with American divisions now coming into action, were in a much better position to replace their losses. The fresh salient in the front line created by Blücher forced Ludendorff to put off a renewed strike against the British and instead to launch an offensive aimed at broadening the salient northwards: the offensive, named Gneisnau, but known to the French as the Battle of the Matz, was launched on 9 June. Despite initial successes, the offensive was called off on 14 June in the face of counter-attacks led by the United States 1st and 2nd divisions.

The section of line on the north-eastern corner of Aval Wood was fairly quiet when it was taken over by 11/East Lancashire on 19 April, and the men took the chance to plunder what food they could find from their surroundings. Percy Crabtree of Z Company remembered the good feeding that followed: 'One effort was a huge potato pie, the crust being made with flour and bacon dripping. It was a great success and the American doctor sent back his plate for more.'

After completing the tour of duty on the night of 27/28 April, the battalion returned to billets where training and reorganization continued while each day 200 men were allocated to work on the Hazebrouck defences.

A further tour of duty from 9–23 May in the Meteren sector was followed by a welcome period of rest. Crabtree recalled how Z Company,

> came out of the line near Caestre on the evening of 23 May, being heavily shelled on the way. Buses were waiting on the main road and these loaded up with men and moved off in the semi-darkness in a westerly direction. Men could hardly believe they were going to a quiet rest camp; they thought 'Jerry' had broken through again and they were going to be rushed to fill the breach. Away the buses rolled through Hazebrouck, Arques, Saint-Omer to Lumbres, the last few miles being in brilliant moonlight with a moon nearly at full.

The battalion rested at Lumbres until 8 June when it left to march to camp at Racquinghem. The march was done in blazing heat and when the exhausted, dust-covered troops reached their destination, many complained of feeling feverish: the influenza epidemic that spread through the battalion effectively put it out of action for several days. After a week of training by company and battalion at Racquinghem, orders were received for 92 Brigade to move up to Wallon-Cappel where it would be ready to reinforce the line should Ludendorff, having broken off his Gneisnau offensive, renew his attack against Hazebrouck. The brigade bivouacked in the open, while officers went forward to reconnoitre the Hazebrouck defences. The immediate threat was short-lived and the battalion moved away from Hazebrouck into billets at Blaringhem only two days after arriving at Wallon-Cappel.

After a short spell in reserve following the Battle of the Lys, LXIV Brigade had returned to action over 5 and 6 May at Mont des Cats, 7 miles north-east of Hazebrouck. Within a matter of days, the brigade was again moved, its guns coming into action near Sec Bois close to the northern edge of Aval Wood on 10 May. C/LXIV suffered two casualties on 16 May when Second Lieutenant Foster and Major Lyne were wounded; Lyne would return to the brigade less than four months later. On 20 May, the brigade side-slipped to the left, moving into new positions 500yd north-west of Grand Sec Bois where they once more covered 1st Australian Division. The brigade's batteries co-operated in the capture of Mont de Merris by 3 Australian Brigade on the night of 2/3 June, the enemy being taken completely by surprise in the middle of a relief. Some of the 250 prisoners taken in the attack reportedly testified to being very impressed by the shooting of the artillery. Major Harold Eaton Hart, who had taken over command of C/LXIV after Lyne's departure, had a further chance to show his battery's mettle when on 5 June he was given the task of responding to a request from the infantry for a farm in enemy hands to be set on fire; Hart's battery carried out a very successful shoot, with which the infantry were said to be very satisfied. The brigade was again in action to support an Australian raid when between 1 and 2am on 13 June forty-eight prisoners, six machine guns and a light trench mortar were captured; the morale of the prisoners was said to be quite good, but they were described as being on the whole 'short and weak, mostly about 19 and 20 years old'. It was evidence that the German army was reaching the limit of its manpower.

The influenza epidemic reached LXIV Brigade at about the same time that it was lifting from 11/East Lancashire, 152 cases being reported in the brigade on both 15 and 16 June. The epidemic gradually passed, and by 27 June only two cases were reported. In the meantime, the epidemic had not prevented the brigade from supporting a successful night-time operation by 3 Australian Brigade to advance the line east of Mont de Merris. While the epidemic had been at its height, Captain Rice joined the brigade and was posted to C Battery.

On 20 June, 5th and 31st divisions received orders to attack on a 6,000yd front east of the Nieppe Forest. The operation was designed both to disrupt any further plans the enemy might have for a renewed offensive, and to push the British lines away from the edge of the wood where they had made an easy target for hostile artillery.

11/East Lancashire went into the front line east of Aval Wood, on the eastern fringe of the Nieppe Forest, for a four-day tour on 21 June then went for a short time into camp near to Grand Hasard before returning to the line on 27 June in readiness for the attack.

In a night-time operation aimed at securing a position from which enfilade fire could be used to support the main attack, two companies of 13/York and Lancaster supported by part of two companies of 18/Durham Light Infantry captured Ankle Farm in the early morning of 27 June. LXIV Brigade co-operated in the attack. Later that day the main attack was practised by 92 Brigade in the area of La Papote, some 3½ miles behind the front line. Conditions were all too realistic. As an East Lancashire regimental historian wryly remarked: 'The closing stages were somewhat marred through the enemy putting down a heavy destructive shoot on the imaginary final objective which gave a touch of reality to the proceedings which was neither helpful nor desired.'

The attacking troops reached their assembly trenches in the quiet early hours of the 28th, unnoticed by the enemy who were not to be forewarned of the attack by a preliminary artillery bombardment. While it is tempting to highlight the undoubted and very considerable advances in battlefield tactics made by the British since the opening of the Battle of the Somme two years earlier, the reality is that the scale of the task confronting 31st Division on 28 June 1918 bore no resemblance to that of 1 July 1916; the German 102nd Regiment holding the line opposite 31st Division was assessed to be only third-rate, its defences comprised no more than shallow trenches and shell holes protected by badly erected wire, while its dugouts were described as being no more than 'rough weather-proof shelters'.

At the far left of the 31st Division front, 15th/17th West Yorkshire of 93 Brigade was to capture and consolidate La Becque Farm – from which the action took its name – before pushing on to Plate Becque stream. To the right of the West Yorkshires were the three battalions of 92 Brigade, 11/East Yorkshire, 11/East Lancashire and 10/East Yorkshire. The two East Yorkshire battalions were each to attack in four waves, with the first two waves expected to go straight through to the final objective. The objectives allocated to 11/East Lancashire included the capture and consolidation of two heavily fortified farms. For this reason, the battalion was to employ a 'leap frog' approach, in which Z Company would halt after capturing Beaulieu Farm, allowing W Company to pass through to capture and hold Gombert Farm; X and Y companies would then move on to the line of the final objective. To the right of 10/East Yorkshire, 5th Division was to attack with five battalions in line.

As an intense shrapnel barrage broke over the enemy front line at 6am on the 28th, the first wave of attacking troops left their trenches and hurried forward through the tall crops. LXIV Brigade again formed part of the artillery support for the attack. The enemy wire was easily passed through – one battalion commander likening it more to trip wire than anything else – and the first wave was able to close up to the barrage before its first lift. On the extreme right of the 31st Division front, a few guns tragically fired short into the right forward company of 10/East Yorkshire, Major Colin Traill MC being among those killed. At the moment the shrapnel barrage lifted, British troops swarmed forward giving the enemy little or no chance to reach machine guns or man parapets before being overrun.

Behind the German lines, gun batteries, road junctions and likely assembly points were being targeted by heavy artillery while the main road through Vieux Berquin was cloaked by a thick smoke screen laid down by Australian artillery.

On the left of the attack, the 15th/17th West Yorkshires encountered only isolated pockets of resistance in driving through to their objectives under the protection of the creeping barrage. In circumstances that were repeated along the length of the front, attacking troops pressing too closely to the barrage were inevitably hit by their own shrapnel, accounting for many of the battalion's 170 casualties.

Lieutenant Colonel Clement Gurney, commanding 11/East Yorkshire, commented that while his battalion faced little resistance from enemy infantry 'individual [enemy] machine gunners put up a splendid fight to the last, which in many cases necessitated enflanking movements'. By 7.25am, both forward companies of the battalion had taken their objectives. Patrols sent out towards the Plate Becque found no enemy west of the stream.

At the centre of 92 Brigade, it was vital that Beaulieu Farm – known to be heavily garrisoned with heavy and light machine guns – was quickly captured by 11/East Lancashire. Pressing closely behind the creeping barrage, Z Company led by Captain Fleischer stormed the farm before many of the guns could be brought to bear. Fleischer personally rushed one of them. To his right, Second Lieutenant Norman Fuller and Lance Corporal Wilfred White – having already overrun one machine gun in the front line – charged at another. White was killed in the attempt, Fuller going on to shoot the enemy gunner with his revolver and take the gun. A third machine gun opened fire on Lance Corporal John Foden's Lewis-gun section, hitting five men. Foden immediately retaliated, shooting the enemy gunner; as man after man bravely tried to take over the machine gun, Foden shot each one down before his section rushed forward to capture it.

Fleischer was awarded the DSO for this action, while Fuller, White and Foden were respectively awarded the MC, MM and DCM. None of the four men had been with the battalion from its formation. Fuller, a 23-year-old from Wandsworth, had been a commercial clerk before the war, and enlisted into the ranks, first going overseas with 23/London in March 1915; he was posted to the East Lancashires on receiving his commission in September 1917. White, a 23-year-old coal miner from Pemberton near Wigan, had joined 11/East Lancashire from the 8th Battalion. Foden was a 20-year-old cotton doffer from Cloughfold, Rawtenstall.

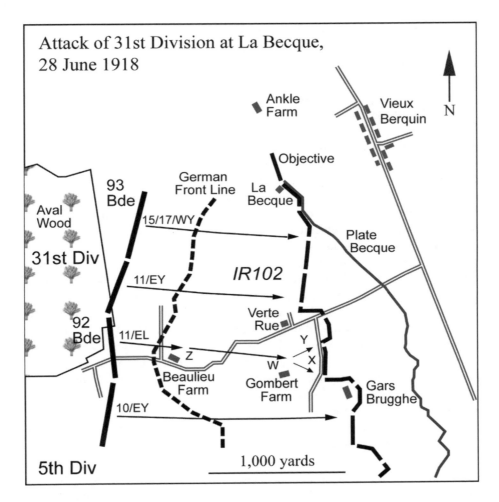

Attack of 31st Division at La Becque, 28 June 1918

With the capture of Beaulieu Farm, W Company led by Captain Cyril McKenzie moved through to press on behind the barrage to Gombert Farm. Although enemy machine guns began to exact a terrible toll as W Company crossed the 1,100yd between the two farms, Gombert Farm was captured shortly after 7am.

Among several acts of gallantry that day for which awards were made of the DCM were those of Corporal James Ashton, a 26-year-old slipper worker from Stacksteads, and Lance Corporal John Ratcliffe, a 23-year-old clerk from Darwen. After passing Beaulieu Farm, Ashton spotted an enemy machine-gun post concealed in a hedge in front. He worked up along another hedge at right angles, until he was close enough to bomb the machine gun out of action. On then discovering that both his platoon officer and sergeant had become casualties, he took command, leading the platoon to its objective where it dug in under heavy shellfire. Ratcliffe, who had joined 11/East Lancashire after recovering from wounds sustained while serving with the 8th Battalion at Arras in April 1917, took command of a Lewis-gun section despite having just been seriously wounded by shellfire and led the section successfully to its objective; he then remained with his men for 5 hours before being ordered to a dressing station.

As W Company consolidated on a line from Gombert Farm to Verte Rue, X and Y companies led by Captain George Bentley forged ahead to the final objective 300yd beyond Gombert Farm. Both companies reached their objectives, though not before X Company had been reduced to just thirty-four men under the command of Sergeant Joshua Beech, a 31-year-old who had been a mule minder in an Oldham cotton mill before the war. Disregarding severe wounds inflicted by shellfire, Company Sergeant Major James Fleming led two platoons of Y Company to their objectives after the loss of their officers.

During their advance across more than 1,500yd of ground, 11/East Lancashire captured ten light machine guns, two heavy machine guns, three trench mortars and two light field guns. The battalion suffered the heaviest casualties in 31st Division with 253 men killed, wounded or missing.

At the right of the 31st Division front, 10/East Yorkshire encountered little resistance in reaching all of their objectives by 7.20am. The enemy were found to have been occupying makeshift defences comprising little more than unconnected slit trenches with adjoining shelters, most if not all of which were not even shrapnel-proof. The battalion's advance was held up only for a short time by machine-gun fire from Gars Brugghe; the farm was soon captured in an outflanking manoeuvre supported by a brief trench-mortar bombardment.

In the operations of 27/28 June, 31st Division reported the capture of 278 men from the German 102nd Regiment along with 3 field guns, 10 heavy machine guns, 29 light machine guns and 9 trench mortars; 223 of the enemy were buried in the area of the advance with more thought to be lying un-discovered in the thick crops. More of the enemy were undoubtedly killed by the barrage of artillery and machine-gun fire placed beyond the line of the objective. All objectives were reached practically on time. To the right of 31st Division, 5th Division was no less successful.

After the retreats of March and April, La Becque was one of several actions to indicate that the tide of war on the Western Front had turned in favour of the Allies: around Chateau-Thierry, the United States 2nd Division completed the capture of Belleau Wood, and took the village of Vaux a few days later; the French Tenth Army (General Charles Emmanuel Marie Mangin) retook higher ground near Soissons over 28–30 June; 11 Australian Brigade supported by units of the United States 33rd Division overran Le Hamel on 4 July; 9th (Scottish) Division attacked successfully at Meteren on 19 July.

The fifth and last German offensive of 1918, a two-pronged attack delivered astride Rheims, was brought to a halt on 17 July. On the following day, Mangin launched a counter-offensive with 18 divisions, including the United States 1st and 2nd divisions, led by more than 300 Renault light tanks. By the end of the day, Mangin had driven the Germans 4 miles back, capturing 15,000 prisoners and 400 guns.

July 1918 was a relatively quiet month for 11/East Lancashire. There were two tours of the line facing Vieux Berquin which accounted for casualties over the month of eight men killed, with one officer and thirty-six men wounded. The remainder of July was largely spent in specialist training, wiring and rifle competitions while in divisional reserve at Grand Hasard; some men were even able to hitch a lift on a lorry into Saint-Omer where they 'had a good day in the old town, finishing with a high tea and trusting to luck to get a lift back to camp'.

For LXIV Brigade, the month of July was mostly taken up with harassing fire and opportunistic shooting. Lieutenant Mayne had joined the brigade on 29 June, and was posted to C Battery. The relief of an Australian infantry brigade in the zone of LXIV Brigade by 40th Division on 18 July was reported alongside the disparaging remark that the new arrivals – which included 13/East Lancashire – consisted of 'B1' men. The month ended with each battery of LXIV Brigade firing more than 1,000 rounds in support of a successful operation by 3 Australian Brigade to capture Merris in the early hours of 30 July.

On 8 August – the day on which Australian and Canadian infantry of Rawlinson's British Fourth Army, covered by over 500 tanks, drove through the German lines at Amiens to a depth of 6 to 8 miles – 11/East Lancashire, then in brigade reserve, went from its billets in Morbecque to a ceremonial parade at which Rickman presented ribbons of the MC, MM and DCM to those whose acts of gallantry during the fighting earlier in the year had been given official recognition. It was about this time that the war-weary battalion was heartened by its first sight of American troops, though some men of Z Company were staggered to be asked if there were 'any good hotels around here?'

In the second of two tours of duty in the front line during August, 11/East Lancashire pursued a policy of 'peaceful penetration' by which the line was moved forward at Vieux Berquin by 200yd between 15 and 19 August; fore-going the support of artillery and machine-gun fire in order to achieve surprise, and by using the tall crops as cover, patrols were able to capture several enemy posts. A heavy bombardment of gas shells on the night of 15/16 August accounted for many of the battalion's casualties during the month: eleven men killed, two officers wounded and eighty-three men either wounded or missing.

To the left of 31st Division, 29th Division had taken over the Merris sector from 1st Australian Division over the nights of 1/2 and 2/3 August. LXIV Brigade moved up into new positions in the sector, south of Strazeele, on

15 August; on the following day, the three 18-pounder batteries registered on Hoegenacker Mill, 1 mile north-east of Outtersteene, in preparation for an operation by 9th Division and 87 Brigade of 29th Division to capture Outtersteene Ridge. The operation began at 11am on 18 August, the brigade's 18-pounder batteries firing an enfilade barrage until the ridge was taken, then two creeping barrages for the capture of Outtersteene village. All objectives were taken by 12.30pm. LXIV Brigade was in action again on the 19th, putting down a 'very good and thick barrage' to aid 86 Brigade of 29th Division to gain further ground south of the ridge. After the enemy pulled back further on 20 and 21 August, the brigade pushed one section from each of C and D batteries 2,000yd forward to a position midway between Merris and Strazeele on the night of 22/23 August. The guns were in constant action over the next two days, firing in retaliation to the heavy hostile bombardments to which the infantry were being subjected. By 29 August the sight of every village behind enemy lines between Kemmel and Estaires on fire was a clear indication that the enemy was preparing to withdraw, and on 30 August the line on the divisional front was advanced by about a mile. The enemy was still withdrawing when LXIV Brigade's guns came out of action on 1 September, and three days later, the brigade marched north to return to the Ypres sector.

Throughout August the Allies had gradually recovered the ground lost since 21 March, taking 150,000 prisoners, 2,000 field guns and 13,000 machine guns in the process. The evacuation of Bailleul, Steenwerck and Nieppe at the end of the month allowed 31st Division to move forward several miles until on the night of 3/4 September 92 Brigade took over the front line between Ploegsteert and Nieppe.

At 8.35am on 4 September, patrols from 10/East Yorkshire began to push towards the Warnave River on a frontage of 2,000yd. On the right, B Company was unable to make any headway as enemy machine-gun fire swept across the open, flat countryside. Despite the absence of any artillery support, some degree of success was achieved on the left and centre of the attack where C and D companies had advanced the front line to around 500yd east of Le Rossignol and Gravier by 11am. A further attack was sent in at 3pm but was soon called off in the face of strong enemy opposition.

11/East Lancashire took over the line during the night and at 4.30am on 5 September patrols were sent out to probe the enemy's defences in front of the Warnave. By noon, Pontceau and Oosthove Farm had been occupied on the right and in the centre, while on the left the enemy had been driven out of Riga Farm. Further progress was prevented by heavy machine-gun fire from the farms and enclosures 400yd west of Soyer Farm.

The attack was renewed at 5pm under cover of a creeping barrage, the platoon occupying Riga Farm having first been withdrawn in order to allow the barrage to move on a north-south line. Z Company attacked on the left with

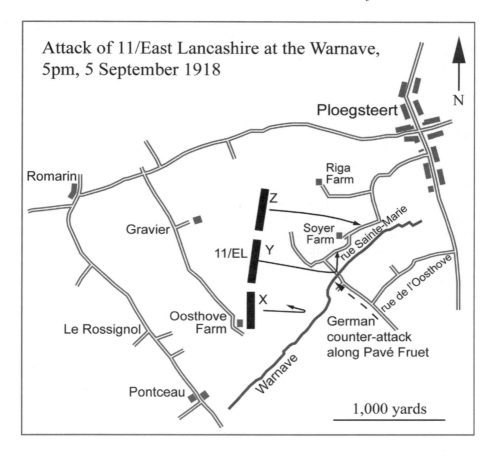

Attack of 11/East Lancashire at the Warnave,
5pm, 5 September 1918

Ploegsteert

N

Romarin

Riga
Farm

Z

Gravier

Soyer
Farm

rue Sainte-Marie

11/EL   Y

rue de l'Oosthove

X

Oosthove
Farm

German
counter-attack
along Pavé Fruet

Le Rossignol

Warnave

Pontceau

1,000 yards

Y Company in the centre and X Company less two platoons on the right. The
first waves moved forward as soon as the barrage fell. At the same time, heavy
enemy machine-gun fire broke out from the right flank. The two platoons
of X Company encountered thick wire almost immediately and lost touch with
Y Company when mounting casualties brought them to a halt. Elsewhere the
enemy quickly abandoned their forward positions, making a moderate stand
200yd to the rear, especially at Soyer Farm where ten prisoners and a machine
gun were taken after coming under enfilade fire from a Lewis-gun team commanded by Corporal Robert Walmsley, a 24-year-old railway clerk from Turton.
Supported by Lewis-gun fire, Y and Z companies reached the line of the
Warnave by 5.40pm and attempted to consolidate. Sergeant Roger Ireland, a
35-year-old house painter from Padiham, won the MM here, having led his
company forward to its objective after all its officers had become casualties.

The gap between X and Y companies had not been closed when the enemy
swiftly counter-attacked up the Pavé Fruet and gradually worked around the
right flank of Y Company killing or capturing the whole of the right platoon.

The remainder of Y Company fell back to the line of the rue Sainte-Marie but there held firm, driving back the enemy with Lewis-gun and rifle fire. Some twenty prisoners and two machine guns had been captured in the day. At least one officer and twenty-eight other ranks of 11/East Lancashire lost their lives; three officers are reported to have been taken prisoner in the battle: Second Lieutenants Harold Duckworth Walmsley, John Marshall and Thomas Crook Atkinson.

As the battalion handed over the line to 11/East Yorkshire during the night of 5/6 September, Soyer Farm slipped back into enemy hands. The loss of the farm was to prove costly, as it held out against repeated attacks by 11 and 10/East Yorkshire on the 6th and 7th.

The East Lancashires occupied the front line on three more days before being withdrawn to divisional reserve north of Hazebrouck on the night of 12/13 September. The battalion then remained at Hazebrouck until the 24th when it moved by train to Bailleul from where it marched to camp in the vicinity of Neuve Église.

Chapter 20

With Great Enthusiasm

Two days after being withdrawn to wagon lines at Vadencourt on 27 April, XLVIII Brigade began a gradual march northwards, passing through Bourdon, Gézaincourt, Lucheux, Grand-Rullecourt, Liencourt, Habarcq, Maroeuil and Anzin-Saint-Aubin to reach Bois de la Haie on 5 May. The brigade's wagon lines moved to Gouy-Servins four days later, while its batteries went into silent positions at Maroc from where they covered 24th Division north of Lens and in front of Loos.

The months of May and June passed largely without incident. Only three men were recorded as being wounded in the entire two-month period and although a large number of men were taken ill with influenza in the latter half of June, the epidemic lasted only a few days.

Shortly before the brigade left its silent role to relieve CXXVI Brigade in action, four bombs dropped at midnight between 6 and 7 July onto the hospital hut at the brigade's wagon lines killed two and wounded ten.

From 9 to 25 July, XLVIII Brigade's guns were engaged in harassing fire while also co-operating with occasional trench raids and firing on opportunistic targets. Beginning on 26 July, the brigade took part in a daily programme of wire-cutting and bombardment employed to mislead the enemy as to the location of the forthcoming British counter-offensive. The Chinese barrage continued until 2 August after which the brigade returned to a normal firing routine with C/XLVIII additionally employed on a number of 'instructional' shoots. On 28 August, XLVIII Brigade side-slipped southwards, replacing XCII Brigade in Liévin. C/XLVIII, less its forward section, was withdrawn to the brigade's wagon lines for training two days later; after the forward section had assisted in a barrage for a raid, it too was withdrawn on 31 August.

For both of the Accrington batteries, C/XLVIII and C/LXIV, the first three weeks or so of September 1918 were largely devoid of remarkable incidents.

C/XLVIII returned to action on 12 September at Liévin from where XLVIII Brigade was covering 73 Brigade (24th Division). Despite being in training, the battery had lost one man wounded on 5 September and a further seven, wounded by gas shells, four days later. During the next two weeks, C/XLVIII reported only one man wounded, though the battery came under occasional bombardment from HE and gas shells. At 5.05am on 27 September, A, C and D/XLVIII co-operated in a Chinese attack by 24th Division designed to delude the enemy as to the location of the next offensive.

LXIV Brigade had, on 4 September, left the Lys front, marching north-wards through Strazeele, Caestre, Eecke, Steenvoorde, Le Droogland and Houtkerque to reach Haandekot, north-west of Poperinghe. C/LXIV moved up into action over the night of 6/7 September, the guns taking up positions west-south-west of Ypres, 500yd south-west of the Cabaret Den Groenen Jager. Major Lyne returned to LXIV Brigade on 10 September, taking over command of A Battery ten days later. The guns were soon on the move again, taking up new positions on the north side of Ypres, near Salvation Corner, between 10 and 12 September. The stay was again a brief one, for the batteries were withdrawn to wagon lines at Hamhoek, on the north side of Poperinghe, over the nights of 18/19 and 19/20 September. On 25 and 26 September, the batteries returned to action 3 miles north of Ypres, 500yd east of Boesinghe, from where they covered the Belgian 6th Division.

A fresh series of Allied offensives opened on 26 September when more than 700 tanks supported by infantry of the French Fourth Army (General Henri Joseph Eugène Gouraud) and United States First Army (General John Joseph 'Black Jack' Pershing) struck on the Meuse–Argonne front. On the 27th, the Hindenburg Line near Cambrai was breached by the British First Army (Lieutenant General Henry Sinclair Horne) and Third Army (Byng). Then, at 5.30am on the 28th, following a 3-hour long bombardment, the Belgian army and British Second Army (Plumer) attacked at Ypres.

In front of LXIV Brigade, the infantry of the Belgian 6th Division made a rapid advance, reaching Poelcapelle by 6.45am. The brigade's four batteries moved forward at 10.30am and were back in action at Poelcapelle 4 hours later. As the battery positions came under heavy shellfire from the Passchendaele–Westroosebeke Ridge, there was a danger that the guns would have to be pulled back towards Langemarck. By 6pm however Passchendaele had been taken by the Belgians and the hostile shelling ceased. Two men of C/LXIV were reported killed by shellfire in the battery position east of Poelcapelle village. Before LXIV Brigade was ordered to withdraw to its wagon lines on 30 September, Moorslede, Westroosebeke, Staden and Dixmude had all been captured.

On the right of the main offensive at Ypres, 11/East Lancashire and 10/East Yorkshire had taken up assembly positions on Hill 63, north-west of Ploegsteert Wood, during the night of 27/28 September.

At 3pm on the 28th, 11/East Lancashire advanced down the eastern slopes of Hill 63 under the cover of a creeping barrage. The battalion immediately came under machine-gun fire from the right. Minutes later, German artillery opened fire. Despite sustaining heavy casualties while moving across ground

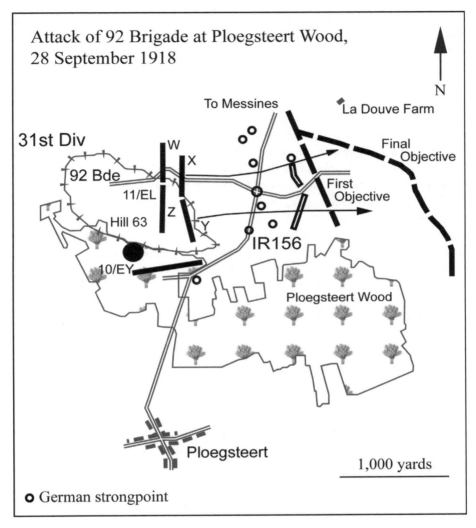

Attack of 92 Brigade at Ploegsteert Wood,
28 September 1918

N

To Messines · La Douve Farm

31st Div

W

X

Final
Objective

92 Bde

11/EL

First
Objective

Z

Hill 63

Y

IR156

10/EY

Ploegsteert Wood

Ploegsteert

1,000 yards

o German strongpoint

tangled with old shell holes, wire, trench systems and concrete emplacements, the East Lancashires managed to make good progress.

On the right of 11/East Lancashire, 10/East Yorkshire was attempting to work along the north-east edge of Ploegsteert Wood prior to pushing through the wood from north to south. In the event, all three company commanders became casualties in the first few minutes of the attack and, in the face of heavy machine-gun fire from the wood, the battalion made little headway.

At 3.34pm X and Y companies of 11/East Lancashire were seen nearing their first objectives. W and Z companies then took over the attack.

By 4pm W Company, led by Captain Duff, was nearing the final objective. Duff then ordered a further attack on La Douve Farm, which was taken and held against heavy counter-attacks. On the right, Z Company – whose commanding officer, Captain Endean, had been severely wounded by a bullet to the right shoulder – was still moving forward but more slowly. The exposed right flank of Z Company, though supported by artillery and machine-gun fire, was struggling to contain German counter-attacks 2 hours later. At 6.20pm the battalion was forced to form a defensive flank facing south along the high ground 400yd north of Ploegsteert Wood. The battalion front then stabilized on or ahead of the line of the final objective on the left, but 400yd short of it on the right. The enemy evacuated Ploegsteert Wood overnight.

The successful advance of 11/East Lancashire, made in spite of both flanks being exposed, came at a heavy cost of 358 killed, wounded and missing. Some fifty prisoners were taken, along with a field gun, seventeen machine guns, two trench mortars and an anti-tank rifle.

On 29 September, the British Fourth Army smashed through the Hindenburg Line. Ludendorff now saw no alternative but to seek an armistice.

In the Lens–Loos sector, 175 Brigade (58th Division) pushed up through Loos on 3 October, covered by the guns of XLVIII Brigade. B and C/XLVIII moved up into Lens on 6 October, followed four days later by A and D/XLVIII. By 13 October, the enemy had withdrawn to the line of the Lens Canal and all four batteries of XLVIII Brigade were able to move up 4½ miles, returning to action at Harnes from where they covered 173 Brigade. At 5.30am on the next day, the brigade fired a barrage in support of an operation to capture the chemical works and distillery which stood on the south bank of the Haute Deûle Canal. The brigade crossed the Lens Canal on 15 October, going into action at Courrières late in the afternoon. The following day saw the brigade march 3 miles to the south-east before returning to action in the evening at Dourges. Over 18–20 October, the brigade marched eastwards 15 miles to reach Bouvignies, where it came under the orders of 8th Division. A further march eastwards of 12 miles on 24 October brought the brigade east of Saint-Amand-les-Eaux to La Croisette where it covered 24 Brigade on the west bank of the Escaut River.

LXIV Brigade had on 3 October marched south through Poperinghe, Reninghelst and Locre to reach its new wagon lines east of Bailleul. By a happy coincidence, the brigade now came under the orders of 31st Division and it is far from fanciful to imagine that over the coming days some reunions took place between Pals and Howitzers. Following the attack on Ploegsteert Wood, 11/East Lancashire had been withdrawn to brigade support on Hill 63. On the day that LXIV Brigade marched south, 11/East Lancashire moved up to relieve 11/East Yorkshire at a forward line of posts on the west bank of the Lys River facing Deûlémont. During both night and day, patrols from the battalion sought to cross the river. 22-year-old Second Lieutenant George Pennington Richards and Sergeant Harry Pursglove, a 23-year-old joiner from Oswaldtwistle, were respectively awarded the MC and DCM for a daring daylight patrol on 4 October which succeeded under hostile trench-mortar and machine-gun fire in crossing the river by means of a half-demolished bridge.

After being relieved over the night of 4/5 October, 11/East Lancashire went briefly into brigade reserve at Neuve Église before 92 Brigade moved into divisional reserve on 6 October and the battalion went into camp near Bailleul. A short distance away from where 11/East Lancashire was using its time in camp for training, a 30yd firing range having been constructed for rifle and Lewis-gun practice, twenty-six men of LXIV Brigade's supply column had the misfortune to be inadvertently poisoned by gas at the hands of their own cook: the hapless individual confessed to the corps chemical adviser that he had used water from a shell hole both to wash dixies and to make tea.

11/East Lancashire returned to the front line in the Ploegsteert sub-sector on the night of 12/13 October. Patrols sent out over the following three days attempted to cross the Lys River and form bridgeheads but invariably encountered heavy machine-gun fire. On the night of 15/16 October, an unusual silence on the east bank of the river suggested that the enemy had withdrawn; patrols stole across the river at Pont Rouge and at a swing bridge 500yd farther south. The main body of the battalion crossed the river on the following day and, without encountering opposition, 11/East Lancashire was able to establish a line about 2½ miles east of the river, near the Quesnoy–Lille railway. The advance of 92 Brigade was continued on 17 October, 11/East Lancashire, now in brigade reserve, crossing the Deûle River in single file by means of a duckboard bridge which the battalion had repaired using floats found nearby. By the end of the day, the battalion was in the area of Bondues and closing in on the city of Tourcoing, having marched an additional 6 miles eastwards.

On 18 October, 11/East Lancashire had the honour of forming the advance guard of 92 Brigade for the march through Tourcoing. The battalion left Bondues at 5am and, with W Company leading the way, passed through the outpost line of 10/East Yorkshire. The battalion war diary records that no opposition was encountered in Tourcoing, the city being 'full of civilians who met the battalion with great enthusiasm'. Major Lyne described LXIV Brigade's entry into the city later in the day:

> It wasn't a march that we made; it was a triumphal entry in the largest sense, amid inhabitants wild with happiness. Mile after mile of frantic civilians, crying, shouting, cheering, and, as the column wound through, we were surrounded by people, kissing the horses, kissing the men, bringing out beer and coffee, clambering on to the guns and wagons with flowers, wreaths and flags.

Having cleared Tourcoing, 11/East Lancashire encountered stiffer resistance on the eastern side of Wattrelos, coming under artillery and machine-gun fire.

The resistance was gradually overcome, and the battalion was able to reach its objective for the day, a line running south from Hersaux to the Roubaix Canal. At Wattrelos four men from the battalion were killed: Sergeant Philip Foster, a 22-year-old spinning machine fitter from Accrington who had been one of the battalion's original E Company recruits, Lance Corporal James Gelling MM, a 20-year-old from Nelson, Walter Grimshaw, a 25-year-old miner from Clayton-le-Moors, and Horace Masser, a 19- or 20-year-old from Newport.

The battalion withdrew to billets between Tourcoing and Wattrelos on the morning of 19 October as 11/East Yorkshire passed through to take over as advance guard of 92 Brigade. With 92 Brigade going into divisional support on the following day, 93 Brigade having taken over the entire 31st divisional front, 11/East Lancashire remained in the Tourcoing area until 25 October carrying out platoon and company training.

After passing through Tourcoing, LXIV Brigade reached Lannoy in the afternoon of 19 October. A further 6 miles to the east, the enemy blew up the last bridge over the Escaut River at 11.30am on 20 October. Only two guns of B/LXIV, which had been detailed as the advanced guard battery of LXIV Brigade, went immediately into action, 1,000yd north-west of Estaimbourg and 2 miles west of the Escaut. C/LXIV returned to action only on 31 October, by which time 31st Division, having been ordered north, had been relieved by 40th Division.

As part of 31st Division's move north, 11/East Lancashire marched 20 miles via Mouscron and Courtrai on 25 October to reach Cuerne, impressing their Corps Commander en route with their turn out and discipline. The next day, the battalion took over a line of posts in the Ingoyghem sector. Although it proved possible to push the line about 700yd forward that same day, it was clear from the volume of hostile artillery and machine-gun fire that the enemy intended to make a stand on the line of the Escaut. Remarkably, despite a high proportion of enemy shells containing mustard gas, Belgian farmers continued to work their land, apparently oblivious to the dangers. The East Lancashires went into billets at Harlebeke on 29 October after being relieved, but only two days later were employed in clearing the battlefield near Ingoyghem; several prisoners were taken, and ten machine guns were among the materiel recovered.

Meanwhile, 25 miles to the south, east of Saint-Amand-les-Eaux, C/XLVIII was pushed forward towards the Escaut on 26 October as the advanced guard battery of XLVIII Brigade. At 10pm on the following day, the battery co-operated in an attempt by 24 Brigade to cross the river; eighteen men from the battery were wounded in the course of the day. 2/Devonshire (23 Brigade) succeeded in crossing the Escaut by rafts three days later. An enemy counter-attack on 31 October was broken up by fire from A, B and C/XLVIII as well as by machine-gun fire. On 3 November, the brigade was withdrawn to divisional reserve.

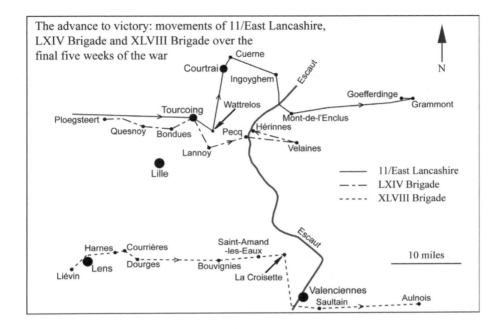

The advance to victory: movements of 11/East Lancashire,
LXIV Brigade and XLVIII Brigade over the
final five weeks of the war

N

——— 11/East Lancashire
– · – · LXIV Brigade
- - - - - XLVIII Brigade

10 miles

On 7 November, 11/East Lancashire moved up from Harlebeke into billets near Kloosterhoek, a tiny hamlet 1½ miles north-west of Avelghem; W Company then moved forward by night and crossed the Den Ryt Gracth Canal at Rugge. The further objective of establishing posts on the east bank of the Escaut proved impossible, not only because of the weight of hostile fire but also because the swiftly flowing river had overflowed its banks on the west side. Yet during the following night, heavy rifle and machine-gun fire from the east bank practically died away to nothing, and patrols sent out at dawn found that the enemy had withdrawn. Y Company crossed the Escaut by the girders of a broken bridge at Rugge, while X Company crossed by rafts at Escanaffles. The end now came quickly. By midday the battalion had covered up to 3 miles more, reaching Mont-de-l'Enclus where it was ordered to halt to allow 11/East Yorkshire to take up the advance. The continuation of the advance by 92 Brigade on 10 November saw 11/East Lancashire march 11 miles forward to billets in the area of Bosstraat. In the early hours of 11 November, the battalion was informed that the enemy had accepted terms on which the Allied governments were prepared to grant an armistice and that hostilities would cease at 11am. Lieutenant Colonel Rickman announced the news to a bewildered battalion as it paraded ready to advance at 9am. At 11am, the battalion had advanced about 6 miles through damp mist and fog but pressed on 4 miles more to reach the Dender River at Grammont. The battalion was later withdrawn to the village of Goefferdinge where it had established a line of posts by midnight.

In front of LXIV Brigade, the enemy had also evacuated the east bank of the Escaut over the night of 8/9 November. All four batteries of the brigade crossed the river at Pecq in the morning and marched on 8 miles to Velaines only to learn that 40th divisional artilley had intended the brigade to be billeted in the area of Hérinnes, just 1½ miles north-east of Pecq on the east bank of the Escaut. The brigade back-tracked, reaching Hérinnes at 11am on 11 November.

XLVIII Brigade had left divisional reserve on 6 November, marching about 12 miles south around the west side of Valenciennes to join 11th Division at Saultain on the 7th. The next day, the brigade advanced another 12 miles to the area of Eugnies, though the bad weather and poor condition of the roads delayed the arrival of some of the batteries until 9 November. The brigade had crossed the border and reached Aulnois, 12 miles farther on, when it received orders to cease firing at 11am on 11 November.

With the cessation of hostilities, the lives of the three units, C/XLVIII, C/LXIV and 11/East Lancashire, were coming to an end.

XLVIII Brigade remained at Aulnois until it returned to Saultain on 30 November, and to Saint-Amand-les-Eaux on 1 December. On the next day, the brigade moved to Péronne where it was billeted until the 19th when it moved on to La Tombe on the north-eastern outskirts of Tournai. Demobilization at La Tombe gradually reduced the brigade to a cadre by the end of March 1919.

Although LXIV Brigade's movements after the Armistice are less well documented, preliminary measures for demobilization were being taken as early as December 1918.

11/East Lancashire left the front two weeks after the Armistice, marching by easy stages to Saint-Omer via Menin, Ypres, Vlamertinghe and Poperinghe. It was at Saint-Omer that the King's Colour was presented to the battalion on 7 February 1919. The process of demobilization was by this time rapidly reducing the strength of the battalion, and Lieutenant Colonel Percy Leigh Ingpen DSO, having taken over command of the battalion on 15 April, had to seek permission to retain four NCOs, Sergeant Sydney Boothman, Company Quartermaster Sergeant D Moss, Warrant Officer II William Swallow MM and Corporal J Mitchell, to form a party to hand over the Colour to the mayor and corporation of Accrington on 18 October 1919. The battalion's life had come to an end.

Chapter 21

Remembrance

Accrington's contribution to the war effort had been considerable. The engineering works of Howard and Bullough had been converted to the manufacture of artillery shells; the chemical works of William Blythe were producing nitric and sulphuric acids which were used by one of the company's adjacent subsidiaries, Coteholme Chemical, to manufacture the explosive picric acid. In the first few days following the declaration of war, Accrington had bade farewell to as many as 500 reservists, 100 men of the St John Ambulance Brigade, the Accrington Company of 5/East Lancashire, and the Church Battery of the East Lancashire Territorial Artillery. Then in the five weeks of the war before recruitment for the Accrington Pals began, more than 500 men volunteered for Army service, finding themselves posted to regiments such as the Cameronians (Scottish Rifles) which had little or no connection to their home town. And, as we have seen, volunteers continued to come forward in large numbers when John Harwood raised the Accrington and Burnley Howitzers in the early months of 1915.

Yet it is generally only the Accrington Pals who are remembered when there is any discussion of Accrington's role in the First World War. The regulars, the reservists, the territorials, the ambulance men, those who rushed to enlist in the heady days of the opening weeks of the war, and the Howitzers, are largely forgotten.

The explanation for this selective remembrance is not hard to find. It lies in the impact felt from one cataclysmic day, the opening day of the Battle of the Somme, 1 July 1916. The first 23 months of the war had accounted for the deaths of about 165 men from Accrington, an average of roughly 7 fatalities per month of the war; the total casualty numbers for Accrington in that period would have approximated to 500. While these might seem to be high numbers, they were by no means exceptional for a British town with a population of 45,000. All that changed in the space of 10 minutes in the morning of 1 July 1916. It was a fact made clear in a lengthy newspaper article of 1919 which reviewed the part played by Accrington in what was then known as 'The Great War':

> As the news came through to Accrington, as one bright young life
> after another was known to have passed, there was a period of agony

and mourning which this district had never before experienced. Never again, though from the district men had gone forth to fall in every unit, in every land, was the sorrow so acutely compressed within the narrow limits of the community.

Even so, the number of service-related fatalities among Accrington men in 1916 was met or exceeded in both 1917 and 1918 (see figure below). Overall, the casualty rate among Accrington's servicemen was about 36 per cent, a number comparable to that for the country as a whole. Equally – at least in literal terms – the casualties of 1 July 1916 hardly amounted to a 'lost generation' in Accrington, the total number representing perhaps 5 per cent of the men in the town who were of recruiting age. The statistics though tell only a part of the story. The men who were killed or maimed – whether physically or mentally – on that fateful day accounted for a disproportionately high share of the bravest and best of a generation; Accrington lost many of its brightest hopes for the future.

The selective remembrance of the Accrington Pals happened despite the best post-war efforts of both John Harwood and Accrington Town Council to see that all the town's dead were honoured equally. Following the ceremonial handover on 18 October 1919 of the King's Colour of 11/East Lancashire to the mayor and corporation of Accrington, the Colour Party and officials were invited by the mayor, Councillor David Walton Moffitt, to lunch at the Railway Hotel. When it came time for John Harwood to make a speech, he took the opportunity to make a point concerning remembrance:

Accrington's war dead by month, 1914–19 (see note to p. 208).

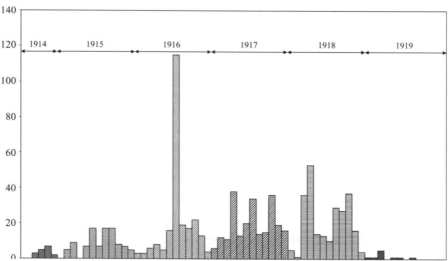

Wooler:	'There will be some genuine. I don't say I agree with all, and we have to question them in a reasonable way, and draw our own conclusions.'
Harwood:	'We don't want sermons here.'
Wooler:	'I dare say it is sometimes overdrawn, but we must give reasonable consideration to their cases.'
Aitken:	'How long have you held these views?'
Applicant:	'I have been an earnest Bible student for about two years.'
Aitken:	'How long have you held the views against war?'
Applicant:	'Since I studied the Bible carefully and particularly during the last few months.'
Harwood:	'I think it a waste of time to argue. We know the Bible probably as well as you and your opinion and ours don't coincide.'

The application for exemption was refused.

John Harwood was to receive no honour from the government in recognition of his extraordinary work to support the war effort. It can only be supposed that political reasons lay behind the negligence.

On 17 December 1923, just four weeks after the death of his wife, Sarah, and three days after his 76th birthday, John Harwood died at his home of Whalley House in Accrington of heart failure brought on by acute bronchitis.

Thomas Yates Harwood, the elder grandson of John Harwood, served as adjutant to 12/East Lancashire from May to September 1916 before being posted overseas to join 1/East Lancashire. He saw action in the Battle of the Somme at Le Transloy in October 1916 and in the Battle of Arras in April 1917. From December 1916 to February 1917 he commanded the battalion's A Company. After being taken ill with influenza on 26 April 1917 he was diagnosed as suffering from heart disease. Following seven months' convalescence, Harwood was posted to 3/East Lancashire at Marske, Yorkshire and remained with the reserve battalion for the rest of the war. Harwood had married 25-year-old Ida Belle Bradley on 29 September 1915 at Accrington; the couple had one son, John Bradley, born in 1921. In civilian life, Harwood worked in the banking profession. He died at the Victoria Hospital, Blackpool on 14 March 1970, aged 78, of a cerebellar haemorrhage brought on by high blood pressure.

The younger grandson of John Harwood, **John Richard Harwood**, was taken ill with septic dermatitis on 26 June 1917 while serving as a gunner with C/XLVIII. On recovering he joined CLXXXIX Brigade on 14 October 1917 but was invalided to England after being wounded by a gas shell on 7 November. He returned to France in March 1918 and served with CLVI Brigade throughout the remainder of the war. Harwood married Elsie Holden, a 24-year-old school teacher, on 30 April 1921 at Accrington; the couple had two children, John Alan Douglas and Sheila Noreen. Although Harwood had returned to his profession as a mechanical draughtsman after the war, he later described himself as a commercial traveller. He died aged 59 on 31 May 1955 at hospital in Lytham St Anne's.

Of the two great-nephews of John Harwood who served as officers with the Howitzers, the elder, **Edmund Mills Harwood**, gained his aviator's certificate from the Royal Aero Club on 18 September 1917 and ended the war with the rank of captain. Harwood married 26-year-old Ruby Madeline Thomas at Penarth on 15 November 1921, the couple departing shortly afterwards for India. They enjoyed only a short time together, for Harwood died in hospital at Bombay on 11 November 1923, at the age of only 29.

The younger great-nephew, **Frank Harwood**, was invalided back to Britain after being wounded on 22 April 1917, the eve of the second Battle of the Scarpe. He remained unfit for GS throughout the remainder of the war, and was granted six months' leave to India in February 1918, departing on 28 March. He relinquished his commission owing to ill health on 18 June 1919 with the rank of lieutenant. On 14 September 1920, he married Valérie Marie Josèphe Gernez, the 20-year-old daughter of an Arras doctor, Armand Benoît Charles Gernez, with whom Harwood had been billeted. The couple had three children, Joan, Edmund and Philip Mills Armand. A merchant in Indian goods in civilian life, Harwood died of a heart attack at the age of 47 when coming off duty with the Home Guard at Purley on 23 February 1944. Valérie died on 8 December 1988 at the age of 89.

Aside from one week's home leave in January 1917, **Percy Allsup** saw continuous service with 11/East Lancashire until he was sent home to recover from the effects of mustard gas in early August 1917. After hospitalization in Scotland, Allsup passed through Sergeants' School before returning to the Western Front. In the remaining months of the war, he survived a wound from machine-gun fire sustained while on night patrol. Allsup returned to civilian life in March 1919 to become a police officer in Blackburn. After marrying in January 1922, he and his wife Annie joined his brothers Arthur, Charles and James in Rhode Island, United States where the Allsup family continues to flourish to this day.

Harold Bancroft returned to Britain on 10 November 1917 after he had been wounded by a gas shell nine days earlier. A Medical Board held at Leith War Hospital, Seafield on 19 December reported that his injuries had included conjunctivitis, vomiting, epigastric pains, first-degree burns and a shell splinter in his leg. There is no record of his returning to active service in the war and, after demobilization in February 1919, he resumed his career with Howard and Bullough. He travelled extensively as a foreign representative for the firm and set up the first textile factory for which Howard and Bullough's supplied the machinery in Australia. During the Second World War, Bancroft played a leading role in the formation of the Home Guard in Accrington and was its first commanding officer. On 9 January 1946, he married Kathleen Mary Hargreaves-Wilson, who was herself a company director. Following his marriage, he became a director and works manager at Taylor and Wilson Limited of Clayton-le-Moors. Bancroft died at his home in Accrington at the age of 61 on 6 October 1951 after an illness that had lasted about fourteen weeks.

After being seriously wounded on the night of 7/8 March 1917, **Reginald St John Beardsworth Battersby** underwent an operation at No. 1 General Hospital, Étretat in which his left leg was amputated at the upper thigh. While convalescing at Devonport Military Hospital in November 1917, he received a letter from the War Office informing him that there was no alternative but that he should relinquish his commission 'on account of ill-health, caused by wounds'. Whereas most would have been glad to accept the decision without argument, the 17-year-old Battersby replied that he would be getting an artificial limb 'about Christmas', that he was 'quite fit in every other way' and that he wished 'to remain in until the end of the war'. Battersby won his battle with the authorities and, after being passed fit for office work on 13 March 1918, he joined the Royal Engineers (Transportation Branch) Record Office in Tavistock Square, London five days later. Following his eventual demobilization on 20 September 1920, Battersby joined his father's vocation, becoming vicar of Chittoe, near Devizes, in 1933. During the Second World War, he organized the Home Guard at Chittoe before serving as chaplain to the Royal Marines at Chatham, an appointment that led to his being made a lifetime honorary member of the Royal Marines Officers Mess. After the war, he returned to his parish at Chittoe but remained active in Civil Defence and was awarded the Civil Defence Medal. Battersby died in 1977 at the age of 77.

Harry Cecil Bloor was wounded in front of the enemy wire on 1 July 1916. He lay in a shell hole until night fell on 2 July, some 38 hours after being hit. He crawled slowly backwards, eventually dropping into the British front line to find it still filled with wounded Pals. The next morning he was seen by an officer and told 'if you want to get out of here, lad, crawl!' It was not until the night of 3/4 July that he finally had his wounds treated at a CCS. Bloor was discharged from the Army in June 1917 and emigrated to Canada before re-settling in Accrington in 1934. The following year he made the first of many pilgrimages to Serre, the last of which was in 1974. Whenever possible, he stood on the site of the British front line at 7.30am on 1 July. Bloor died on 1 January 1976 at the age of 77, and was buried in Accrington Cemetery.

Robert (Bob) Bullen was severely wounded in the right hand and leg by machine-gun fire on 1 July 1916. The *Burnley Express and Advertiser* of 12 July 1916 reported that Bullen lay on the battlefield for two days before he was carried back to the British lines. Following amputation of his leg, he was invalided home and transferred to Huddersfield Military Hospital where his parents were able to visit him on Sunday, 9 July. At 8 o'clock on the following morning, Bullen died of his wounds. He lies buried in Padiham Cemetery.

Tom Coady waited to go over the top on the morning of 1 July 1916 alongside Frank Thomas. In a letter that Thomas wrote a few weeks later, he described how Coady went to his death:

> We chatted all the time as if there was nothing going on, but I think he knew his end was near. Five minutes before the order came to go he said to me – 'We will just say a prayer' – and we did. Then in the last half minute we shook hands and these were the last words I heard him say – 'God bless you, Frank, and if we die we will die fighting'.

Coady lies buried in Queens Cemetery at Serre.

Although he would never be free of the disability caused by the bullet wound to his right shoulder on 28 September 1918, **Bart Endean** became a highly skilled stonemason after returning to civilian life. He died on 28 December 1986 at the age of 93.

Percy Harrison Fawcett left CLVIII Brigade on 4 December 1916 to take command of 48th Heavy Group, Royal Garrison Artillery. In February 1917 he was appointed Counter Battery Staff Officer to VI Corps, a position that he retained until his demobilization with the rank of lieutenant colonel two years later. In the course of the war, Fawcett had been awarded the DSO, and on four occasions had been mentioned in dispatches. With his Army career once more at an end, Fawcett returned to his quest for ancient South American civilizations. Although he was brought close to bankruptcy by two aborted expeditions in 1920/1, he was able to raise the finance for a further expedition once the North American Newspaper Alliance agreed to purchase the story rights. On 25 January 1925, Fawcett and his 21-year-old son, Jack, together with Jack's closest friend, 23-year-old Raleigh Rimell, reached Rio de Janeiro on board the steamship *Vauban*. By early March, the trio had moved on to Cuiabá, the capital of Mato Grosso, 1,000 miles deep into the continent. The expedition left Cuiabá on 20 April, heading north to reach the settlement of Bakairí Post on 15 May. A fortnight later, Fawcett wrote to his wife, Nina, that he was at Dead Horse Camp, 'the spot where my horse died in 1920: only his white bones remain. My calculations anticipate contact with the Indians in about a week or ten days.' Nothing further was ever heard of Fawcett's party.

Cecil Douglas Gay joined 10/East Lancashire at Wareham on 4 September 1916, two months after being wounded in the neck at Serre with 11/East Lancashire. He remained at Wareham until he reported for duty with 1/East Lancashire on 18 September 1917, the day before the battalion entrained for the Ypres salient. During the Battle of Broodseinde on 4 October, Gay won the MC for organizing and leading an attack to capture an enemy strong point. On the night of 17/18 August 1918, Gay – by this time promoted to the acting rank of captain – was in the front line on the edge of the Nieppe Forest when he was caught in the explosion from a direct hit by an enemy trench mortar. After receiving early treatment for severe wounds to the legs and hands at a CCS at Aire-sur-la-Lys, Gay was taken by canal barge to Calais. On 28 August he was returned to Britain and admitted to the Prince of Wales' Hospital for Officers in Marylebone, London. He was still convalescing at Marylebone when the war ended on 11 November. Following his demobilization with the rank of captain on 25 April 1919, Gay returned to Trinity College, Cambridge to study engineering. In 1924 he joined Alfred Herbert Limited and shortly afterwards founded with Axel Wickman the Coventry machine tool company of A C Wickman. He married Charlotte Rose in 1930, and eight years later was able to purchase Nailcote Hall at Berkswell for his family, which by then included a son and daughter. During the Second World War, Gay worked closely with the Ministry of Supply with responsibility for meeting the country's machine-tool needs. After retiring from Wickman's in 1945 to take up farming, Gay served for many years on the board of governors of Studley Agricultural College and as a magistrate at Coventry and Solihull. In 1962 he sold Nailcote to Wickman's, but continued to live nearby for the remainder of his life. In late life, as a widower, he married Rosa Nancy Plumb. Gay died of heart failure at his home in Berkswell on 26 October 1980 at the age of 85.

Following the onset of cardiac problems, **Gerald Thomas (Gerry) Gorst** was invalided back to Britain in November 1916. Once pronounced fit for light duty, he became an instructor with No. 15 Officer Cadet Battalion at Hare Hall, Gidea Park, Romford before being released for service in the Colonial Office with effect from 24 April 1918. After leaving the Colonial Office in August 1919, Gorst was employed as a clerk with N M Rothschild & Sons until he decided to study law. He was admitted as a solicitor on 1 March 1924, and shortly after became a partner in the firm of Reynolds & Sons specializing in commercial law. On 30 June 1928 he married 26-year-old Mary Katherine Joyce Tolcher at Thurlestone. While serving as an air-raid warden for the Borough of Richmond in the summer of 1940, Gorst successfully applied for registration in the Army Officers' Emergency Reserve. His application was supported by his uncle, Charles Lloyd Carson, and by N L Macaskie, a King's Counsel. Macaskie described Gorst as,

> a man of singular charm, good temper and impurturbability. I can vouch for his integrity, competence and reliability. If he has a fault it is that he is inclined to remain in the background and not to assert himself, possibly the defect of a somewhat gentle nature. He

is not weak, on the contrary he follows unswervingly the path he sets out on.

On 5 August 1940, Gorst was commissioned into 10/Devonshire (Home Defence) at Plymouth with the rank of lieutenant. A little under two years later, he was posted to 22/Devonshire (Home Guard) for duty as adjutant with the acting rank of captain, a promotion that was confirmed on 17 October 1942. From 8 December 1942 until his demobilization on 24 August 1944, he was on attachment to 17/Devonshire (Home Guard). Gorst died at his home in St Buryan, Cornwall on 18 February 1968 at the age of 72.

Fred Hacking died at his home in Jubilee Street, Oswaldtwistle on 15 September 1915 of pneumonia after returning home to attend the funeral of his mother, Susannah.

In a letter to his parents and sisters that **Samuel Davies (Sam) Hardman** wrote on 30 June 1916, he asked them to keep their hearts up if they didn't hear from him for a while. He was killed in action on the following morning and lies buried in Queens Cemetery at Serre.

Just as he expected, **William Hill** returned to 11/East Lancashire after only a short stay in hospital to recover from the wound he sustained during the fighting of 11–13 April 1918. On 29 June 1918 he died of wounds and lies buried at Longuenesse (St Omer) Souvenir Cemetery.

Although wounded in the neck, arm and hand with 11/East Lancashire near Meteren on 21 May 1918, **Ernest David Kay** had less than one month's recuperation before being pronounced fit for GS after three weeks' leave. Kay was transferred to the newly formed Royal Army Ordnance Corps and took part in the Baltic mission against the Bolsheviks before leaving service on 21 December 1919. Kay set himself up as an importer, bought a wool-merchandizing firm and for several years owned a cutlery works in Sheffield. In 1925, he was first elected as a director of Burnley Football Club; despite losing his seat four years later, he re-joined the board in 1937 and was chairman from 1948 to 1952. Kay died in hospital at the age of 80 on 10 June 1956.

Wilfred (Wilf) Kitchen was killed in action with 11/East Lancashire on 28 June 1918. He lies buried in Aval Wood Military Cemetery, Vieux-Berquin.

Otto Lais survived the war to become a prominent artist. He was aged 90 when he died at Merbeck in Germany on 5 March 1988.

George Lee was promoted to regimental quartermaster sergeant in October 1914 and continued to serve with 11/East Lancashire until, suffering from rheumatism, he was invalided home from France on 25 May 1916. After leaving hospital, he spent short spells with both 10 and 12/East Lancashire before being discharged from the Army on 10 August. After the war, Lee returned to the West Country where he died at Devonport on 4 August 1936 at the age of 75.

Chapter 4

page

25–6   'practically the whole Company had been destroyed': *Papers of Brigadier General H C Rees,* vol. 1 of typed transcript of memoirs, IWM 77/179/1 (hereafter Rees V1), p. 38.

26   'I got away with about a dozen men': *ibid.,* p. 39.

26   'I confess to being very badly shaken': *ibid.,* p. 40.

26   'advance without delay and deliver a counter-attack': *Official History of the Great War DVD-ROM, Military Operations France and Belgium* (The Naval & Military Press, 2010), 1914, Vol. 2, p. 323.

26–7   'man-handled the gun out on to the road': Rees V1, pp. 42–3.

27   awarded the Distinguished Service Order (DSO): *London Gazette,* 1 December 1914, p. 10187.

27   'there was nothing to stop them': Rees V1, p. 43.

27   'standing in masses in the rear of the German front': Haig, p. 323.

Chapter 5

page

28   'misapprehension and mistake of a man or two': *Accrington Observer and Times,* 26 September 1914, p. 8.

28   the entire battalion of 1,100 men was present: *Accrington Observer and Times,* 29 September 1914, p. 2.

28   with Harwood's agreement, remained at home: William Turner, *Pals: The 11th (Service) Battalion (Accrington) East Lancashire Regiment* (Wharncliffe, 1987) (hereafter Turner, 1987), p. 40.

28   outdated Lee-Metfords: *Accrington Observer and Times,* 10 October 1914, p. 8.

29   from 8.30am until 9.30pm day after day: *Accrington Observer and Times,* 10 November 1914, p. 2.

29   'received with the upmost pleasure': *Accrington Observer and Times,* 29 September 1914, p. 2.

29   expressed their anger: *Accrington Observer and Times,* 3 October 1914, p. 3.

29   'practically all fully equipped': *Accrington Observer and Times,* 8 December 1914, p. 2.

29   Kitchener blue: Simkins, p. 263.

29–30   'ten weeks without uniform': *Chorley Guardian,* 28 November 1914, p. 5.

30   3s 11d per day with back pay: *ibid.*

30   sanctioned an allowance of 8s 6d: Simkins, p. 261.

30   a grievance concerning their transport: *Accrington Observer and Times,* 12 December 1914, p. 6.

30   'we want to be there': quoted in *Accrington Gazette,* 7 November 1914, p. 5.

30   'echoed through the woodlands': Sayer, p. 50.

31   'a small hot-pot for one of the men': *Accrington Observer and Times,* 28 November 1914, p. 5.

31   all the evidence pointed to suicide: *Accrington Observer and Times,* 21 November 1914, p. 5.

31   twenty-two officers gazetted to the battalion: *Accrington Observer and Times,* 14 November 1914, p. 7.

31   resigned his position: *Accrington Gazette,* 7 November 1914, p. 5.

31   between 1,600 and 1,700 men from Accrington alone had enlisted: *Accrington Gazette,* 14 November 1914, p. 5.

31   thirty or forty men had enlisted: *Accrington Gazette,* 12 December 1914, p. 5.

32   gratefully accepted: *Accrington Observer and Times,* 26 December 1914, p. 4.

32   a concert at Accrington Town Hall: *ibid.*

32   'Following the Christmas break': *Accrington Gazette,* 2 January 1915, p. 8.

33   wounded soldiers from Baxenden Military Hospital: *Accrington Gazette,* 9 January 1915, p. 5.

33   a local artillery brigade: *Accrington Gazette*, 16 January 1915, p. 4.
33   the period from 1 to 5 July 1916: *Soldiers Died in the Great War 1914–1919*, CD ROM Version 1.1 (The Naval & Military Press, 1998).
33   the deaths of two Pals from pneumonia: *Accrington Gazette*, 6 February 1915, p. 4.
33   eight more officers had been appointed: *Accrington Observer and Times*, 13 February 1915, p. 7.
33   three promotions had been announced: *Accrington Gazette*, 6 February 1915, p. 4.
33   official instructions were received: *Accrington Gazette*, 20 February 1915, p. 5.
33   hosted by Mr James Sumner: *Chorley Guardian*, 20 February 1915, p. 8.
34   unable to gain admission: *Accrington Gazette*, 27 February 1915, p. 4.
34   the time came for the battalion to leave its home towns: for newspaper reports of the battalion's departure see: *Accrington Gazette*, 27 February 1915, p. 8; *Accrington Observer and Times*, 27 February 1915, p. 5; *Burnley Express and Advertiser*, 24 February 1915, p. 2; *Burnley News*, 24 February 1915, p. 3; *Chorley Guardian*, 27 February 1915, p. 6.
34   'part and parcel of the life of the town': *Accrington Observer and Times*, 27 February 1915, p. 5.
35   'the billets were excellent': quoted in *ibid.*
35   'a time of our lives': undated postcard sent by Fred Hacking to his aunt, Mrs Jamieson of Accrington.
35–6   'all the people in Carnarvon speak Welsh': letter from Sam Hardman to his parents and sisters, dated 3 March 1915.
36   the home of the Ensor sisters: *1911 Census for England and Wales*.
36   'a piano in the front room': quoted in *Accrington Observer and Times*, 1 May 1915, p. 7.
36   'The place is so dead': *Accrington Observer and Times*, 13 March 1915, p. 6.
36–7   'We have been here over a fortnight now': *Accrington Observer and Times*, 20 March 1915, p. 6.
37   'We have a grand field for drilling in': *Accrington Observer and Times*, 2 March 1915, p. 1.
37   warned their girls not to be seen talking to a soldier: *Accrington Observer and Times*, 20 March 1915, p. 8.
37   'association of our girls with the soldiers': quoted in *Accrington Observer and Times*, 27 March 1915, p. 5.
37   Lieutenant Colonel Arthur Wilmot Rickman: Army service record of Arthur Wilmot Rickman, TNA WO 374/57451.
37   a lively personality: private communication from Neil Erskine.
37   the marriage broke down: *The Times*, 15 October 1915, p. 3; *The Times*, 9 May 1916, p. 4.
38   'We have got a new Colonel this week': undated letter from Robert Bullen to his brother, Jack.
38   A typical day: *Accrington Observer and Times*, 13 March 1915, p. 5.
38   'under the influence of Liquor': Army service record of Edward Jones, TNA WO 339/22590.
38   'an opportunity of redeeming his fault': *ibid.*; Jones eventually resigned his commission – the resignation was gazetted on 30 July 1917 – and was subsequently posted to the Army Service Corps.
38   'their behaviour is excellent': quoted in *Accrington Observer and Times*, 20 March 1915, p. 6.
38   the excellent conduct of the men: *Accrington Observer and Times*, 20 March 1915, p. 8.
38   'better at drill than football': quoted in *Accrington Observer and Times*, 16 March 1915, p. 2.
38   an XI drawn entirely from Z Company: *Accrington Observer and Times*, 6 April 1915, p. 2; the XI were James Sullivan, Charles Hargreaves, William Ingham, James Kendall, Benjamin Duckworth, William Boden, James O'Mara, Willie Riley, Ernest Clegg, Francis Kendall and Samuel Wilson.

38   wins of 3–2 and 3–0: *Accrington Observer and Times*, 13 March 1915, p. 5; *ibid.*, 20 March 1915, p. 8.

38   a promising flyweight: Mike Sherrington, *Despatch*, Issue 3 (May 2009), pp. 2–3 (Western Front Association, Lancashire North Branch) at www.wfanlancs.co.uk/despatch/May09 PDFs/FinalMay09.pdf.

39   his impressions of George Formby Snr: *Accrington Observer and Times*, 18 July 1916, p. 1.

39   mock night-time attacks: *Accrington Observer and Times*, 6 April 1915, p. 2.

39   a shopping list of field instruments: *Accrington Gazette*, 10 April 1915, p. 1.

39   'into a bog two or three feet away': *Accrington Gazette*, 20 March 1915, p. 4.

39–40 'much pleased': quoted in *Accrington Observer and Times*, 10 April 1915, p. 5.

40   a concert provided for the Pals: *ibid.*; *Accrington Gazette*, 10 April 1915, p. 5.

40   the funeral of a young woman: *Accrington Observer and Times*, 6 April 1915, p. 2.

40   'making rapid progress with our training': letter from Richard Ormerod to his sister, Polly, 16 April 1915.

40   'more work these last three weeks': quoted in *Accrington Observer and Times*, 24 April 1915, p. 5.

40   exceptionally clean and polished appearance: quoted in *Accrington Observer and Times*, 1 May 1915, p. 7.

41   'a sound of revelry by night': *Accrington Observer and Times*, 15 May 1915, p. 5.

41   posted to the reserve company: *ibid.*, p. 5; Frank Birtwistle, Thomas Yates Harwood, Charles Douglas Haywood, Edward Jones, James Ramsbottom and William Slinger were probably also posted to the reserve company at this time.

41   recent experience of trench warfare: Army service record of William Faulkner, TNA WO 339/27526.

41   a chance encounter: private communication from Diccon Nelson-Roberts.

41   'kissed him in full view of the crowd': *Accrington Observer and Times*, 15 May 1915, p. 5.

Chapter 6
page

42   gained no appreciable ground at a cost of 90,000 casualties: John Keegan, *The First World War* (Hutchinson, 1998) (hereafter Keegan), p. 197.

42   not be surpassed even in 1917: Shelford Bidwell and Dominick Graham, *Fire-power: The British Army: Weapons & Theories of War 1904–1945* (Pen & Sword, 2004), p. 73.

42   accomplished its destructive work well: General Sir Martin Farndale KCB, *History of the Royal Regiment of Artillery: Western Front 1914–18* (The Royal Artillery Institution, 1986) (hereafter Farndale), pp. 88–90.

42   into Neuve-Chapelle at about 8.50am: *Official History of the Great War DVD-ROM, Military Operations France and Belgium* (The Naval & Military Press, 2010), 1915, Vol. 1, p. 96.

43   able to move across no-man's-land: *ibid.*, p. 100.

43   blown out of its position by friendly artillery fire: Nicholson, p. 126.

43   'a reminder of what an advance really is': *Accrington Observer and Times*, 15 May 1915, p. 12.

43   'Isn't it good news': letter from Gerry Gorst to his sister, Betty, 13 March 1915.

44   'the last place I expected or wanted to be in': letter from Gerry Gorst to his sister, Betty, *c.* 20 March 1915.

44   'there aren't enough men born to clear Belgium': *ibid.*

44   The experience of 2/East Lancashire: Nicholson, pp. 130–2.

44   only 20 per cent of the intensity: Robin Prior and Trevor Wilson, *Command on the Western Front: The Military Career of Sir Henry Rawlinson 1914–1918* (Pen & Sword, 2004) (hereafter Prior and Wilson), p. 85.

44–5 just over 11,000 casualties: *ibid.*, p. 91.

45   losses had mounted to 100,000 men: Terraine, 1983, p. 68.
45   paralysis of the extensor muscles: Army service record of Gerald Thomas Gorst,
      Ministry of Defence.

Chapter 7
page
46   an invitation from the War Office: *Accrington Gazette*, 16 January 1915, p. 4.
46   an offer to raise a howitzer artillery brigade: *Accrington Observer and Times*,
      23 January 1915, p. 6.
46   'grateful acceptance': *Accrington Gazette*, 30 January 1915, p. 5.
46   not alone in responding: see list of *Locally Raised Units*, TNA PRO 30/57/73.
46   unable to find the time: *Accrington Observer and Times*, 2 February 1915, p. 2.
47   a number of provisional appointments: *Accrington Gazette*, 6 February 1915, p. 4.
47   Thomas Purvis Ritzema: *Accrington Observer and Times*, 9 February 1915, p. 2; Army
      service record of Thomas Purvis Ritzema, TNA WO 374/57794.
47   dental treatment: *Accrington Observer and Times*, 13 February 1915, p. 6.
47   'men of the mechanic class': *Accrington Gazette*, 13 February 1915, p. 5.
48   John Richard Harwood: Army service record of John Richard Harwood, TNA WO
      363/H1356.
48   should line the streets: *Accrington Observer and Times*, 20 February 1915, p. 6.
48   issued with new khaki overcoats and caps: *Accrington Gazette*, 27 February 1915,
      p. 4.
48   the fourth battery was nearing completion: *Accrington Observer and Times*,
      27 February 1915, p. 6.
48   a missionary in British Columbia: *Burnley Express and Advertiser*, 24 February 1915,
      p. 5.
49   Harwood refused to rest: *Accrington Observer and Times*, 27 February 1915, p. 6.
49   'not a battalion or a brigade of its own': *Accrington Observer and Times*, 20 March
      1915, p. 6.
49   Accrington claimed to have supplied the ammunition column: *Accrington
      Observer and Times*, 13 March 1915, p. 11.
49   1,300 of the 2,000 men: *Accrington Gazette*, 12 June 1915, p. 7.
50   'our hearts were in the same place as theirs': *Accrington Observer and Times*,
      13 March 1915, p. 6.
50   'try running up the breast of Moleside': *Accrington Observer and Times*, 27 March
      1915, p. 6.
50   the route march to Whalley: *Accrington Observer and Times*, 3 April 1915, p. 6.
51   'with about fifty a side': *Accrington Observer and Times*, 1 May 1915, p. 6.
51   'very smart brigade': *Accrington Gazette*, 17 April 1915, p. 4.
51   'neither child nor elder escaped the contagion': *Accrington Observer and Times*,
      24 April 1915, p. 6.
52   increased its complement to about 148 men: see the list of officers and men of
      B Battery published in the *Accrington Observer and Times* of 22 May 1915, p. 12.
52   'in the most approved music hall style': *Accrington Observer and Times*, 22 May 1915,
      p. 12.
52   absent on munitions work: *Accrington Gazette*, 29 May 1915, p. 4.
52   'hearty cheers': *Accrington Gazette*, 5 June 1915, p. 6.
52   'I shall come to see you at Weeton': quoted in *Accrington Gazette*, 12 June 1915, p. 6.
52   large numbers of well-wishers: *Burnley Express and Advertiser*, 9 June 1915, p. 5.
52   arrived by motor car: *Accrington Observer and Times*, 15 June 1915, p. 2.
53   'Though little had been said': quoted in *Accrington Gazette*, 12 June 1915, p. 7.
53   resigned the presidency: *Accrington Gazette*, 3 July 1915, p. 3.
53   assistance in raising a pioneer battalion: *Accrington Observer and Times*, 14 August
      1915, p. 7.

53–4   **a letter written to relatives in Accrington by Robert Higgin**: *Accrington Observer and Times*, 26 June 1915, p. 5.

54   **jibbed, reared and kicked**: *Accrington Observer and Times*, 13 July 1915, p. 1.

55   **an eagerly anticipated half-day holiday**: *Accrington Observer and Times*, 10 July 1915, p. 5.

55   **a great number of visitors**: *Accrington Observer and Times*, 27 July 1915, p. 1.

55   **bantam battalions**: see Martin Middlebrook, *Your Country Needs You* (Pen & Sword, 2000), p. 75.

56   **'rang out a clarion note'**: *Accrington Observer and Times*, 7 August 1915, p. 7.

56   **'soon after darkness has come'**: *Accrington Observer and Times*, 24 August 1915, p. 2.

56   **'a roaring trade'**: *Accrington Observer and Times*, 17 August 1915, p. 2.

57   **'it is not bad'**: *Accrington Gazette*, 25 September 1915, p. 4.

57   **said to have made a good impression**: *Accrington Observer and Times*, 4 September 1915, p. 7.

57   **previously commanded XXX Brigade**: Lieutenant Colonel H M Davson, *The History of the 35th Division in the Great War* (Sifton Praed, 1926) (hereafter Davson), p. 4.

57   **damaged his right knee**: Army service record of Thomas Wilde Rice, TNA WO 339/26293.

57   **in India when war broke out**: *The Times*, 5 August 1916, p. 9.

58   **took place on 2 December**: www.1914-1918.net/rfa_units.htm.

58   **orders to embark for France**: *CLVIII Brigade War Diary*, 26 January 1916, TNA WO 95/2474.

58   **officers at embarkation**: *CLVIII Brigade War Diary*, 31 January 1916, TNA WO 95/2474.

Chapter 8

page

59   **born on 31 August 1867**: Army service record of Percy Harrison Fawcett, TNA WO 138/51 (hereafter Fawcett Service Record).

59   **Fellow of the Royal Geographical Society**: *1881 Census for England and Wales*.

59   **'devoid of parental affection'**: Colonel P H Fawcett, *Exploration Fawcett* (Phoenix Press, 2001) (hereafter Fawcett), p. 15.

59   **'grand times'**: *ibid.*, p. 16.

59   **course in surveying**: see David Grann, *The Lost City of Z* (Simon & Schuster, 2009) (hereafter Grann), pp. 58–65; Grann dates the start of 'more than a year of course work' as 4 February 1900.

59   **a secret service assignment in Morocco**: Grann, p. 70.

59   **'loathed army life'**: Fawcett, p. 15.

59   **left for South America in May 1906**: *ibid.*, p. 20.

59   **'a bearded ruffian'**: *ibid.*, p. 107.

59   **the start of the obsession**: *ibid.*, pp. 113–14.

59   **about 1,200 square miles of border territory were secured for Bolivia**: *ibid.*, p. 125.

60   **'for a wage less than that of most curates'**: *ibid.*, p. 138.

60   **'itching to make'**: *ibid.*, p. 172.

60   **'an orgy of beer drinking'**: *ibid.*, p. 206.

60   **'arrived back in Britain early in December'**: see letter of 17 November 1914 from Nina Fawcett to John Scott Keltie in which she writes of Fawcett being due to arrive at Bristol on 7 December, RGS/PHF/2/2a.

60   **with 4/Rifle Brigade on 20 December 1914**: British Army WW1 Medal Rolls Index Card, Henry James Costin at www.ancestry.co.uk.

60   **re-joining the Army in January 1915**: Fawcett Service Record.

60   **went overseas in September 1915**: *ibid.*

60   **Cecil Eric Lewis Lyne**: according to his birth certificate, Lyne was born Eric Cecil Lewis Lyne at Llanhennock on 16 May 1893.

60   'a most colourful personality': Private Papers of C E L Lyne, Memoirs, IWM 80/14/1 (hereafter Lyne Memoirs), p. 10.

60   'a superb villa': Private Papers of C E L Lyne, Typed Transcripts of Letters, IWM 80/14/1 (hereafter Lyne Letters), 22 October 1915.

60   at the age of 24: Sir Lawrence Bragg, Major General A H Dowson, Lieutenant Colonel H H Hemming, *Artillery Survey in the First World War* (Field Survey Association, 1971), p. 19.

60   'the nastiest man I have ever met': H H Hemming, *My Story: Part II, At War* (unpublished manuscript held at The Liddle Collection, University of Leeds, GS 0740), p. 85.

61   'owned a Ouija Board': *ibid.*

61   While home on leave: see letter of 2 March 1916 from Nina Fawcett to John Scott Keltie, RGS/PHF/2/2a.

Chapter 9
page

62   'arrived here safe': *Accrington Gazette*, 15 May 1915, p. 5.

63   'expressed his appreciation': quoted in *Accrington Gazette*, 22 May 1915, p. 4.

63   formal takeover: *Accrington Gazette*, 5 June 1915, p. 5.

63   4,000 men turned out to fight fires: *Burnley Express and Advertiser*, 26 May 1915, p. 2.

63   'It is a terrible place up here': letter from Richard Ormerod to his sister, Polly, 21 June 1915.

63   4 days leave: *Accrington Gazette*, 29 May 1915, p. 4.

64   'We would follow our Colonel anywhere': quoted in *ibid.*

64   keen for the battalion to have its own band: *Accrington Gazette*, 12 June 1915, p. 4.

64   the loan of instruments: *Accrington Observer and Times*, 26 June 1915, p. 5.

64   the work's comic jazz band: H Crossley, *Accrington Pals*, unpublished manuscript.

64   'contributed to the collection': *Accrington Observer and Times*, 3 July 1915, p. 10.

64   No explanation has survived: Nicholson, p. 512.

64   the battalion's ranks were being depleted: *Accrington Gazette*, 7 August 1915, p. 2.

65   four men were recommended for commissions: *Accrington Observer and Times*, 26 June 1915, p. 6.

65   friend of the Harwood family: Ernest Edgar Ritchie was born in Cawnpore, India; in 1910 he and his wife had a son whom they named Edgar Harwood Ritchie.

65   'its discipline when severely tested was fully maintained': quoted in *Accrington Gazette*, 17 July 1915, p. 5.

65   'take those young shirkers with you': *Chorley Guardian*, 31 July 1915, p. 5.

66   disappointed at the absence of a civic welcome: *Accrington Gazette*, 7 August 1915, p. 5.

66   the march on to Accrington: an excerpt from film of the battalion captured by a cinematographer during the march from Blackburn to Accrington can be seen at www. pals.org.uk/film/film1.htm.

66   almost silent: *Accrington Gazette*, 7 August 1915, p. 5.

66   'cheer upon cheer broke from the crowd': *Accrington Gazette*, 7 August 1915, p. 7.

66   'absolutely stunned': quoted in *Accrington Gazette*, 7 August 1915, p. 2.

66   'beaming with pride': *Accrington Gazette*, 7 August 1915, p. 5.

66   'to correct an impression': *Accrington Gazette*, 7 August 1915, p. 2.

66   'he looked after them and cared for them': *ibid.*

66   'a bit ratty or hot-tempered': *ibid.*

67   'the happiest lot that ever existed': Major Thomas Rawcliffe MC interviewed by William Turner in November 1981; North West Sound Archive, Recording Number 1994.0102.

67   'packed from end to side': *Accrington Gazette*, 7 August 1915, p. 5.

67 **below 72,000 in September:** *Statistics of the Military Effort of the British Empire During the Great War, 1914–1920* (HMSO, 1922), p. 364.

67 **National Registration Act:** see Simkins, pp. 144–8.

67 **accomplished mostly by teachers:** *Accrington Observer and Times*, 7 September 1915, p. 2.

68 **'quite a garden city':** *Accrington Observer and Times*, 14 August 1915, p. 7.

68 **'so smart a body of men':** quoted in *Accrington Gazette*, 14 August 1915, p. 5.

68 **highly satisfactory results:** *Accrington Gazette*, 4 September 1915, p. 4.

68 **'we are now progressing with our training':** letter from Richard Ormerod to his sister, Polly, August 1915.

69 **'exceeded all his expectations':** quoted in *Accrington Gazette*, 11 September 1915, p. 4.

69 **'all the brighter for their promise':** *Accrington Observer and Times*, 11 September 1915, p. 6.

69 **closed the door on accepting the mayoralty:** *ibid.*

69 **a new khaki overcoat:** *Burnley Express and Advertiser*, 15 September 1915, p. 2.

69 **unwounded out of the Battle of Neuve-Chapelle:** *The Times*, 21 December 1921, p. 14.

69 **'by no means above the average':** Army service record of Raymond St George Ross, TNA WO 339/16465.

69 **'frequently appealed':** *ibid.*

70 **'most cheerfully given':** *Accrington Gazette*, 9 October 1915, p. 5.

70 **Derby Scheme:** see Simkins, pp. 150–2.

70 **only 40 had turned up:** *Accrington Gazette*, 13 November 1915, p. 5.

70 **'feel rather keenly':** *Accrington Gazette*, 11 December 1915, p. 4.

71 **'He is "some" Colonel':** *Accrington Gazette*, 20 November 1915, p. 4.

71 **only one absentee:** *Accrington Gazette*, 11 December 1915, p. 5.

71 **sent to Le Havre:** Nicholson, p. 521.

71 **handed back its detailed maps:** *Accrington Gazette*, 18 December 1915, p. 5.

71 **captured on film:** an excerpt from the film can be seen at www.pals.org.uk/film/film2.htm.

71 **a dinner was given:** *Burnley Express and Advertiser*, 18 December 1915, p. 12.

71 **transferred to the Machine Gun Corps:** *Chorley Guardian*, 15 July 1916, p. 5.

Chapter 10
page

72 **put forward the bold idea:** Peter Chasseaud and Peter Doyle, *Grasping Gallipoli* (Spellmount, 2005), p. 34.

73 **casualties over the campaign:** Terraine, 1983, p. 82.

73 **a strategic reserve was assembled:** Sir James E Edmonds, *Military Operations: France and Belgium 1916 V1* (London, Macmillan, 1932) (hereafter Edmonds, 1916 V1), p. 22.

73 **pre-fabricated in Germany:** Keegan, pp. 238–40.

73 **embarked onto troopships:** *11/East Lancashire War Diary*, 19 December 1915, TNA WO 95/4590.

73 **splendid quarters:** *Accrington Observer and Times*, 18 January 1916, p. 2.

74 **crowded hammocks:** diary of Richard Ormerod, Lancashire Infantry Museum collection (hereafter Ormerod Diary), 20 December 1916.

74 **'dozens of small boats':** *Accrington Gazette*, 15 January 1916, p. 5.

74 **shortly after 1pm:** *The Times*, 3 January 1916, p. 11.

74 **loss of 334 lives:** A J Tennent, *British Merchant Ships Sunk by U-Boats in World War One* (Periscope Publishing, 2006), p. 182.

74 **'suddenly the ship canted over':** Percy Crabtree and Fred Sayer, *The History of Z Company* (unpublished manuscript) (hereafter Crabtree and Sayer), p. 21.

74 **by only 100ft:** *11/East Lancashire War Diary*, 31 December 1915, TNA WO 95/4590.

75   **unsuccessful campaign by Harwood and Rickman**: British Army WW1 Medal Rolls Index Card, Arthur Wilmot Rickman at www.ancestry.co.uk.

75   **'widespread relief'**: *Accrington Gazette*, 8 January 1916, p. 5.

75   **'our spare money goes in buying eatables'**: *Accrington Gazette*, 29 January 1916, p. 4.

75   **'best dinner since arrival'**: Ormerod Diary, 20 January 1916.

76   **'hardest day since enlistment'**: *ibid.*, 25 January 1916.

76   **'reminder of ancient Egypt'**: Crabtree and Sayer, p. 23.

76–7 **'away from all civilization'**: Crabtree and Sayer, p. 25.

77   **excavation to a width of 24ft**: Lieutenant Colonel W D Lowe, DSO, MC, *War History of the 18th (S.) Battalion Durham Light Infantry* (Oxford University Press, 1920) (hereafter Lowe), p. 22.

77   **'a tough march back to El Ferdan'**: Crabtree and Sayer, p. 25.

77   **midnight before tents were pitched**: Ormerod Diary, 20 February 1916.

77   **'a great favourite'**: *Accrington Gazette*, 11 March 1916, p. 4.

77   **'won the hearts of his men'**: Crabtree and Sayer, p. 25.

77   **gas gangrene**: Army service record of Henry Harrison Mitchell, TNA WO 339/22592.

77   **fallen exhausted by the wayside**: Ormerod Diary, 22 February 1916.

78   **possible to reduce the strategic reserve**: Edmonds, 1916 V1, p. 23.

78   **31st Division to embark for France**: *31st Division War Diary*, 26 February 1916, TNA WO 95/4589.

78   **left for France at 10pm**: Ormerod Diary, 2 March 1916.

78   **'cheery, singing, and laughing'**: quoted in *Accrington Gazette*, 18 March 1916, p. 4.

Chapter 11

page
79   **'alarming rumours'**: *Accrington Observer and Times*, 5 February 1916, p. 6.

79   **'wines and beer are very cheap'**: *Accrington Observer and Times*, 19 February 1916, p. 6.

79   **greetings and best wishes**: *Accrington Observer and Times*, 19 February 1916, p. 7.

79   **inspected by Kitchener and GOC XI Corps**: Davson, pp. 8–9.

79   **the engines of one were heard**: *CLVIII Brigade War Diary*, 19 February 1916, TNA WO 95/2474.

79   **a Zeppelin dropped fifteen bombs**: *CLVIII Brigade War Diary*, 20 February 1916, TNA WO 95/2474.

80   **suffering from myopia in both eyes**: Army service record of Gilbert Grimshaw, TNA WO 339/27226.

80   **awarded the Founder's Medal**: Grann, p. 163.

80   **'quite efficient'**: see letter of 11 March 1916 from Nina Fawcett to John Scott Keltie, RGS/PHF/2/2a.

80   **'impossibly backward'**: *ibid.*

80   **'content and keen'**: *ibid.*

80   **the first raid undertaken by the division**: Davson, p. 14.

81   **C Battery came under heavy shellfire**: *CLVIII Brigade War Diary*, 28 March 1916, TNA WO 95/2474.

81   **allowed to resign his commission**: Army service record of Harold Gray, TNA WO 339/29147.

81   **a colonial farmer**: Army service record of Stanley Knocker, TNA WO 339/55184.

81   **'cheerful in spite of all!'**: *Accrington Gazette*, 27 May 1916, p. 7.

81   **a fine and clear day**: *CLVIII Brigade War Diary*, 2 April 1916, TNA WO 95/2474.

81   **'minor strafe'**: *CLVIII Brigade War Diary*, 10 April 1916, TNA WO 95/2474.

82   **played football every evening**: *Accrington Observer and Times*, 12 August 1916, p. 8.

82   **raiding party of one officer and sixteen men**: *23/Manchester War Diary*, 8 May 1916, TNA WO 95/2484.

82   **the nearby burst of an enemy shell**: *CLVIII Brigade War Diary*, 8 May 1916, TNA WO 95/2474.

82 'comforts': *Accrington Gazette*, 3 June 1916, p. 8.
82 'the undoing of the Boche': *Accrington Observer and Times*, 10 June 1916, p. 5.
83 both the Military Cross (MC) and the Distinguished Flying Cross (DFC): Army service record of Harold Aubrey Pearson, TNA AIR 76/396.
83 practically obliterating the front line: *CLVIII Brigade War Diary*, 31 May 1916, TNA WO 95/2474.
83 discarded shovels and unexploded bombs: Davson, p. 21.
83 a letter to John Harwood: *Accrington Observer and Times*, 17 June 1916, p. 4.
83 recommended for gallantry: *CLVIII Brigade War Diary*, 31 May 1916, TNA WO 95/2474.
83 recommended for devotion to duty: *ibid*.
83 a successful raid: Davson, pp. 22–3.
84 two officers and four men killed, and twelve men wounded: *CLVIII Brigade War Diary*, 8 June 1916, TNA WO 95/2474.
84 several superficial HE shell wounds: Army service record of William Chambers, TNA WO 339/25126.
84 to stiffen the 61st divisional artillery: *CLVIII Brigade War Diary*, 10 June 1916, TNA WO 95/2474.
84 'died on the way to hospital': *Burnley News*, 17 June 1916, p. 10.
85 as many as 2,000,000 casualties: Terraine, 1983, p. 90.
85 145,000 casualties in Champagne and nearly 50,000 more in Artois: *ibid*., p. 93.
85 'greatest Allied internment camp': see, for example, Terraine, 1983, p. 86.
85 conclusions from the conference: Edmonds, 1916 V1, pp. 7–8.
85 dropped by Joffre on 14 February: *ibid*., p. 29.
85 von Hötzendorf's offensive: see Terraine, 1983, p. 114.
86 three armies each of sixteen divisions: William Philpott, *Bloody Victory* (Abacus, 2010) (hereafter Philpott), p. 115.
86 'They want a bayonet running through them': *Accrington Gazette*, 25 March 1916, p. 4.
87 in exchange for a few coppers: *Accrington Gazette*, 1 April 1916, p. 5.
87 lying on damp soil: Ormerod Diary, 30 March 1916.
87–8 'it is really nothing to worry about': *Accrington Gazette*, 15 April 1916, p. 4.
88 in charge of two machine-gun crews: Ormerod Diary, 4 April 1916.
88 dead French soldiers were uncovered: *ibid*., 9 April 1916.
88 kept a diary: diary of Percy B Allsup, IWM 1388 87/17/1.
89 'a miserable affair': quoted in Nicholson, p. 523.
89 'It was like a perfect Hell': letter from Richard Ormerod to his sister, Polly, 18 April 1916.
89 a fall from a horse: Army service record of Harry Clegg, TNA WO 339/41306.
89 list of the battalion's officers: handwritten document from the private collection of Lieutenant Colonel Arthur Wilmot Rickman. Curiously, the original document included the late Lieutenant Mitchell of Z Company; otherwise, the list has been transcribed in full.
90 four weeks shy of his 15th birthday: Army service record of Reginald St John Beardsworth Battersby, TNA WO 339/34889; private correspondence from Anthony Battersby.
90 'Scratching and scraping': Fred Sayer, *Solidus* (unpublished autobiography), p. 147.
90 member of the Burnley Lads' Club: *Burnley News*, 13 May 1916, p. 6.
90 'By the time you get this': *Accrington Observer and Times*, 6 May 1916, p. 5.
91 'God straff England': Ormerod Diary, 30 April 1916; almost certainly a mistranscription by Ormerod of 'Gott strafe England'.
91 'to sit and enjoy the sunshine': Crabtree and Sayer, p. 29.
91 'heaps of tobacco and cigarettes': *Accrington Gazette*, 6 May 1916, p. 4.
91–2 'very nerve trying': *Accrington Gazette*, 1 July 1916, p. 4.
92 accidentally shot: William Turner, *Accrington Pals Trail* (Leo Cooper, 1998) (hereafter Turner, 1998), pp. 29–31.

92   **'blown up by a shell'**: Army service record of John Charles Palmer, TNA WO 339/35550.

92   **an unusual conclusion**: Army service record of Harry Bury, TNA WO 339/15855.

93   **'socks go so quickly out here'**: *Accrington Observer and Times*, 10 June 1916, p. 5.

93   **'a very good battalion'**: letter from Gerry Gorst to his sister, Betty, 29 May 1916.

93   **fell out of the march in large numbers**: Ormerod Diary, 5 June 1916.

94   **'a hundred or two wire-cutters'**: *Accrington Gazette*, 10 June 1916, p. 4.

94   **'I had dinner with the 1st [Battalion] last week'**: letter from Gerry Gorst to his sister, Betty, 7 June 1916.

94   **'stew, stew, stew'**: *Accrington Gazette*, 17 June 1916, p. 4.

94   **taken 12 hours**: Ormerod Diary, 16 June 1916.

95   **'discovered he has hammer toes'**: see also Army service record of Philip John Broadley, TNA WO 339/16458.

95   **'Ruttle is also in hospital'**: Lieutenant Jack Ruttle left the battalion on 12 June 1916 suffering from pneumonia (Army service record of John Henry Ruttle, TNA WO 339/64917).

95   **trench fever**: Army service record of John Charles Shorrock, TNA WO 339/22595.

95   **'We are in the line at the moment'**: letter from Gerry Gorst to his sister, Betty, 22 June 1916.

95   **'Aren't the Rooshians great'**: *ibid.*

96   **injured by a German HE shell**: Army service record of Walter Affroville Lewino, TNA WO 339/39486.

96   **served as a battery quartermaster sergeant**: Army service record of William Barrett, TNA WO 339/65285.

96   **'time for a hasty one'**: letter from Arnold Tough to his sister, Christina, 29 June 1916.

96   **'my love to Tom and Peg'**: Arnold Tough's sister, Margaret (Peg), had married Tom Graham in 1915. Tough was trying to dissuade his brother-in-law from enlisting; Tom Graham went on to serve with the RAMC, and was blinded by enemy gas.

Chapter 12
page

97   **initial plan for the offensive**: *Official History of the Great War DVD-ROM, Military Operations France and Belgium, 1916 Appendices 1* (The Naval & Military Press, 2010) (hereafter *1916 Appendices 1*, pp. 64–71.

98   **formal response to the Fourth Army plan**: *1916 Appendices 1*, pp. 72–5.

99   **his amended plan dated 19 April**: *1916 Appendices 1*, pp. 76–82.

99   **memorandum from GHQ dated 16 May**: *1916 Appendices 1*, p. 83.

99   **planned according to a strict timetable**: although the author has been unable to locate an original version of the battalion orders for the attack on Serre by 11/East Lancashire, a translation into German dated 3 July 1916 was made from documents taken from a dead British officer (most likely to have been Captain Harry Livesey) and is available at the Generallandesarchiv Karlsruhe: *Übersetzung des englischen Angriffbefehls auf Serre: Operationsbefehl von Oberstlt. A. W. Rickman, Kommandeur des XI / E. Lan. R.*; the author's description of the plan for the battalion's attack has also drawn on *94th Infantry Brigade (Preliminary) Operational Order No. 45* (23 June 1916), its amendment (29 June 1916) and corrigenda (30 June 1916), TNA WO 95/2363.

101   **it was known**: a dugout deep under the German front line at Serre was reported to be similar to one in Monk Trench which, until June 1915, had been in German hands (*Report to 94 Infantry Brigade* by Captain Douglas C Allen, 5 July 1916, TNA WO 95/2363); a successful trench raid by 1/Lancashire Fusiliers had discovered dugouts and tunnels that were 'more or less bombardment proof' (Major Ian C Grant, Brigade Major 86 Brigade, 29th Division, TNA CAB 45/189).

101   **only one heavy per 57yd**: Gordon Corrigan, *Mud, Blood and Poppycock* (Cassell, 2004), p. 260.

101   **at 5am on 24 June**: author's own translation from the War Diary of 169th (8th Baden) Infantry Regiment held at the Generallandesarchiv Karlsruhe (hereafter *IR169 Diary*), 24 June 1916; note that all times have been converted to those in use by British forces on the Western Front, as German forces operated on a time 1 hour ahead.

102   **'would drive us mad'**: Otto Lais, *Erlebnisse badischer Frontsoldaten, Band 1: Maschinengewehre im Eisernen Regiment (8. Badisches Infanterie-Regiment Nr.169)* (G. Braun, Karlsruhe 1935) (author's translation; hereafter Lais), p. 2.

102   **disquieting news**: *31st Division War Diary*, 28 June 1916, TNA WO 95/2341.

102   **for all to hear**: *Papers of Brigadier General H C Rees*, vol. 2 of typed transcript of memoirs, IWM 77/179/1 (hereafter Rees V2), p. 89.

102   **had not been cut**: *31st Division War Diary*, 29 June 1916, TNA WO 95/2341.

102   **merited use of a Bangalore torpedo**: report of wire examining patrol on night of 29/30 June, TNA CAB 45/191.

102   **'very full of men'**: *18/West Yorkshire War Diary*, 29 June 1916, TNA WO 95/2362.

103   **forced to withdraw**: *12 and 13/Royal Sussex War Diaries*, 30 June 1916, TNA WO 95/2582.

103   **'a glowing letter of praise'**: *Accrington Observer and Times*, 19 August 1916, p. 8.

103   **an electrical engineer from Barnoldswick**: Army service record of James Farnworth, TNA WO 363/F71.

103   **'how cheerful we were'**: *Accrington Observer and Times*, 22 July 1916, p. 7.

103–4   **a tin disc tied with string**: description of the kit taken from *Scheme of Attack issued by Headquarters 94 Infantry Brigade to OC 11/East Lancashire on 8 June 1916* and *Supplement to 94 Infantry Brigade (Prelim) Operation Order No. 45, 23 June 1916*, TNA WO 95/2363; the idea behind the tin disc was that light reflected from the metal would help observers to follow the progress of the attack.

104   **the communication trench named Central Avenue**: according to Turner, 1987 (p. 139) the Accrington Pals entered the trench system on the night of 30 June southeast of Colincamps at the ruins of the Sugar Factory; Rickman's *Report on Operations* (TNA WO 95/2366) (hereafter Rickman), Rees V2 and battalion orders deposited with the *94 Brigade War Diary* (TNA WO 95/2363) make it clear that the point of entry was north of Colincamps.

104   **intercepted an order**: Jack Sheldon, *The German Army on the Somme 1914–1916* (Pen & Sword, 2005), pp. 132–3.

104   **'lively activity'**: translation of *lebhafte Bewegung* from *IR169 Diary*, 1 July 1916.

105   **'twenty minutes to go, boys'**: *Burnley Express and Advertiser*, 22 July 1916, p. 9.

105   **'badly hurt'**: *Burnley News*, 5 August 1916, p. 3; Bart Endean's own account of this event can be found in Turner, 1998, pp. 35–6.

105   **bullets tore at the sandbags**: personal correspondence from Ross Davies; confirmation that there were machine guns from IR169 firing at this time can be found in the *IR169 Diary*.

105   **inexplicably 5 minutes ahead of schedule**: Lieutenant Colonel J I A McDiarmid, Brigade Major VIII Corps Heavy Artillery, TNA CAB 45/190.

105   **1,150 rounds onto the German front line**: *94 Brigade Light Trench Mortar Battery War Diary*, 1 July 1916, TNA WO 95/2366.

105–6   **'terrific hail of steel'**: Rees V2, p. 91.

106   **'from shell-hole to shell-hole'**: Lais, p. 2.

106   **thought to have reached 30 per cent**: *14/York and Lancaster War Diary*, 1 July 1916 TNA WO 95/2365.

106–7   **'how that choir of hell sang'**: *Burnley Express and Advertiser*, 19 August 1916, p. 9.

107   **'tried to keep the line together'**: Edward G D Liveing, *Attack: an Infantry Subaltern's Impression of July 1st, 1916* (Macmillan, 1918) at www.gutenberg.org/files/28145/28145-h/28145-h.htm, p. 15.

107   **'the heaviest barrage I have seen'**: Rees V2, p. 91.

107–8   **'lucky for us that the sun's shining in their eyes'**: Lais, p. 3.

108   **hit by a shell burst and killed**: Ralph Gibson and Paul Oldfield, *Sheffield City Battalion* (Wharncliffe, 1988), p. 153.

108   **where there were gaps in the wire**: *12/York and Lancaster War Diary*, 1 July 1916, TNA WO 95/2365.

108   **fatally hit**: see letters from Jack Haining, Captain Anton Peltzer and Lieutenant Colonel Arthur Rickman published in the *Accrington Gazette*, 15 July 1916, p. 8.

108   **'thought I was done for'**: undated letter from Frank Thomas to his father, John.

108   **hit just below the right ear lobe**: Army service record of Cecil Douglas Gay, Ministry of Defence P/82925.

109   **suffered up to 50 per cent casualties**: by analogy with numbers reported for 12/York and Lancaster (*12/York and Lancaster War Diary*, 1 July 1916, TNA WO 95/2365).

109   **Riley was killed by machine-gun fire**: Army service record of Henry Davison Riley, TNA WO 339/14340.

109   **wounded in the right calf**: Army service record of George Gabriel Williams, TNA WO 339/66402.

109   **'got in a shell-hole'**: *Accrington Gazette*, 15 July 1916, p. 5.

109   **last seen leading a bombing party**: Army service record of Charles Elam, TNA WO 339/21709.

109–10 **'proud to belong to them'**: letter from Gerry Gorst to his sister, Betty, 10 July 1916.

110   **'it's quickly filled!'**: Lais, p. 3.

110   **infantry reach the German second-line trench**: *CLXV Brigade War Diary*, 1 July 1916, TNA WO 95/2349.

110   **penetrated in Sector S2**: *IR169 Diary: 9.0 Vorm. Meldung Abschnitt Rechts, dass Gegner im ersten Graben S2 anscheinend eingedrungen.*

110–11 **'the enemy fire dies out here as well'**: Lais, p. 3.

111   **never to be seen again**: Jon Cooksey, *Barnsley Pals* (Wharncliffe, 1986), p. 206.

111   **sighted over the fourth line**: *CLXV Brigade War Diary*, 1 July 1916, TNA WO 95/2349.

111   **infantry were seen in Serre itself**: *CLXV Brigade War Diary*, 1 July 1916, TNA WO 95/2349; *31st Division War Diary*, 1 July 1916, TNA WO 95/2341.

111   **persuaded by reports**: Rees V2, p. 92.

111   **no news whatsoever**: Rickman.

111   **again in possession of Sectors S1 and S2**: *IR169 Diary: 10.15 Vorm. Meldung an Brigade. Major Berthold meldet, dass S2 wieder in unserer Hand, ebenso wie immer S1.*

111–12 **'I reached our own lines'**: *Accrington Observer and Times*, 15 July 1916, p. 4.

112   **'sent me to the dressing station'**: undated letter from Frank Thomas to his father, John.

112   **'stuck to his gun to the last'**: *Accrington Observer and Times*, 5 August 1916, p. 8.

112   **'very courageous of him'**: *Accrington Observer and Times*, 11 July 1916, p. 1.

112–13 **'as soon as I was hit'**: *Accrington Gazette*, 15 July 1916, p. 5.

113   **'a good deal rattled'**: Rickman.

113   **584 were killed, wounded or missing**: Nicholson, p. 527.

113   **'the number has reached overwhelming proportions'**: *Accrington Observer and Times*, 1 August 1916, p. 2.

114   **3,600 killed, wounded, missing or taken prisoner**: Edmonds, 1916 V1, p. 448.

114   **591 killed, wounded or missing**: *IR169 Diary*.

114   **19,240 were counted as having been killed in action or died of wounds**: Edmonds, 1916 V1, p. 483.

Chapter 13
page

115   **to relieve the pressure on Verdun**: Haig, p. 189.

115   **to bring the offensive to an end**: A H Farrar-Hockley, *The Somme* (Pan, 1964), pp. 196–7.

115   an acrimonious meeting on 3 July: Haig, p. 198.
115   eighteen times that of 1 July: Philpott, p. 238.
115   along a front of 6,000yd: Wilfrid Miles, *Military Operations: France and Belgium 1916 V2* (London, Macmillan, 1938) (hereafter Miles, 1916 V2), p. 88.
117   would have preferred to adopt a 'creeping barrage': Brigadier General W B Staveley, *35th Divisional Artillery Operations 21st to 30th July inclusive 1916*, 2 August 1916 (in *30th Division War Diary*, TNA WO 95/2310).
117   'had to be constantly relaid for the last 500 yards': Neil Fraser-Tytler, *Field Guns in France* (The Naval & Military Press reprint) (hereafter Fraser-Tytler), p. 97.
117   remnants of the left and centre companies: Miles, 1916 V2, pp. 139–40.
117   improved their defensive tactics: Robin Prior and Trevor Wilson, *The Somme* (Yale University Press, 2006) (hereafter Prior and Wilson, 2006), p. 150.
118   managed to stop the horses: *Accrington Observer and Times*, 1 August 1916, p. 1.
118   'our progress will be slow but sure': *Burnley Express and Advertiser*, 5 August 1916, p. 4.
118   arrived in the same post: *Burnley News*, 5 August 1916, p. 3.
118   wounded in the wrist and stomach: *CLVIII Brigade War Diary*, 24 July 1916, TNA WO 95/2474.
118–19   'taken away to a dressing station': *Burnley Express and Advertiser*, 2 September 1916, p. 4.
119   'with utter disregard of personal danger': *Supplement to the London Gazette*, 20 October 1916, p. 10184.
119   'I doubt very much if I deserved it': *Accrington Observer and Times*, 23 September 1916, p. 5.
119   orders to assist in an operation: *35th Divisional Artillery Order No. 34*, 26 July 1916 in *CLVIII Brigade War Diary*, TNA WO 95/2474.
119   125,000 shells weighing 4.5 million pounds: Prior and Wilson, 2006, pp. 150–1.
119   about 50yd inside the northern edge of the wood: Miles, 1916 V2, p. 158.
120   'a mighty hot shop': *Accrington Observer and Times*, 8 August 1916, p. 2.
120   The fire plan for the 35th divisional field guns: *35th Divisional Artillery Order No. 35*, 29 July 1916 in *CLVIII Brigade War Diary*, TNA WO 95/2474.
120   overwhelmed by German counter-attacks: Miles, 1916 V2, p. 165.
121   'like the battle pictures of Nelson's day': Fraser-Tytler, p. 183.
121   five enemy aeroplanes: *CLVIII Brigade War Diary*, 31 July 1916, TNA WO 95/2474.
121   left the safety of a dugout: Davson, p. 43.
121   'died of shock an hour later': Fraser-Tytler, p. 103.
121   'a very gallant, efficient, and valuable officer': Fawcett quoted in Davson, p. 43.
121   'never regained consciousness': *Burnley Express and Advertiser*, 16 August 1916, p. 2.
122   died from their wounds in hospital at Corbie: *Burnley Express and Advertiser*, 23 August 1916, p. 2.
122   sudden and intense lifting barrages: Miles, 1916 V2, p. 176.
123   'a devilish hot time for us': *Burnley Express and Advertiser*, 26 August 1916, p. 9.
123   The infantry attack that started at 4.20am: Miles, 1916 V2, pp. 177–80.
124   the infantry attack of 18 August: *ibid.*, pp. 190–2.
124   typhoid fever: Army service record of Harry Renham, TNA WO 339/30391.
124   colitis: Army service record of Robert Mercer, TNA WO 339/25147.
125   ranging a howitzer battery: *Supplement to the London Gazette*, 20 October 1916, p. 10182.
125   had been with Frank Harwood: *Accrington Observer and Times*, 3 October 1916, p. 1.
125   repairing broken wires under shellfire: *Supplement to the London Gazette*, 20 October 1916, p. 10205.
125   throughout a 6-hour enemy bombardment: *Accrington Observer and Times*, 2 December 1916, p. 6.

125   'sooner go through any strafe and say nowt': *Accrington Observer and Times*, 14 October 1916, p. 7.
126   to rest as many of its men as possible: *CLXIII Brigade War Diary*, 2 August 1916, TNA WO 95/2475.
126   enfilade fire from Falfemont Farm: Miles, 1916 V2, pp. 200–1.

Chapter 14

page
127   'picked out as an NCO': Allsup Diary, 7 July 1916.
127   'a bitter blow': Rees V2, p. 95.
127   relieved by 6/Gloucester: *11/East Lancashire War Diary*, 4/5 July 1916, TNA WO 95/2366.
127   'slept first class': Allsup Diary, 9 July 1916.
127   'very exhausting and rather heart-breaking': letter from Gerry Gorst to his sister, Betty, 10 July 1916.
127   'a great success so far': letter from Gerry Gorst to his sister, Betty, 16 July 1916.
128   brought on by influenza: Army service record of Frank Bailey, TNA WO 339/14336.
128   'the Kaiser's travelling menagerie': Allsup Diary, 26 July 1916.
128   shot himself in the left hand: Army service record of Gordon Peter Raeburn, TNA WO 339/44032.
128–9 'an infernal machine': letter from Gerry Gorst to his sister, Betty, 12 August 1916.
129   an unsuccessful attempt to desert: Army service record of Richard Scholes, TNA WO 364/3594.
129   the opposition of Lieutenant Colonel Ritzema to his transfer: Army service record of Samuel Taylor, TNA WO 339/53469.
129   'a very nice fellow named Duff': letter from Gerry Gorst to his sister, Betty, 22 August 1916.
129   supported by the South African High Commissioner: Army service records of John Shire Duff, TNA WO 339/52613, and Spencer Richard Fleischer, TNA WO 339/52614.
130   a store manager in Russia: Army service record of Harold Wilton, TNA WO 339/41217.
130   'the old Hun is of the Saxon variety': letter from Gerry Gorst to his sister, Betty, 21 September 1916.
130   'quite as close as I care about': *ibid.*
130–1 'never made a sound': letter from Gerry Gorst to his sister, Betty, 28 September 1916.
131   took on the role of head of operations: Keegan, p. 337.
131   'isn't the news from the south good?': letter from Gerry Gorst to his sister, Betty, 28 September 1916.
131   use by signallers of flares and ground-shutters: *11/East Lancashire War Diary*, 8–18 October 1916, TNA WO 95/2366.
131   'somewhere on familiar ground': letter from Gerry Gorst to his sister, Betty, 6 October 1916.
131–2 'the joyous ring of Lancashire voices': Crabtree and Sayer, p. 47.
132   'beastly in the extreme': *ibid.*, p. 48.
132   'the excruciating pain of Trench Feet': *ibid.*, p. 50.
133   the intended point-of-entry: at map reference 57dNE3 (Hebuterne) K.23.b.6.0.
133   to identify the units holding the enemy line: *94 Infantry Brigade Order No. 90*, 16 November 1916, TNA WO 95/2363.
133   no record of what followed: the copies of the battalion war diary held at TNA (WO 95/2366) and at the Lancashire Infantry Museum inexplicably make no mention of the trench raid. It may be that one or more pages have been lost from the diary. The war diary of 31st Division (TNA WO 95/2341) records only that the attempt to enter the enemy trenches failed.

134   'one of the best': *Accrington Gazette*, 13 January 1917, p. 5.

134   a system that was criticized: Nicholson, p. 531.

134   covered with ice to a depth of between 12 and 18in: *Accrington Gazette*, 10 February 1917, p. 8.

134   a gift from the battalion's friends: Nicholson, p. 533.

134–5   'the old spirit still there': Sayer, p. 216.

135   on the fourth day of the course: documents from the subsequent Court of Inquiry can be found in the Army service record of George Joseph Beaumont, TNA WO 339/39491.

135   died of a gangrenous appendix: Army service record of George Wentworth Dimery, TNA WO 339/87704.

135   rumours were rife: Crabtree and Sayer, p. 53.

135   'it points to the evacuation of Serre': *21/Manchester Patrol Report 24 February 1917*, TNA WO 95/1668.

136   Serre had final fallen: *21/Manchester Report on Operations 25 February 1917*, TNA WO 95/1668.

136   the German retreat of 16–19 March: see Irina Renz, Gerd Krumeich and Gerhard Hirschfeld, *Scorched Earth: The Germans on the Somme 1914–1918* (Pen & Sword Military, 2009).

136–7   'a German patrol found us and took us in': Army service record of Frederic James Wild, TNA WO 339/45628.

137   a direct hit on Y Company headquarters: Nicholson, p. 534.

137   the bodies of several men who had been reported missing: *ibid.*

137   'thankless and unenviable task': *Accrington Observer and Times*, 24 March 1917, p. 4.

Chapter 15

page

138   reorganization of the divisional artillery: Davson, p. 58.

138   a complicated transition: *CLVIII Brigade War Diary*, 8 September 1916, TNA WO 95/2474; note the erroneous diary entry 'D/163 joined the Brigade & becomes C/163'.

138   a raid by 15/Cheshire: Davson, pp. 60–2; *CLVIII Brigade War Diary*, September 1916, Appendix 1, TNA WO 95/2474.

139   a raid made by 15/Sherwood Foresters: Davson, pp. 68–70; *CLVIII Brigade War Diary*, October 1916, Appendix 1, TNA WO 95/2474.

139   co-operated with 17/West Yorkshire: Davson, p. 71.

139   a raid north-east of Roclincourt: Davson, pp. 77–8; *CLVIII Brigade War Diary*, November 1916, Appendix 2, TNA WO 95/2474.

140   killing him instantly: *Accrington Gazette*, 9 December 1916, p. 5.

140   unable to find Slinger's body: letter from Lieutenant J H Hanrick to Major G N Slinger dated 14 December 1916.

140   in the grounds of the Château d'Immercourt: private communication from Sue Baker Wilson.

141   CLVIII Brigade was broken up: *CLVIII Brigade War Diary*, 8, 10 and 11 January 1917, TNA WO 95/2474.

142   forced a delay of 24 hours: Jonathan Nicholls, *Cheerful Sacrifice: The Battle of Arras 1917* (Leo Cooper, 1990) (hereafter Nicholls), p. 54.

142   'nothing but a wilderness of broken stone remained': Lyne Letters, 8 April.

142   'a mass of flames': *ibid.*

142   damaged by shellfire over Bullecourt: Trevor Henshaw, *The Sky Their Battlefield* (Grub Street, 1995), p. 156.

142   the attack of 51st (Highland) Division: Captain Cyril Falls, *Military Operations: France and Belgium 1917*, Vol. 1 (London, Macmillan, 1940) (hereafter Falls, 1917 V1), p. 234.

142   saw it destroyed: *LXIV Brigade War Diary*, 9 April 1917, TNA WO 95/295.

143   'an impossible task': quoted in Nicholls, p. 117.
143   stopped by heavy machine-gun fire from the right: *XLVIII Brigade War Diary*, 9 April 1917, TNA WO 95/455.
143–4 'ceased to hope for anything better': Lyne Letters, 17 April 1917.
144   134,000 in the first 10 days alone: Colonel G W L Nicholson, *Official History of the Canadian Army in the First World War: Canadian Expeditionary Force, 1914–1919* (Duhamel, 1964) at www.cmp-cpm.forces.gc.ca/dhh-dhp/his/docs/CEF_e.pdf, p. 243.
144   'a fearful strafing all day': Lyne Letters, 23 April 1917.
144   described in the brigade war diary as useless: *LXIV Brigade War Diary*, 22 April 1917, TNA WO 95/295.
145   'now on his way to England': Lyne Letters, 23 April 1917.
145   'walls of dead some five feet high': Lyne Letters, 24 April 1917.
145   an average of 13,000 rounds per brigade: Falls, 1917 V1, p. 400.
145   'not cut and pretty heavy': *LXIV Brigade War Diary*, 28 April 1917, TNA WO 95/295.
146   only two could be regarded as rested: Nicholls, p. 196.
146   quickly lost the creeping barrage: Falls, 1917 V1, pp. 446–7.
146   'a much more serious loss': Lyne Letters, 4 May 1917.
146   'a lively day in the shell line': *ibid.*
147   'a wonderful scheme afoot': Lyne Letters, 10 May 1917.
147   'found to be quite dead': *Accrington Observer and Times*, 19 May 1917, p. 8.
147–8 drove back an enemy raid: *11/East Lancashire War Diary*, 12 May 1917, TNA WO 95/2366.
148   Lott led a bombing party: *11/East Lancashire War Diary*, 13/14 May 1917, TNA WO 95/2366.
148   50yd north of the junction: *94 Infantry Brigade War Diary*, 14 May 1917, TNA WO 95/2363.
149   a 20-minute bombing duel: Nicholson, p. 536.
149   a 'very hot' action: *94 Infantry Brigade War Diary*, 15 May 1917, TNA WO 95/2363.
149   further advance along the trench was impossible: *94 Infantry Brigade War Diary*, 17 May 1917, TNA WO 95/2363.
149   ten killed, thirty-six wounded and one missing: *11/East Lancashire War Diary*, 16 May 1917, TNA WO 95/2366.
149   average daily rate of British casualties: John Terraine, *The Smoke and the Fire: Myths and Anti-Myths of War, 1861–1945* (Sidgwick and Jackson, 1980) (hereafter Terraine, 1980), p. 46.
149   kept his remaining guns in action: *Supplement to the London Gazette*, 16 August 1917, p. 8387.
149   three objectives: see *Report on Operations Carried Out by 31st Division on June 28th, 1917*, TNA WO 95/2342 (hereafter *31st Division Report 28 June 1917*), p. 1.
149   a marked system of trenches at Brunehaut Farm: *Report of the Attack on the German Front Line Trenches between Gavrelle and Oppy Wood, on June 28th 1917, by the 94th Infantry Brigade*, TNA WO 95/2342 (hereafter *94 Brigade Report 28 June 1917*).
151   a short but heavy searching barrage: *94 Infantry Brigade War Diary*, 27 June 1917, TNA WO 95/2363.
151   repeated at 5pm on the 28th: *94 Brigade Report 28 June 1917*.
151   dropped short: Nicholson, p. 538.
151   a double-banked creeping barrage: *31st Division Report 28 June 1917*, p. 3.
151   a 300-round Thermite barrage: *ibid.*, p. 4; Thermite were incendiary bombs based on the chemical reaction between iron (III) oxide and aluminium.
151   as near as 60yd: *ibid.*, p. 3.
151   reported no casualties at all: *12th S. Battalion York and Lancaster Regiment – Part Taken by this Battalion in the Offensive Operations of 28th June 1917*, TNA WO 95/2365.
151   led his platoon into the enemy's trench: *Supplement to the London Gazette*, 17 September 1917, p. 9558.

151 took over command of the platoon: *Supplement to the London Gazette*, 17 September 1917, p. 9600.
151 eight killed and forty-two wounded: *11/East Lancashire War Diary*, 30 June 1917, TNA WO 95/2366.
152 two killed, thirty-six wounded and two missing: *13/York and Lancaster War Diary*, 28 June 1917, TNA WO 95/2365.
152 increased in intensity over the next 18 minutes: *94 Brigade Report 28 June 1917.*
152 'coolness and disregard of danger': *Supplement to the London Gazette*, 17 September 1917, p. 9576.
152 'pluck and determination': *ibid.*
152 fired an SOS signal: *94 Brigade Report 28 June 1917.*
152 soon dispersed by heavy fire: *ibid.*
152 29 killed and 160 wounded: *ibid.*

Chapter 16
page
153 526,000 tons of British shipping: John Terraine, *Douglas Haig: The Educated Soldier* (Hutchinson, 1963), p. 260.
153 impossible for Britain to continue the war: Haig, p. 301.
154 95,600lb of ammonal: Alexander Barrie, *War Underground: The Tunnellers of the Great War* (Tom Donovan, 1962), p. 251; ammonal is composed of 65 per cent ammonium nitrate, 17 per cent aluminium, 15 per cent trinitrotoluene and 3 per cent charcoal (F Bostyn in *Fields of Battle: Terrain in Military History*, edited by Peter Doyle and Matthew R Bennett (Springer, 2011), p. 226).
154 'the hottest show we have been in yet': Lyne Letters, 3 June 1917.
154 severely wounded: *Accrington Observer and Times*, 9 June 1917, p. 5.
155 'Rather fine of him, wasn't it?': Lyne Letters, 3 June 1917.
155 'a perfect deluge of debris': Lyne Letters, 4 June 1917.
156 felt distinctly in London: Brigadier General Sir James E Edmonds, *Military Operations: France and Belgium 1917 V2* (London, HMSO, 1948) (hereafter Edmonds, 1917 V2), p. 55.
156 'never been seen before': Lyne Letters, 10 June 1917.
156 'Talk about Belle Vue fireworks! My word!': *Accrington Observer and Times*, 14 July 1917, p. 5.
156 3,561,530 rounds had been fired: Edmonds, 1917 V2, p. 49.
156 captured from the enemy: *ibid.*, p. 87.
156–7 Gough asked on 14 June: *ibid.*, p. 89; Frank E Vandiver in *Passchendaele in Perspective: The Third Battle of Ypres*, edited by Peter H Liddle (Leo Cooper, 1997), p. 35.
157 'a terror of a day': Lyne Letters, 26 June 1917.
157 'and occasionally exploded': *ibid.*
157 'withdrew to wagon lines': *LXIV Brigade War Diary*, 25 June 1917, TNA WO 95/295.
157 3,106 guns combined to fire almost 3 million shells: Farndale, p. 195.
158 pigeons or runners to send back messages: *LXIV Brigade War Diary*, 31 July 1917, TNA WO 95/295.
159 exploded in the entrance to the dugout: *Accrington Observer and Times*, 6 October 1917, p. 5; *Burnley Express and Advertiser*, 6 October 1917, p. 4.
159–60 defended by a hundred men and five machine guns: Edmonds, 1917 V2, p. 196.
160 a belt of swamp and water-filled shell holes: *ibid.*, p. 265.
161 900yd south-west of the Frezenberg crossroads: *LXIV Brigade War Diary*, 2 October 1917, TNA WO 95/295.
161 hit in the head and leg: *Accrington Observer and Times*, 20 October 1917, p. 5.
161 digging in on the line of their final objective: *LXIV Brigade War Diary*, 4 October 1917, TNA WO 95/295.

161   at a conference with Haig on 7 October: Edmonds, 1917 V2, p. 325.
161   on either side of the road to Wieltje: *LXIV Brigade War Diary*, 6 October 1917, TNA WO 95/295.
161   muzzle-deep in mud: Edmonds, 1917 V2, p. 328.
162   LXIV Brigade learned at 9.45am: *LXIV Brigade War Diary*, 9 October 1917, TNA WO 95/295.
162   apparently unchanged at 12.50pm: *LXIV Brigade War Diary*, 12 October 1917, TNA WO 95/295.
162   a bomb dropped from an enemy aeroplane: *LXIV Brigade War Diary*, 18 October 1917, TNA WO 95/295.
162   following the amputation of his leg: *Burnley Express and Advertiser*, 7 November 1917, p. 3.
162   confirmed to LXIV Brigade by the firing of Very flares: *LXIV Brigade War Diary*, 26 October 1917, TNA WO 95/295.
163   17,900 rounds of ammunition: *LXIV Brigade War Diary*, 27–9 October 1917, TNA WO 95/295.
163   raised the number to 244,897: Edmonds, 1917 V2, p. 361.
163   evacuated with gas poisoning: *XLVIII Brigade War Diary*, 1 November 1917, TNA WO 95/455.
163   'Steenbeek positions constantly shelled': *XLVIII Brigade War Diary*, 4 November 1917, TNA WO 95/455.
164   'as opportunity permits': *XLVIII Brigade War Diary*, 5 November 1917, TNA WO 95/455.
164   west of the road to Saint-Julien: *XLVIII Brigade War Diary*, 14 November 1917, TNA WO 95/455.
164   by attaching a buoy to its spade: *ibid.*
164   wounded in the head by a shell: *Accrington Observer and Times*, 8 December 1917, p. 10.
164   died at a CCS: *LXIV Brigade War Diary*, 24 November 1917, TNA WO 95/295.
165   direct hit from a shell on a dugout: *Accrington Observer and Times*, 5 January 1918, p. 8.

Chapter 17
page
166   reorganized into three fighting companies: *11/East Lancashire War Diary*, 4–13 July 1917, TNA WO 95/2366.
166   'might have aroused Fritz's suspicions': *Accrington Gazette*, 28 July 1917, p. 4.
166   causing 2,014 casualties: Edmonds, 1917 V2, p. 137, n. 4.
167   while leading a working party up to the lines: *Accrington Observer and Times*, 4 August 1917, p. 5.
167   held during the German attacks of 1918: *Accrington Observer and Times*, 26 July 1919, p. 3.
167   wounding 5 officers and 114 other ranks: *11/East Lancashire War Diary*, 4–5 September 1917, TNA WO 95/2366.
167   while in brigade support east of Willerval: *11/East Lancashire War Diary*, 12 and 16 October 1917, TNA WO 95/2366.
167   again came under bombardment from HE and gas shells: *11/East Lancashire War Diary*, 13 November 1917, TNA WO 95/2366.
167   served with the Ceylon Engineer Volunteers: Army service record of Basil Arthur Horsfall, TNA WO 339/45724.
168   changed his name by deed poll: *London Gazette*, 1 October 1915, p. 9693.
169   294,000 prisoners and 3,136 guns: David Stevenson, *1914–1918: The History of the First World War* (Penguin, 2005) (hereafter Stevenson), p. 379.
169   disbanding or merging no less than 153 battalions: Nicholls, p. 212.
169   20 officers and 400 other ranks from 8/East Lancashire: *8/East Lancashire War Diary*, 1 February 1918, TNA WO 95/2537.

170	**only five US divisions**: Terraine, 1983, p. 166.
170	**raised from 147 to 191**: Stevenson, p. 399.
170	**to co-ordinate the activities of the Allied armies**: Sir James E Edmonds, *Military Operations: France and Belgium 1918*, Vol. 2 (Macmillan, 1937) (hereafter Edmonds, 1918 V2), p. 1.
171	**resumed command**: *11/East Lancashire War Diary*, 21 March 1918, TNA WO 95/2358.
171	**a very strong attack**: *Narrative of Operations of 31st Division between March 22nd and April 1st, 1918*, TNA WO 95/2343.
172	**no wire was available**: *Narrative of the Operations round Ervillers & the Aerodrome, from March 23rd to 27th inclusive*, TNA WO 95/2356.
172	**short-falling British artillery fire**: *ibid*.
173	**first infantry attack on the 92 Brigade front at 11.17am**: *11/East Lancashire War Diary*, 27 March 1918, TNA WO 95/2358.
173	**11/East Yorkshire was forced back**: *ibid*.
173	**renewed at noon and at 12.20pm**: Nicholson, p. 546.
173	**again recovered the position**: VC citation, Second Lieutenant Basil Arthur Horsfall, *Supplement to the London Gazette*, 22 May 1918, p. 6058 (hereafter Horsfall VC citation).
173	**stopped short by heavy machine-gun fire**: Nicholson, p. 546.
173	**a foothold on the ridge**: *31st Division War Diary*, 27 March 1918, TNA WO 95/2343.
173	**by pigeon**: *ibid*.
173	**said he could have held on**: Horsfall VC citation.
174	**killed, wounded or missing**: *11/East Lancashire War Diary*, end of March 1918, TNA WO 95/2358.
174	**anticipation of an enemy breakthrough**: *LXIV Brigade War Diary*, 10 March 1918, TNA WO 95/295.
174	**under orders to hold the line of the Ancre River**: Edmonds, 1918 V2, p. 30.
174–5	**three machine guns on a crest**: *XLVIII Brigade War Diary*, 28 March 1918, TNA WO 95/455.
175	**attempting to repair one of the battery's guns**: *Accrington Observer and Times*, 23 April 1918, p. 1 and 27 April 1918, p. 7.
175	**'Marto'**: *The Times*, 2 April 1924, p. 1.

Chapter 18

page

176	**woken by the sound of heavy gun fire**: Lyne Letters, 3 May 1918.
176	**raid by two companies**: Edmonds, 1918 V2, p. 171.
176	**moved up across the Lys River**: *LXIV Brigade War Diary*, 6 April 1918, TNA WO 95/295; Lyne in his memoirs incorrectly remembers the battery being positioned near Froid Nid Farm.
176	**From 4.15am**: Edmonds, 1918 V2, p. 164.
176	**Lyne soon received an urgent wire**: Lyne Letters, 3 May 1918.
176	**the headquarters had been hit by shellfire**: *LXIV Brigade War Diary*, 9 April 1918, TNA WO 95/295.
176	**Lieutenant Stanley Knocker**: Stanley Knocker is referred to as 'K' in Lyne's letter of 3 May 1918, but can be identified from the letters of 10 June 1917 and 23 April 1918.
176	**crossed the river by foot**: Lyne Letters, 3 May 1918.
176	**At 8am**: Edmonds, 1918 V2, p. 167.
177	**suffering from low morale before the battle**: Haig, p. 400.
177	**Lyne later recalled**: Lyne Memoirs, p. 22.
177	**The race to the guns**: Lyne Letters, 3 May 1918.
177–8	**the gun teams hurriedly left the scene**: Lyne Memoirs, p. 23.
178	**awarded a Bar to his MC**: *Supplement to the London Gazette*, 16 September 1918, p. 10896.

178   in action at Bac Saint-Maur for between 1 and 2 hours: Lyne Letters, 3 May 1918.
178   the permanent bridge at Bac Saint-Maur was blown up: Edmonds, 1918 V2, p. 181.
178   followed orders to pull back: *LXIV Brigade War Diary*, 9 April 1918, TNA WO 95/ 295.
178   At around 4pm: Edmonds, 1918 V2, p. 182.
178   At the same time, LXIV Brigade was returning to action: *LXIV Brigade War Diary*, 9 April 1918, TNA WO 95/295.
178   Commanding 150 Brigade was Brigadier General Hubert Rees: *Papers of Brigadier General H C Rees*, vol. 3 of typed transcript of memoirs, IWM 77/179/1, pp. 32–44.
178   the night of 9–10 April: Edmonds, 1918 V2, p. 184.
179   Foch had earlier declined: Edmonds, 1918 V2, p. 186.
179   'the best and bravest fellow': Lyne Letters, 3 May 1918.
179   At about 7.30am: Edmonds, 1918 V2, p. 197.
179   breakthrough in the Bac Saint-Maur sector: *ibid.*, p. 199.
179   began to withdraw to the north: *LXIV Brigade War Diary*, 10 April 1918, TNA WO 95/295.
179   'didn't want to go and feared to stay': Lyne Letters, 15 May 1918.
179   Returning to action at about 3pm: *ibid.*
179   'a sleepless night of singular misery': *ibid.*
179   rebuilding and training at Bailleul-aux-Cornailles: *11/East Lancashire War Diary*, 10 April 1918, TNA WO 95/2358.
180   By 9am: Edmonds, 1918 V2, p. 228.
180   92 Brigade was pushed forward: *92 Brigade Operations 10–15 April 1918*, TNA WO 95/2356.
180   succeeded in re-taking La Becque and La Rose Farm: *93 Brigade Diary of Operations*, 10–15 April, TNA WO 95/2360.
180   forcing 86 and 87 brigades to pull back: *Narrative of Operations of 29th Division*, 9–14 April 1918, TNA WO 95/2284.
180   he and Monk went forward: Lyne Letters, 15 May 1918; note that the typed transcript of this letter places the events of 12 April 1918 before those of 11 April 1918.
180   At 4pm, LXIV Brigade retired: *LXIV Brigade War Diary*, 11 April 1918, TNA WO 95/295.
180–1 'never a chance of getting their wounds dressed': Lyne Letters, 15 May 1918.
181   'no other course open to us': Edmonds, 1918 V2, p. 512.
181   'rivers of muck and blasted manure dumps': Crabtree and Sayer, p. 81.
181   At daybreak on 12 April: Edmonds, 1918 V2, pp. 231–3.
181   149 Brigade was soon being driven back: *ibid.*, p. 263.
181   At Bleu, where LXIV Brigade's batteries were now firing: Lyne Letters, 15 May 1918.
182   a gap had opened up: *10/East Yorkshire Report on Operations*, 11–13 April 1918, TNA WO 95/2357.
182   ordered to start withdrawing to the north-west: *ibid.*; *11/East Yorkshire War Diary*, 12 April 1918, TNA WO 95/2357.
182   some not more than 2,500yd away: Lowe, p. 113.
182   Lieutenant Harold Wilton: Wilton's Army service is summarized in TNA WO 339/ 41217, his MC citation is recorded in the *Supplement to the London Gazette*, 16 September 1918, p. 11036, and the *1911 Census for England and Wales* shows him to be 'en route to Russia'.
182   the battalion received orders to withdraw: Nicholson, p. 550.
182   formed from brigade details and stragglers: *Report on Operations, 10–14 April 1918*, Lieutenant Colonel C H Gurney DSO, TNA WO 95/2357.
182   swung around its left to face east: *10/East Yorkshire Report on Operations, 11–13 April 1918*, TNA WO 95/2357.

182   came under machine-gun fire from Outtersteene: *LXIV Brigade War Diary*, 12 April 1918, TNA WO 95/295.

183   so as to make contact with 29th Division: *11/East Lancashire War Diary*, 12 April 1918, TNA WO 95/2358.

183   succeeded in reaching the two companies: MM citation for Charles Edwin Nutt; though dated 13 April 1918, the citation clearly describes an action that took place on the previous day.

183   evacuated owing to loss of blood: *Supplement to the London Gazette*, 16 September 1918, p. 10945.

183   in a cellar in Le Paradis: Nicholson, p. 550.

184   Lance Corporal William Albert Stuart: *Accrington Observer and Times*, 20 July 1918, p. 5.

184   dug in west of Merris: *92 Brigade Operations 10–15 April 1918*, TNA WO 95/2356.

184   an ammunition dump caught fire: *2/Royal Fusiliers War Diary*, TNA WO 95/2301.

184   Sergeant Walter Beckett: *Burnley News*, 1 June 1918, p. 3.

184   sent a gun down the road towards Vieux Berquin: *LXIV Brigade War Diary*, 13 April 1918, TNA WO 95/295.

184   Kay was to be awarded the MC for his actions: *Supplement to the London Gazette*, 16 September 1918, p. 19074.

184   blown out of its positions at La Couronne: *31st Division War Diary*, 13 April 1918, TNA WO 95/2343.

184   launched a fresh attack at 2.35pm: *92 Brigade Operations 10–15 April 1918*, TNA WO 95/2356.

184   11/East Lancashire held its positions: the line, however, must have come perilously close to being broken; the War Diary of 2/Royal Fusiliers (TNA WO 95/2301) claims that the staff captain of 86 Brigade had to rally faltering troops on the battalion's left (11/East Lancashire).

185   streaming north out of Vieux Berquin: *92 Brigade Operations* and *Narrative 10–15 April 1918*, TNA WO 95/2356.

185   promptly sent: Nicholson, p. 551.

186   respectively awarded the DSO and the MC: *Supplement to the London Gazette*, 16 September 1918, pp. 10868 and 10981.

186   the left front of 4 Guards Brigade had been broken: *31st Division War Diary*, 13 April 1918, TNA WO 95/2343.

186   Acting Captain Thomas Tannatt Pryce MC: *Supplement to the London Gazette*, 22 May 1918, pp. 6057–8.

186   ordered to withdraw his battalion: *92 Brigade Narrative, 10–15 April 1918*, TNA WO 95/2356.

186   Second Lieutenant John Cyprian Lott: Army service record of John Cyprian Lott, TNA WO 339/61046; *Supplement to the London Gazette*, 17 September 1917, p. 9576.

187   aimed at gaining the Strazeele Ridge: Edmonds, 1918 V2, p. 307.

187   successful local attack at Merris: *LXIV Brigade War Diary*, 16 April 1918, TNA WO 95/295.

187   'perhaps the Yankees will polish them off': letter from William Hill to his father, John, 28 April 1918.

187   'we had a pretty hot time': letter from Wilf Kitchen to Robert and Rose Jones, the parents of his best friend, Harold, 12 May 1918, held at The Liddle Collection, University of Leeds, GS 0903.

Chapter 19

page

188   British Army casualties in the months of April and May 1918 totalled 316,889: *Statistics of the Military Effort of the British Empire During the Great War* (HMSO, 1922), p. 267.

188   **303,450 casualties reported in the 3 main assaulting armies:** Keegan, p. 435.
188   **'the key of the Chemin des Dames position':** Sir James E Edmonds, *Military Operations: France and Belgium 1918*, Vol. 3 (Macmillan, 1939), p. 52 (hereafter Edmonds, 1918 V3).
188   **fired an estimated 2 million shells:** Holger H Herwig, *The First World War: Germany and Austria-Hungary 1914–1918* (Arnold, 1997), p. 415.
188   **The infantry assault began at 3.40am:** Edmonds, 1918 V3, pp. 49–50.
188   **ceased to exist by 8am:** *ibid.*, p. 53.
189   **'sent back his plate for more':** Crabtree and Sayer, p. 82.
189   **'came out of the line near Caestre on the evening of 23 May':** *ibid.*, p. 83
190   **very impressed by the shooting of the artillery:** *LXIV Brigade War Diary*, 3 June 1918, TNA WO 95/295.
190   **said to be very satisfied:** *LXIV Brigade War Diary*, 6 June 1918, TNA WO 95/295.
190   **'short and weak, mostly about 19 and 20 years old':** *LXIV Brigade War Diary*, 14 June 1918, TNA WO 95/295.
190   **5th and 31st divisions received orders to attack:** *31st Division Report on Operations 27 and 28 June 1918*, TNA WO 95/2343 (hereafter *31st Division Report 27–28.06.18*).
191   **a night-time operation:** *ibid.*
191   **wryly remarked:** Nicholson, p. 553.
191   **'rough weather-proof shelters':** Edmonds, 1918 V3, fn. 2 on p. 196.
191   **a 'leap frog' approach:** *Narrative of the Operations carried out by the 31st Division on the 28th June, east of Foret de Nieppe*, TNA WO 95/2356.
191   **The enemy wire was easily passed through:** *10/East Yorkshire Report on Operations East of Forest de Nieppe on 28 June 1918*, TNA WO 95/2357 (hereafter *10/East Yorkshire Report 28.06.18*).
191   **a few guns tragically fired short:** *ibid.*
192   **On the left of the attack:** Everard Wyrall, *The West Yorkshire Regiment in the War 1914–1918, Volume 2* (John Lane, 1924), pp. 282–3.
192   **'put up a splendid fight to the last':** *Report on Operations carried out by 11/East Yorkshire at the Forest de Nieppe 28th to 30th June 1918*, TNA WO 95/2357.
192   **Fleischer personally rushed one of them:** *Supplement to the London Gazette*, 15 October 1918, p. 12053.
192   **Fuller going on to shoot the enemy gunner:** *Supplement to the London Gazette*, 15 October 1918, p. 12073.
192   **Foden immediately retaliated:** *Supplement to the London Gazette*, 30 October 1918, p. 12820.
193   **W Company led by Captain Cyril McKenzie:** Nicholson, p. 554.
193   **Ashton spotted an enemy machine-gun post:** *Supplement to the London Gazette*, 30 October 1918, p. 12809.
194   **X and Y companies led by Captain George Bentley:** Nicholson, p. 554.
194   **11/East Lancashire captured:** *11/East Lancashire War Diary*, 28 June 1918, TNA WO 95/2358.
194   **10/East Yorkshire encountered little resistance:** *10/East Yorkshire Report on Operations East of Forest de Nieppe on 28th June 1918*, TNA WO 95/2357.
194   **31st Division reported the capture:** *31st Division Report on Operations 27th and 28th June 1918*, TNA WO 95/2343.
195   **capturing 15,000 prisoners and 400 guns:** Terraine, 1983, p. 173.
195   **specialist training, wiring and rifle competitions:** *11/East Lancashire War Diary*, 16–22 July 1918, TNA WO 95/2358.
195   **'a good day in the old town':** Crabtree and Sayer, p. 85.
195   **consisted of 'B1' men:** *LXIV Brigade War Diary*, 18 July 1918, TNA WO 95/295.
195   **'any good hotels around here?':** Crabtree and Sayer, p. 85.
195   **'peaceful penetration':** Nicholson, p. 554.

196   '**very good and thick barrage**': *LXIV Brigade War Diary*, 19 August 1918, TNA WO 95/295.

196   **patrols from 10/East Yorkshire began to push towards the Warnave River**: *10/East Yorkshire War Diary*, 4 September 1918, TNA WO 95/2357.

196   **11/East Lancashire took over the line during the night**: *Report on Operations carried out by 11/East Lancashire 5 September 1918*, TNA WO 95/2356 (hereafter *11/East Lancashire Report 05.09.18*).

196   **The attack was renewed at 5pm**: *ibid.*

197   **enfilade fire from a Lewis gun team commanded by Corporal Robert Walmsley**: MM citation, private communication from Ryan Walmsley.

197   **after all its officers had become casualties**: citation for MM award to Sergeant Roger Ireland, private communication from David Ingham.

197   **the enemy swiftly counter-attacked**: *11/East Lancashire Report 05.09.18*.

198   **twenty prisoners and two machine guns had been captured**: *11/East Lancashire War Diary*, 5 September 1918, TNA WO 95/2358.

198   **three officers are reported to have been taken prisoner**: *List of British Officers taken prisoner in the various Theatres of War between August 1914 and November 1918* (Cox and Co., 1919).

198   **held out against repeated attacks**: Everard Wyrall, *The East Yorkshire Regiment in the Great War 1914–1918* (Harrison & Sons, 1928), pp. 366–7.

Chapter 20

page
199   **killed two and wounded ten**: *XLVIII Brigade War Diary*, 7 July 1918, TNA WO 95/455.

200   **Passchendaele had been taken**: *LXIV Brigade War Diary*, 28 September 1918, TNA WO 95/295.

201   **the battalion made little headway**: *10/East Yorkshire War Diary*, 28 September 1918, TNA WO 95/2357.

201   **nearing the final objective**: *Report of Operations Carried Out by the 92nd Infantry Brigade from 27th September to 4th October 1918*, TNA WO 95/2356 (hereafter *92 Brigade Operations 27.9.18–4.10.18*).

201–2   **held against heavy counter-attacks**: MC citation, Captain John Shire Duff MC, *Supplement to the London Gazette*, 30 July 1919, p. 9693.

202   **forced to form a defensive flank**: *92 Brigade Operations 27.9.18–4.10.18*.

202   **358 killed, wounded and missing**: *11/East Lancashire War Diary*, 28 September 1918, TNA WO 95/2358.

202–3   **a daring daylight patrol on 4 October**: DCM citation, Sergeant H Pursglove, *Supplement to the London Gazette*, 11 March 1920, p. 3086; MC citation, Second Lieutenant George Pennington Richards, *Supplement to the London Gazette*, 30 July 1919, p. 9768.

203   **inadvertently poisoned by gas**: *LXIV Brigade War Diary*, 11 October 1918, TNA WO 95/295.

203   '**with great enthusiasm**': *11/East Lancashire War Diary*, 18 October 1918, TNA WO 95/2358.

203   '**flowers, wreaths and flags**': Lyne Letters, 21 October 1918.

204   **the last bridge over the Escaut River**: *LXIV Brigade War Diary*, 20 October 1918, TNA WO 95/295.

204   **apparently oblivious to the dangers**: Nicholson, p. 558.

205   **overflowed its banks on the west side**: *ibid.*

205   **announced the news to a bewildered battalion**: *Burnley Express and Advertiser*, 11 November 1931, p. 8.

206   **moved to Péronne**: Péronne is believed to be Péronne-en-Mélantois, south-east of Lille.

Chapter 21
page
207 **explosive picric acid**: the *Accrington Observer and Times* of 30 October 1976 carried an account of an explosion that took place at the Coteholme Chemical Company on 28 April 1917, resulting in blown-out windows and cracked plaster across Church and even beyond. PC James Hardacre who was killed in the blast was credited with preventing an even bigger explosion by slamming shut the door to a magazine that contained stored explosives.

207–8 **'sorrow so acutely compressed within the narrow limits of the community'**: *Accrington Observer and Times*, 19 July 1919, p. 9.

208 **met or exceeded in both 1917 and 1918**: based on an analysis of 836 entries out of 875 on Accrington's war memorial in Oak Hill Park for which the author has established a date of death.

208 **about 36 per cent**: author's own estimate.

208 **comparable to that for the country as a whole**: see Terraine, 1980, notes.

209 **'every reason to be proud in Accrington'**: *Accrington Observer and Times*, 21 October 1919, p. 1.

209 **much disagreement**: *Accrington Observer and Times*, 3 February 1920, p. 2.

209 **three sons who lost their lives in the war**: Captain Harry Hargreaves Bolton, Lieutenant John Bolton and Captain Maurice Baldwin Bolton MC.

209 **'the name of some lost one'**: *Accrington Observer and Times*, 4 July 1922, p. 1.

209 **a dinner for thirty officers at the Holborn Restaurant in London**: *Accrington Observer and Times*, 5 July 1919, p. 7.

210 **the names of the winning players**: the *Accrington Observer and Times*, 26 July 1919, p. 3 lists them as Second Lieutenant C H Mallinson, Sergeant J Sullivan, Corporal J Quinn, Corporal H Taylor, Private E Baldwin, Corporal W Brindle, Privates W Fuller, H Hitchen, F Lewis, J T Hacking and W Waring.

210 **at the drill hall in Argyle Street, Accrington**: *Accrington Observer and Times*, 9 April 1935, p. 5.

210 **no credible account**: William Turner has claimed that the 1935 reunion had its origins in the death of Major Ross, described as 'a bachelor with no family' (Turner, 1987, p. 188); in fact, Ross, a married man, lived until 1944.

210 **repeated in subsequent years**: reunions were held on 25 April 1936, 20 March 1937, 26 March 1938 and 25 March 1939.

210 **ceremonially transferred on 6 November 1938**: *Accrington Observer and Times*, 8 November 1938, p. 1.

210 **called for there to be some official remembrance**: *Accrington Observer and Times*, 11 June 1966, p. 9.

210 **more than 300 attended the service**: *Accrington Observer and Times*, 5 July 1966, p. 5.

210 **only seven former Pals were identified as being present**: a number of former Pals, one of which was Harry Bloor, missed the service through attending the fiftieth anniversary commemorations on the Somme.

Chapter 22
page
212–13 **tribunal meeting of 3 March 1916**: see *Accrington Gazette*, 4 March 1916, p. 5.

213 **Thomas Yates Harwood**: biographical notes for Thomas Yates Harwood were compiled with the aid of his Army service record, TNA WO 339/15858.

213–14 **John Richard Harwood**: biographical notes for John Richard Harwood were compiled with the aid of his Army service record, TNA WO 363/H1356.

214 **Edmund Mills Harwood**: biographical notes for Edmund Mills Harwood were compiled with the aid of his Army service record, TNA WO 339/30840.

214 **Frank Harwood**: biographical notes for Frank Harwood were compiled with the aid of his Army service record, TNA WO 339/25137.

214   **with whom Harwood had been billeted**: private correspondence from Pen Harwood.

214   **coming off duty with the Home Guard**: *ibid.*

214   **Percy Allsup**: biographical notes for Allsup come largely from personal correspondence with his son, Percy B Allsup.

214–15   **Harold Bancroft**: biographical notes for Bancroft were compiled with the aid of his Army service record, TNA WO 339/29027.

215   **its first commanding officer**: *Accrington Observer and Times*, 9 October 1951, p. 1.

215   **St John Battersby**: biographical notes for Battersby were complied from his Army service record, TNA WO 339/34889, and with the help of his son, Anthony Battersby.

215   **Harry Cecil Bloor**: biographical notes for Bloor were compiled with the help of Ross Davies.

216   **'if we die we will die fighting'**: *Accrington Observer and Times*, 5 August 1916, p. 8.

216   **Bart Endean**: biographical notes for Endean were compiled with the aid of his Army service record, TNA WO 339/39944, and with the help of Peter Bell.

216   **'contact with the Indians in about a week or ten days'**: *The Times*, 6 February 1928.

216–17   **Cecil Douglas Gay**: biographical notes for Gay were compiled from his Army service record, held by the Ministry of Defence, *Coventry Evening Telegraph*, 27 October 1980, p. 4, and with the help of his son, David Gay.

217–18   **Gerald Thomas (Gerry) Gorst**: details of Gorst's post-war career were largely taken from his Army service record, held by the Ministry of Defence.

218   **after returning home to attend the funeral of his mother**: *Accrington Gazette*, 18 September 1915, p. 5.

218   **fit for GS after three weeks' leave**: Army service record of Ernest David Kay, TNA WO 339/84716.

218   **chairman from 1948 to 1952**: *Burnley Express and News*, 13 June 1956, p. 2.

218   **George Lee**: biographical notes for Lee were compiled from his Army service record, TNA WO 97/3277, and with the help of Dennis Hounsell.

219   **found employment as a munitions inspector**: *Will Marshall: North West Sound Archive 1985.0038A*.

219   **four of his grandsons were serving**: *Accrington Observer and Times*, 7 March 1942, p. 4.

219   **'I shall have died for a noble cause'**: *Accrington Observer and Times*, 29 July 1916, p. 5.

219   **caught in the flywheel of an electricity generator**: *Accrington Observer and Times*, 20 October 1925, p. 3.

219–20   **the distinguished nature of his military service**: *The Salisbury and Wiltshire Journal*, 23 October 1925, p. 11.

220–1   **Raymond St George Ross**: biographical notes for Ross were compiled from his Army service record, TNA WO 339/16465, and with the help of Nelly and Jacquie Ainslie and Martin Bird.

221   **George Nicholas Slinger**: biographical notes for Slinger were compiled from his Army service record, TNA WO 339/16466, the *Accrington Observer and Times*, 18 December 1923, p. 5, and with the help of Walter Slinger and John Slinger.

221   **'conspicuous gallantry and devotion to duty'**: *Supplement to the London Gazette*, 17 September 1917, p. 9600.

221   **stayed with the firm until his retirement**: *Accrington Observer and Times*, 10 November 1959, p. 5.

221   **from the hearse to the Manchester train**: *Accrington Gazette*, 13 March 1915, p. 4.

221–2   **Frank Thomas**: biographical notes for Thomas were compiled with the help of his son, Ian Thomas.

222   **a bomb dropped from an enemy aeroplane**: *No. 5 Field Ambulance War Diary*, 6 October 1918, TNA WO 95/1337.

Index